FOR ORGANS, PIANOS & ELECTRONIC KEYBOARDS

126

the best of
BARRY MANILOW

Contents

7777 W. BLUEMOUND RD. P.O. BOX 13819 MILWAUKEE, WI 53213

Can't Smile Without You

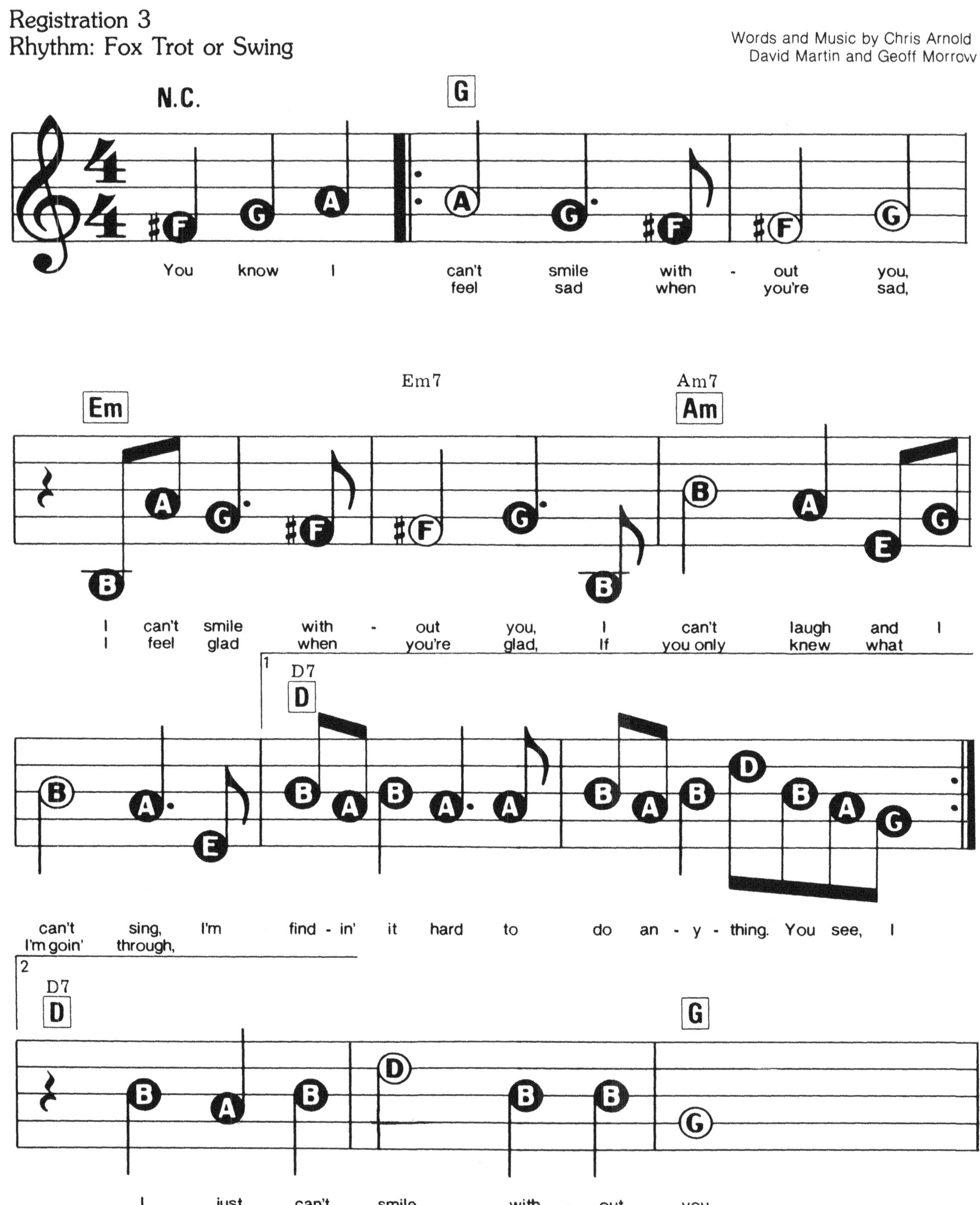

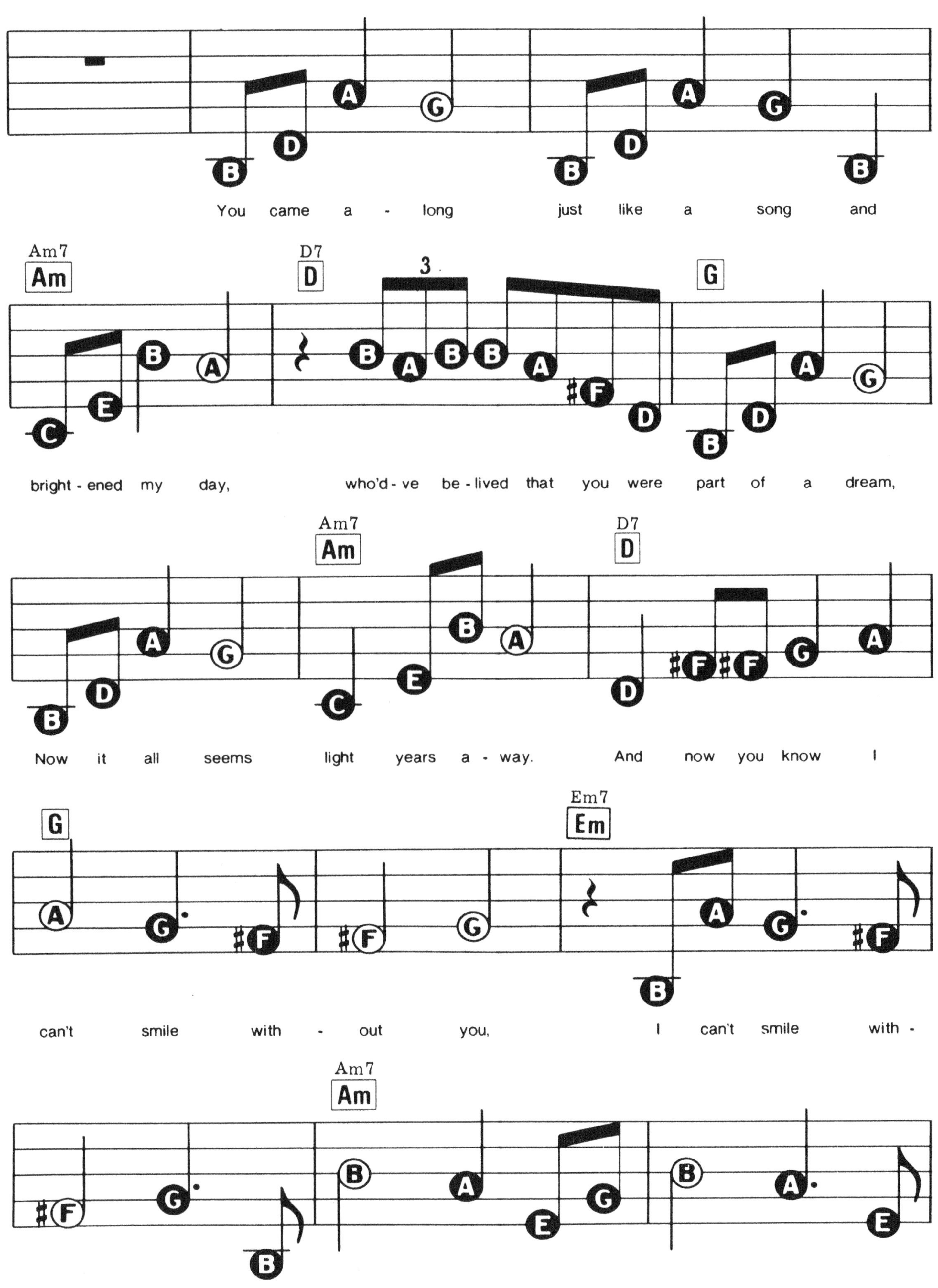
You came a - long just like a song and
Am7 Am D7 D 3 G
bright - ened my day, who'd - ve be - lived that you were part of a dream,
Am7 Am D7 D
Now it all seems light years a - way. And now you know I
G Em7 Em
can't smile with - out you, I can't smile with -
Am7 Am
out you, I can't laugh and I can't sing, I'm

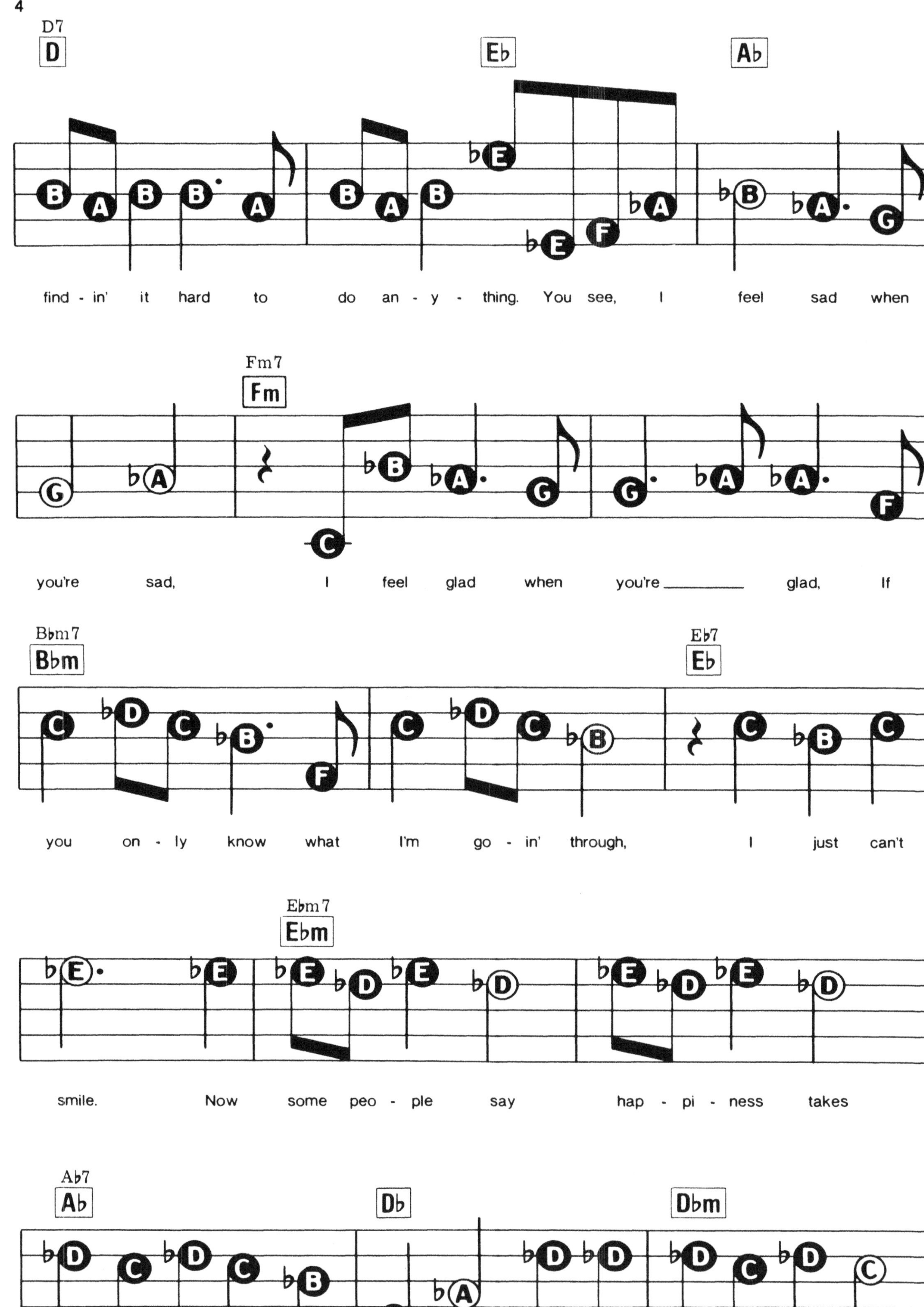
D7
D
Eb
Ab
find - in' it hard to do an - y - thing. You see, I feel sad when
Fm7
Fm
you're sad, I feel glad when you're glad, If
Bbm7
Bbm
Eb7
Eb
you on - ly know what I'm go - in' through, I just can't
Ebm7
Ebm
smile. Now some peo - ple say hap - pi - ness takes
Ab7
Ab
Db
Dbm
so ver - y long to find. Well, I'm find - in' it hard

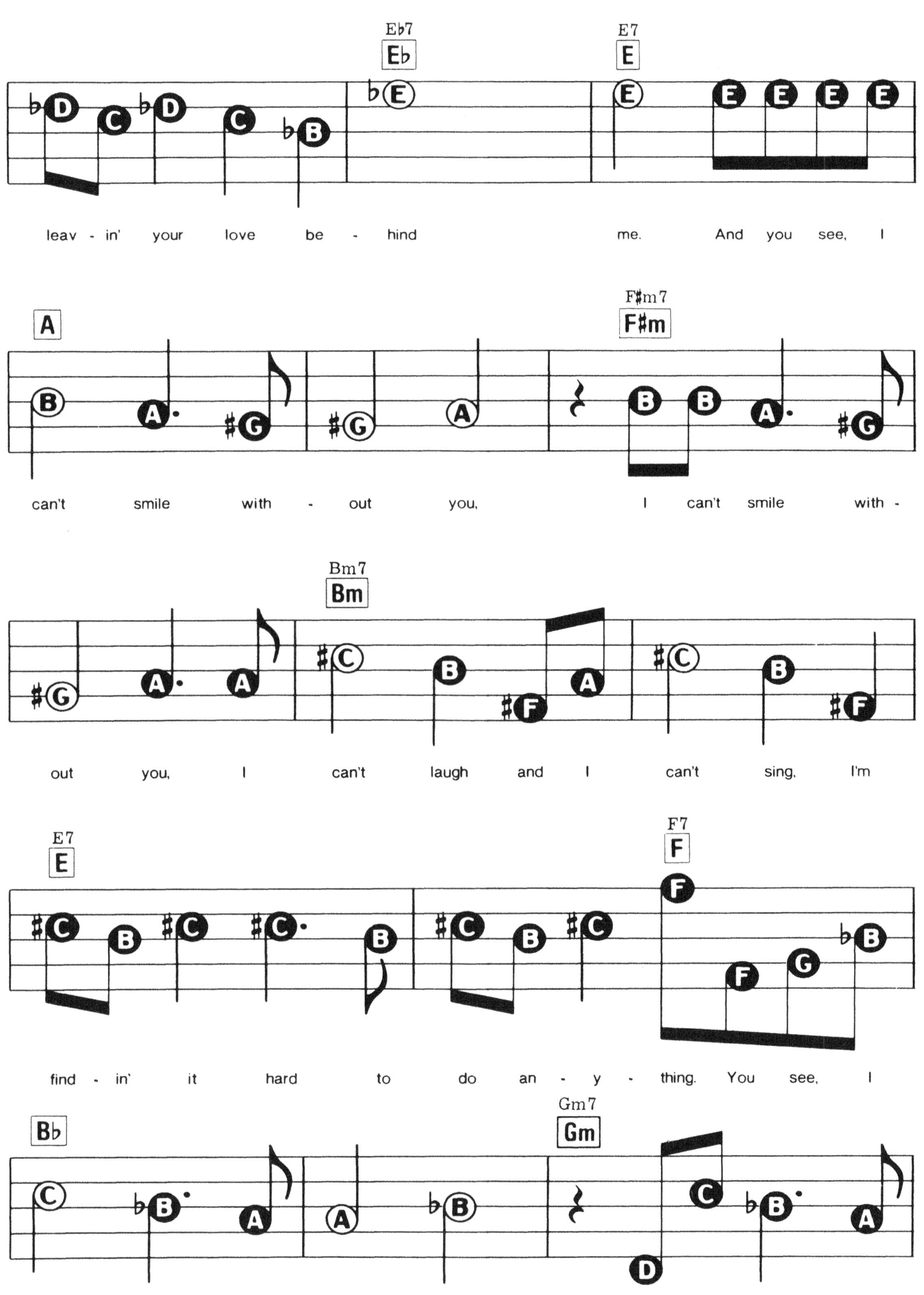
E♭7
E♭
E7
E
D C D C B E E E E E E
leav - in' your love be - hind me. And you see, I
A
F♯m7
F♯m
B A G G A B B A G
can't smile with - out you, I can't smile with -
Bm7
Bm
G A A C B F A C B F
out you, I can't laugh and I can't sing, I'm
E7
E
F7
F
C B C C B C B C F F G B
find - in' it hard to do an - y - thing. You see, I
B♭
Gm7
Gm
C B A A B D C B A
feel glad when you're glad, I feel sad when

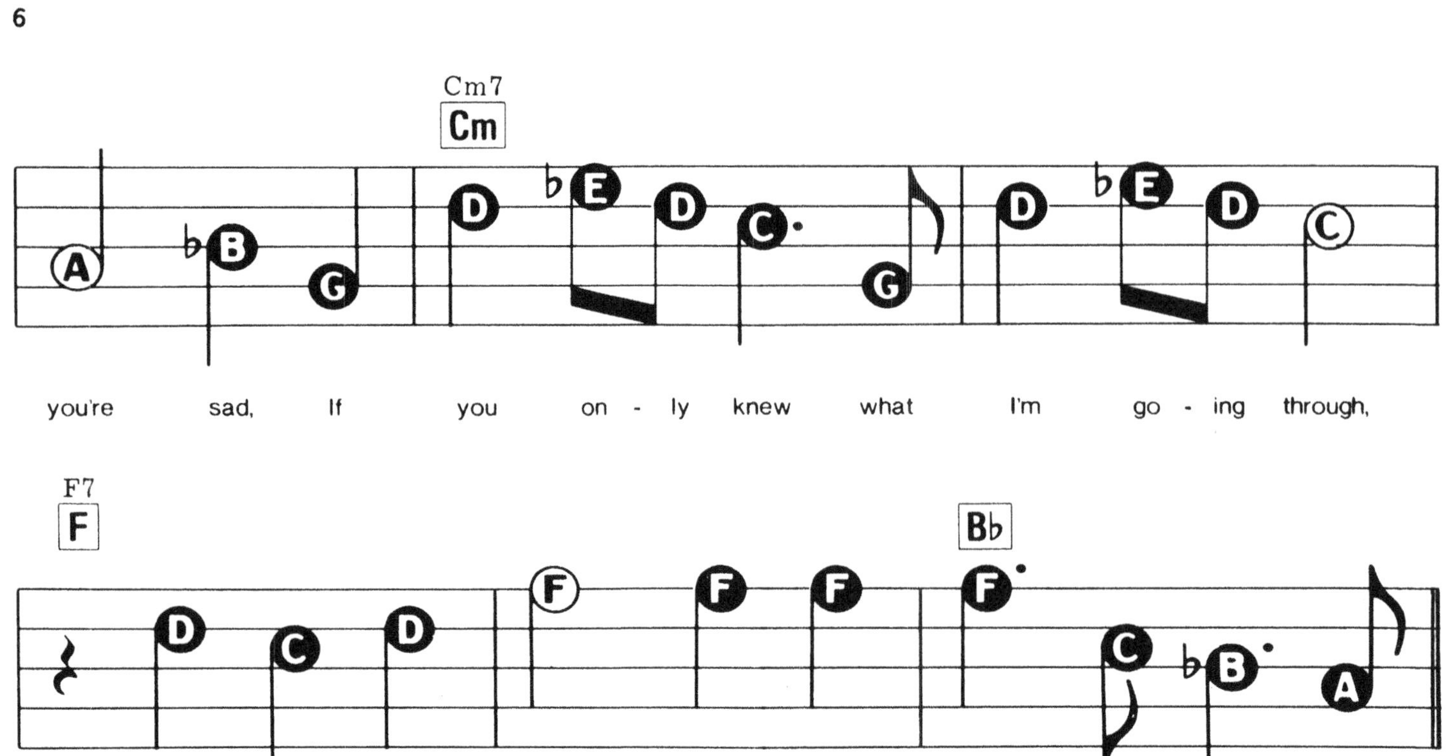
Cm7
Cm
A ♭B G D ♭E D C G D ♭E D C
you're sad, If you on - ly knew what I'm go - ing through,

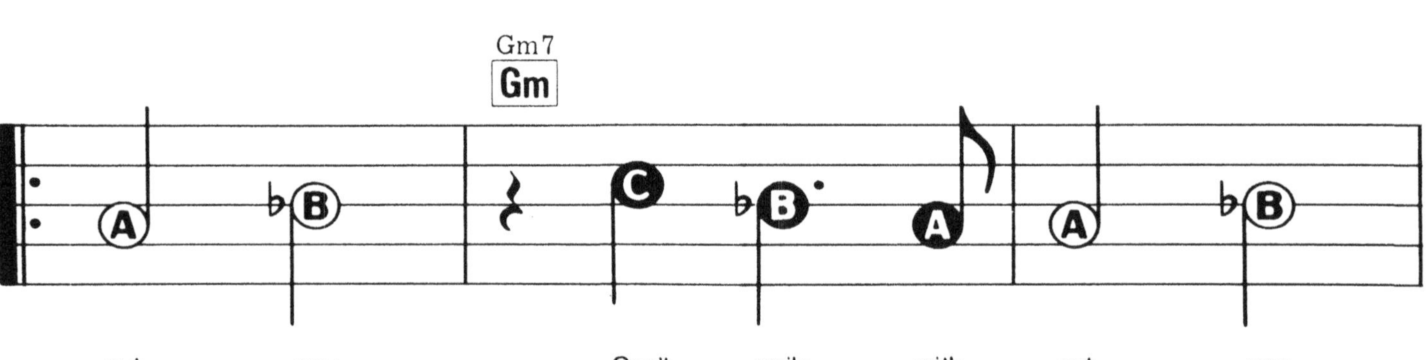
F7
F
Bb
D C D F F F F C ♭B A
I just can't smile with - out you, Can't smile with -

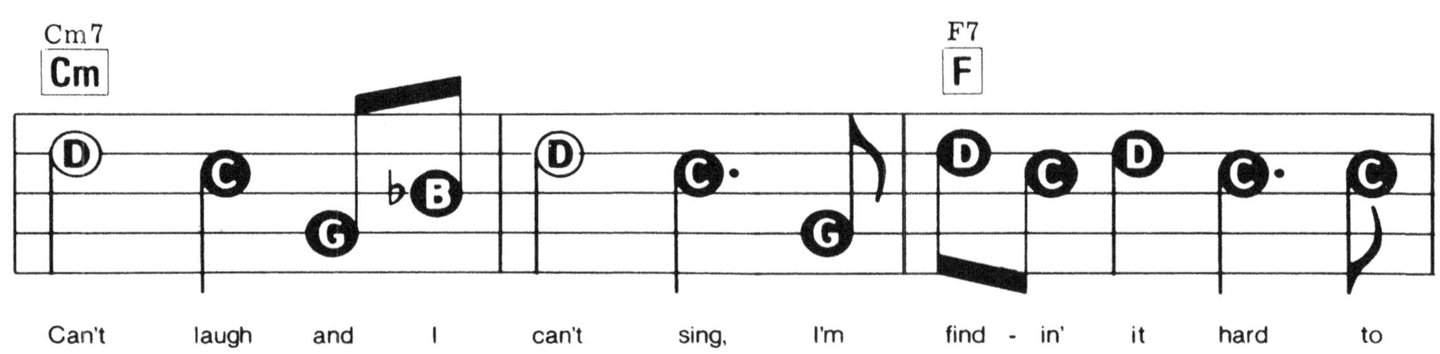
Gm7
Gm
A ♭B C ♭B A A ♭B
out you Can't smile with - out you,

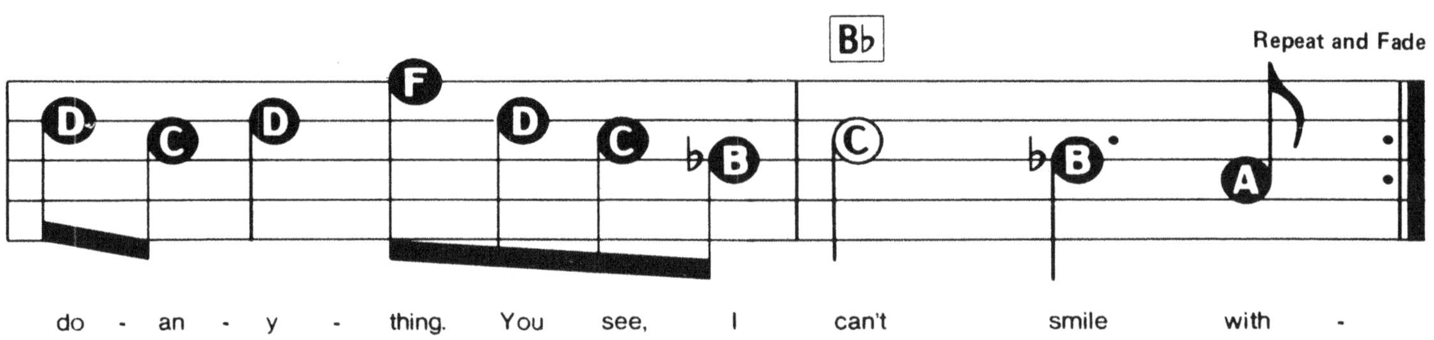
Cm7
Cm
F7
F
D C G ♭B D C G D C D C C
Can't laugh and I can't sing, I'm find - in' it hard to
Bb
Repeat and Fade
D C D F D C ♭B C ♭B A
do - an - y - thing. You see, I can't smile with -

Copacabana
(At The Copa)

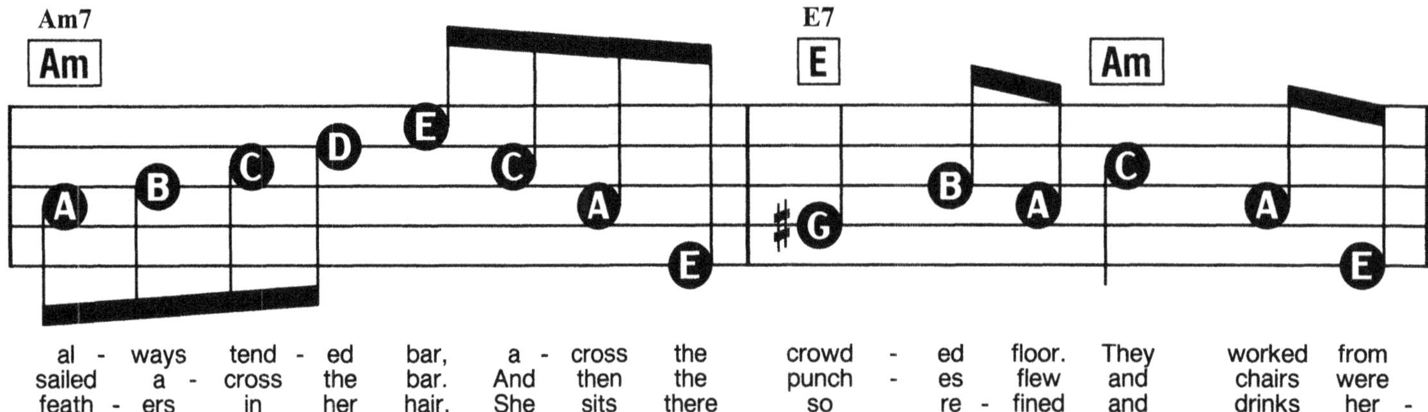
Am7 Am E7 E Am
al - ways tend - ed bar, a - cross the crowd - ed floor. They worked from
sailed a - cross the bar. And then the punch - es flew and chairs were
feath - ers in her hair, She sits there so re - fined and drinks her -

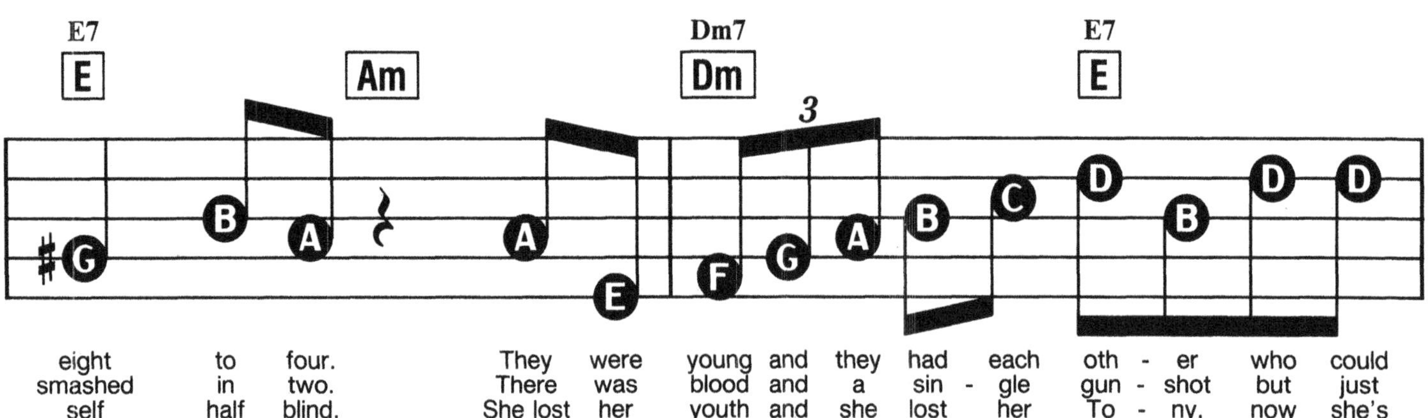
E7 E Am Dm7 Dm E7 E
3
eight to four. They were young and they had each oth - er who could
smashed in two. There was blood and a sin - gle gun - shot but just
self half blind. She lost her youth and she lost her To - ny, now she's

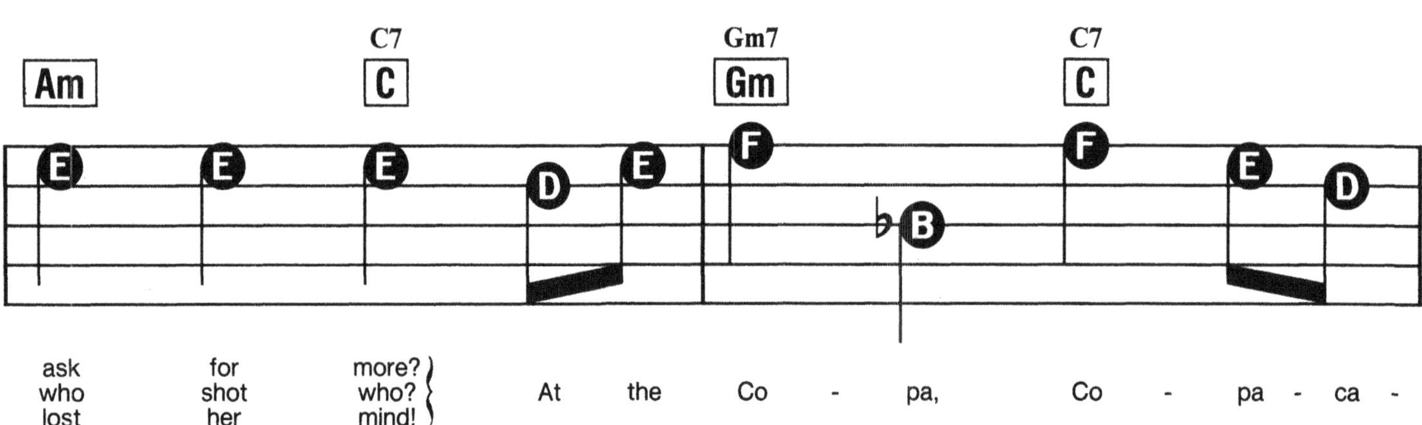
Am C7 C Gm7 Gm C7 C
ask for more?
who shot who?
lost her mind!
At the Co - pa, Co - pa - ca -

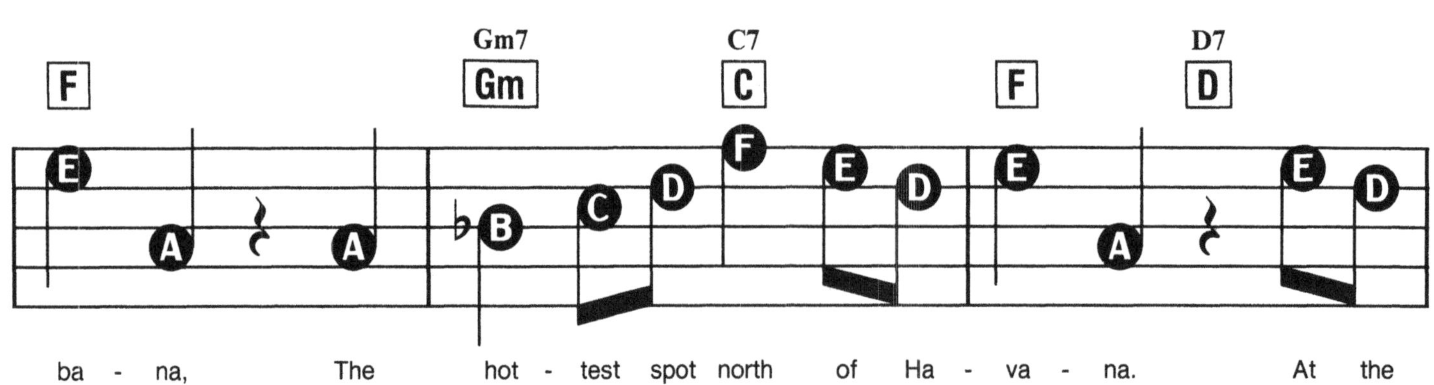
F Gm7 Gm C7 C F D7 D
ba - na, The hot - test spot north of Ha - va - na. At the

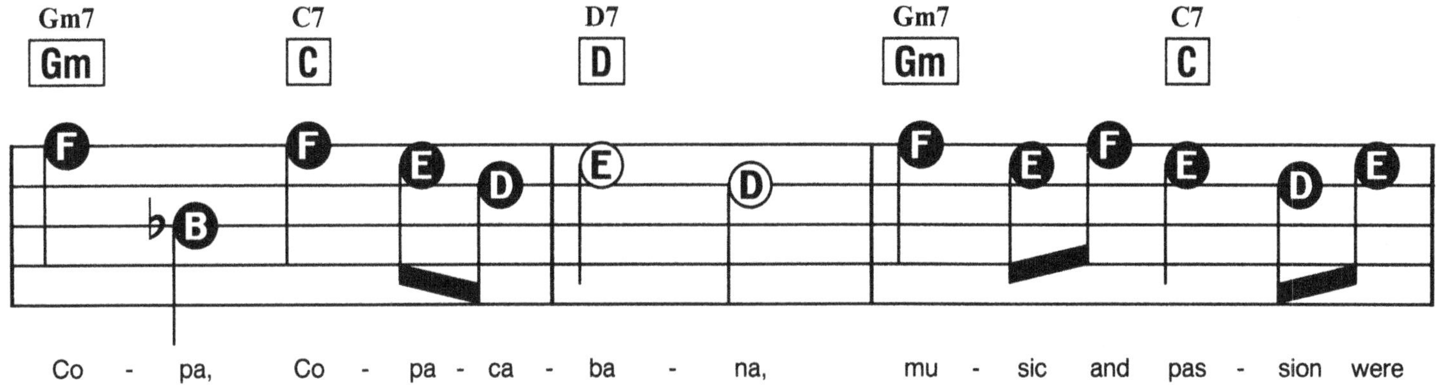
Gm7
Gm
C7
C
D7
D
Gm7
Gm
C7
C
F
B
F
E
D
E
D
F
E
F
E
D
E
Co - pa, Co - pa - ca - ba - na, mu - sic and pas - sion were

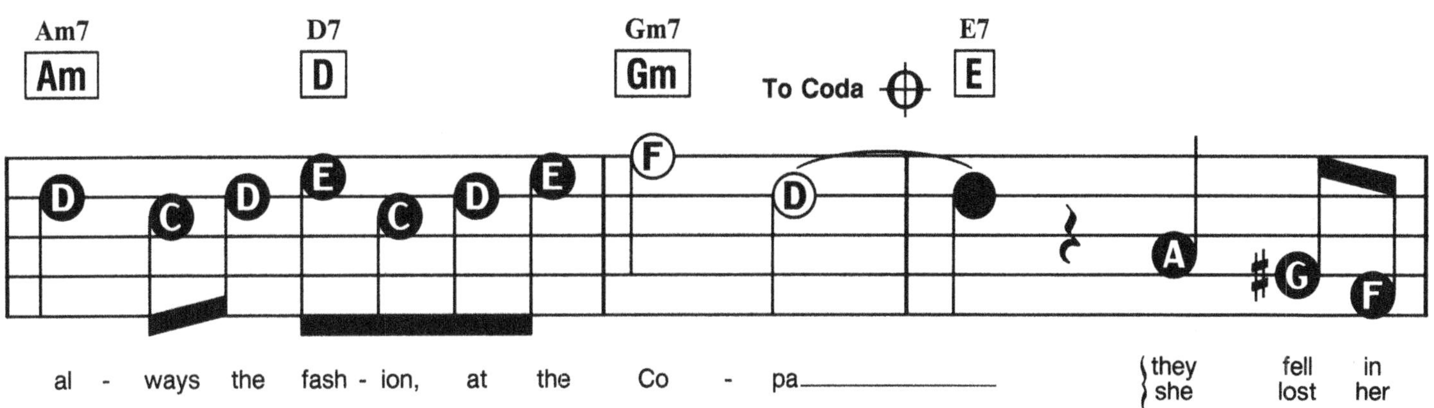
Am7
Am
D7
D
Gm7
Gm
To Coda
E7
E
D
C
D
E
C
D
E
F
D
A
G
F
al - ways the fash - ion, at the Co - pa
they fell in
she lost her

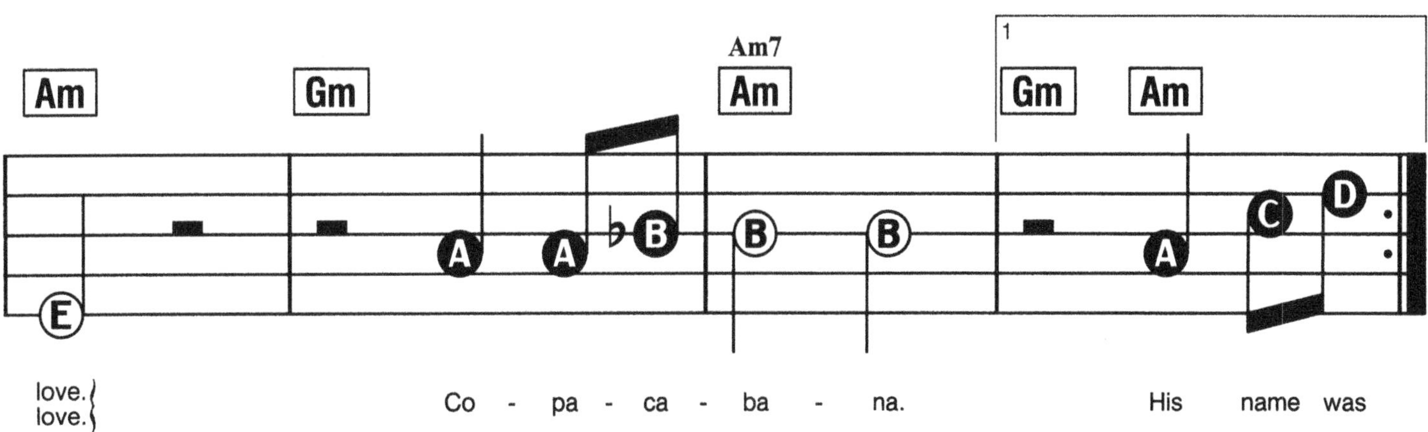
Am
Gm
Am7
Am
1
Gm
Am
E
A
A
B
B
B
A
C
D
love.
love.
Co - pa - ca - ba - na.
His name was

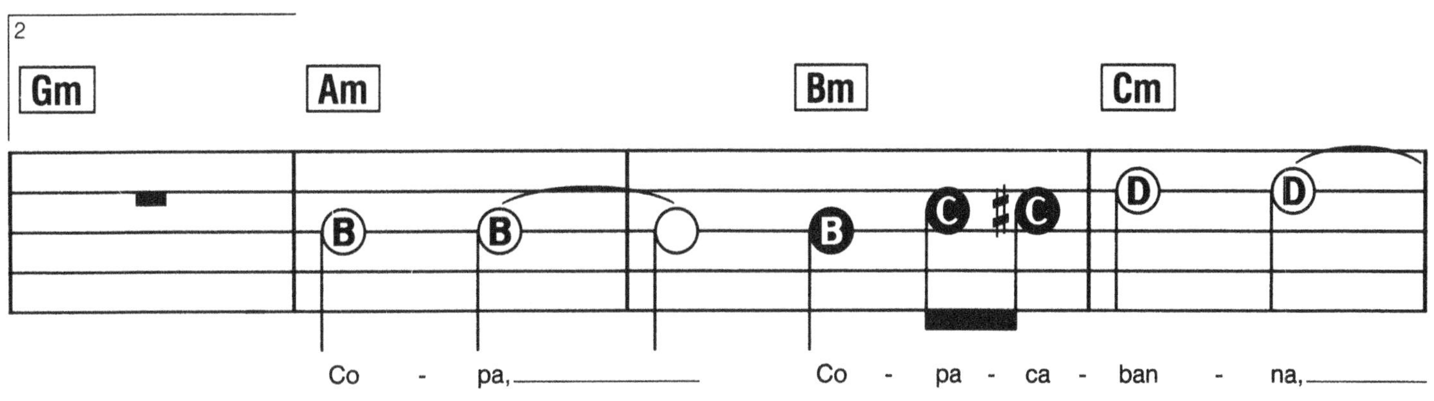
2
Gm
Am
Bm
Cm
B
B
B
C
C
D
D
Co - pa,
Co - pa - ca - ban - na,

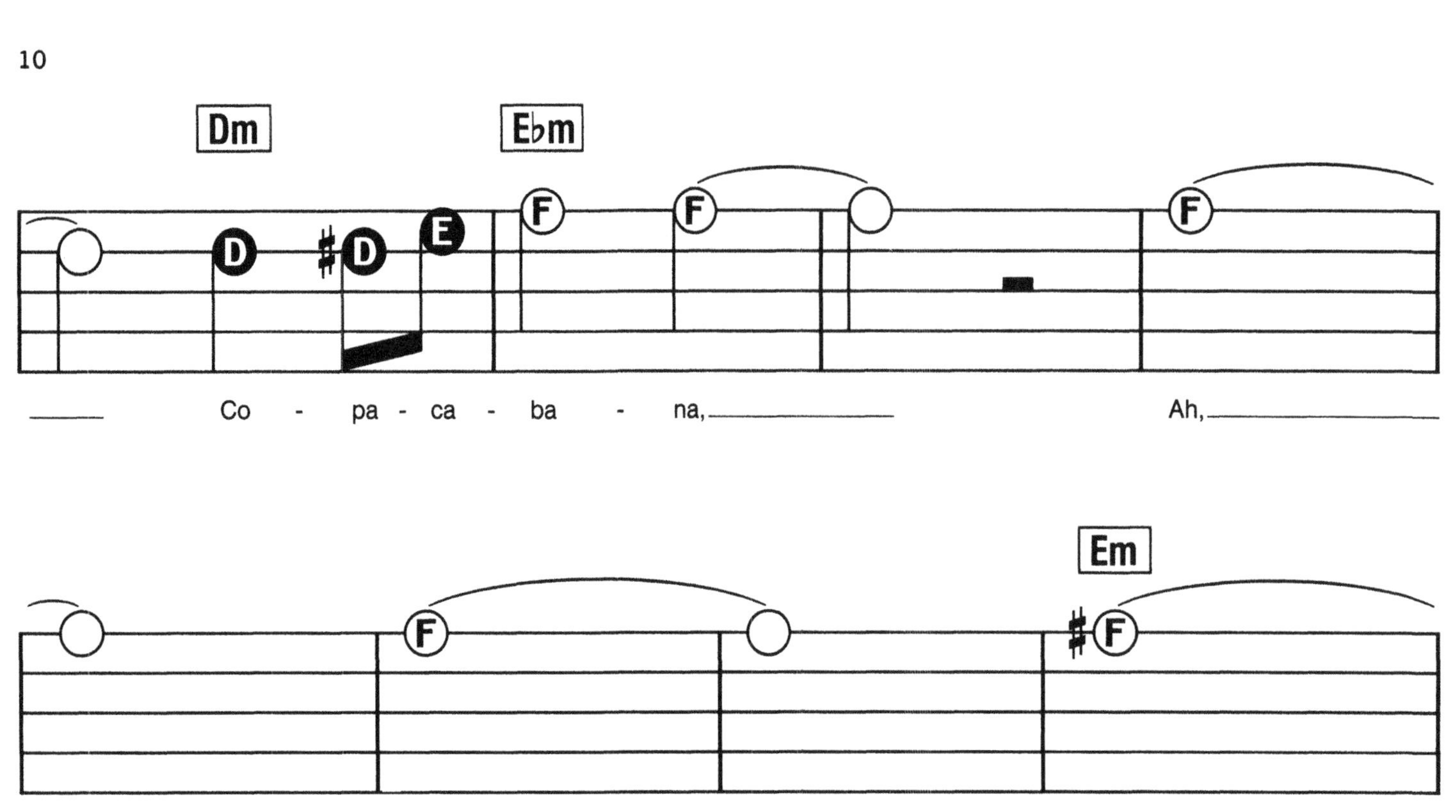
Dm
Eb m
D
♯D
E
F
F
F
Co - pa - ca - ba - na,
Ah,
Em
F
F
♯F
Ah,
Ah,

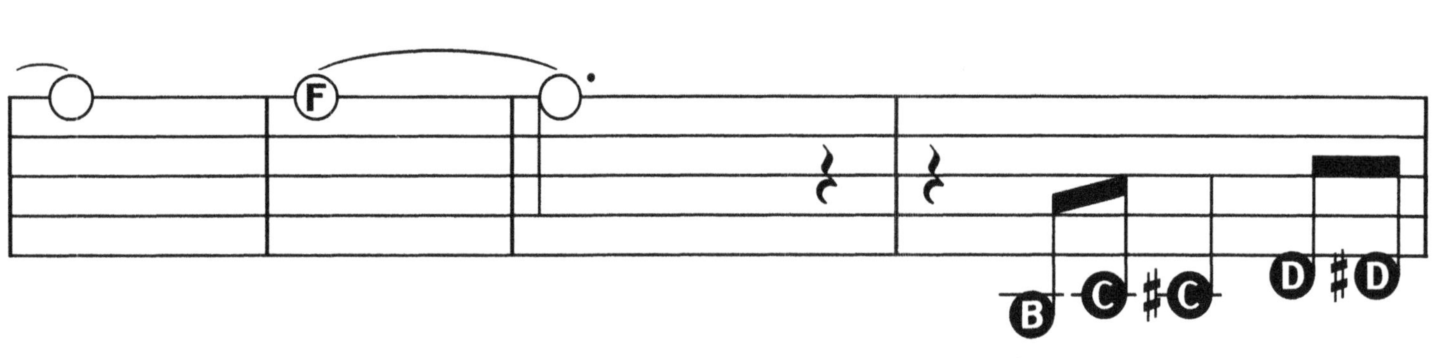
F
B
C
♯C
D
♯D
Ah.
Ah.

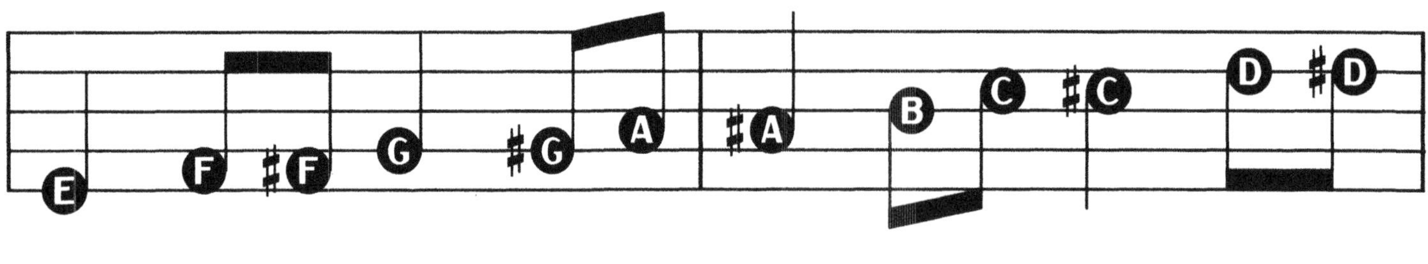
E
F
♯F
G
♯G
A
♯A
B
C
♯C
D
♯D

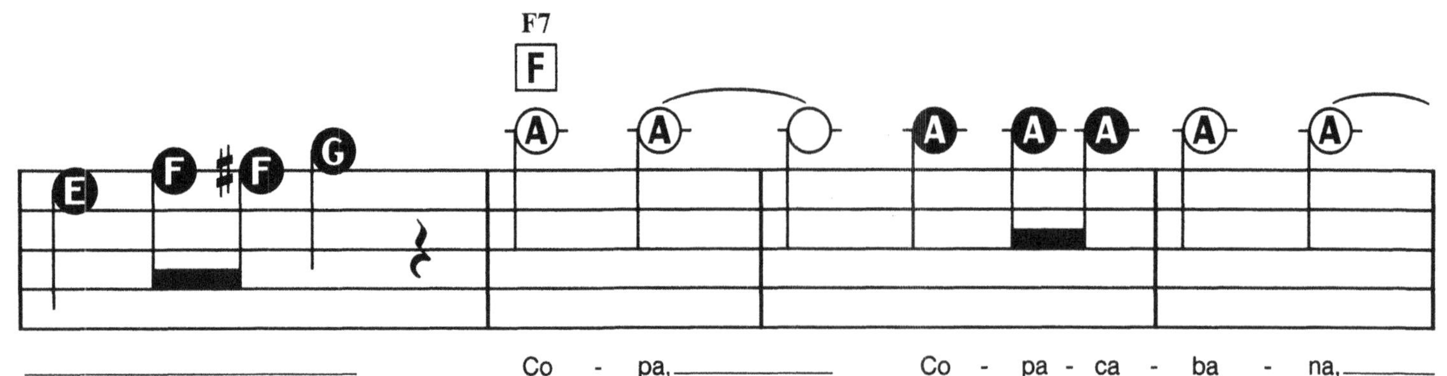
F7
F
E
F
♯F
G
A
A
A
A
A
A
A
Co - pa,
Co - pa - ca - ba - na,

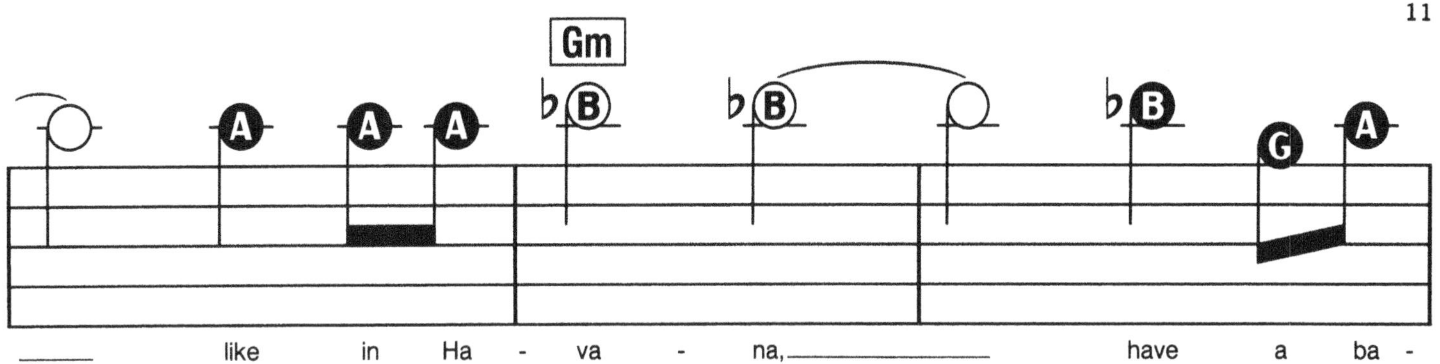
Gm
like in Ha - va - na,
have a ba -

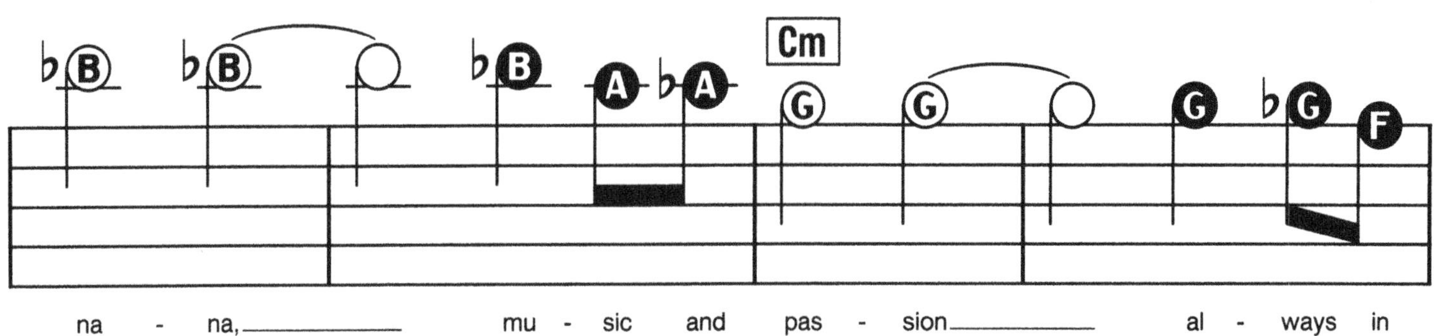
Cm
na - na,
mu - sic and pas - sion
al - ways in

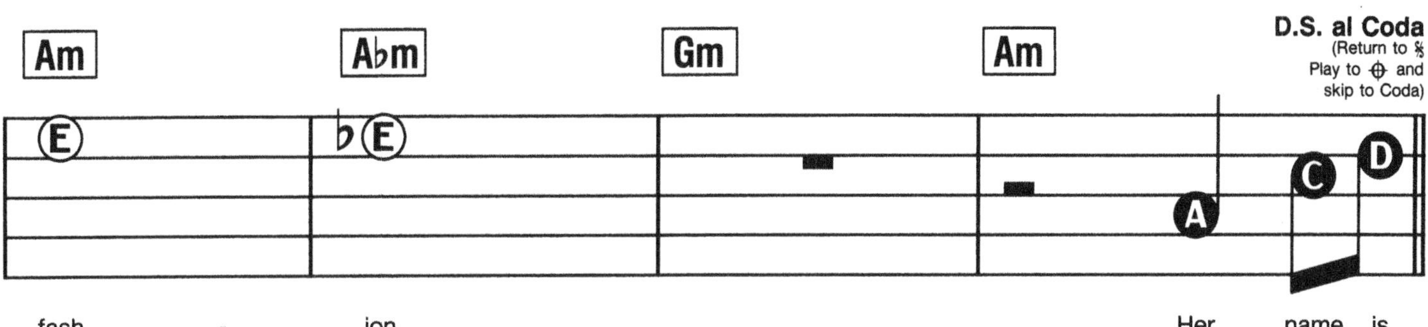
Am
A♭m
Gm
Am
D.S. al Coda
(Return to 𝄋
Play to ⊕ and
skip to Coda)
fash - ion.
Her name is

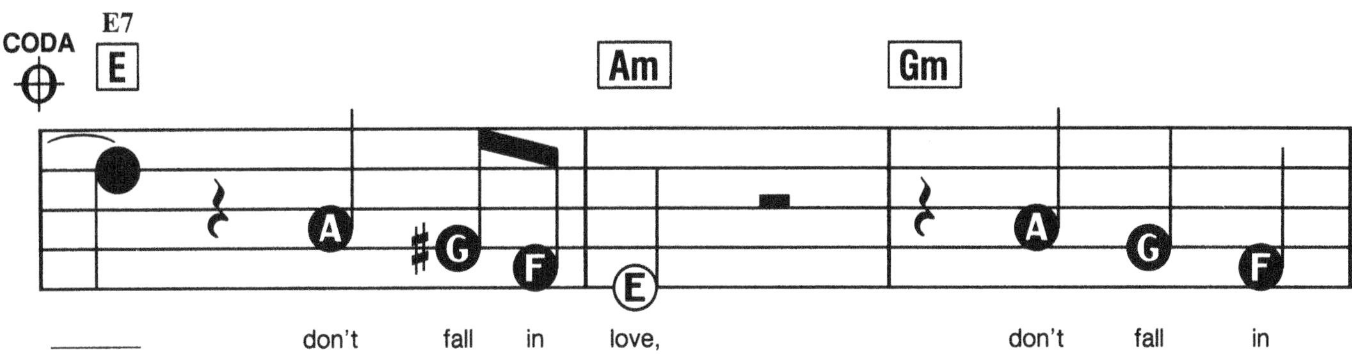
CODA
E7
E
Am
Gm
don't fall in love,
don't fall in

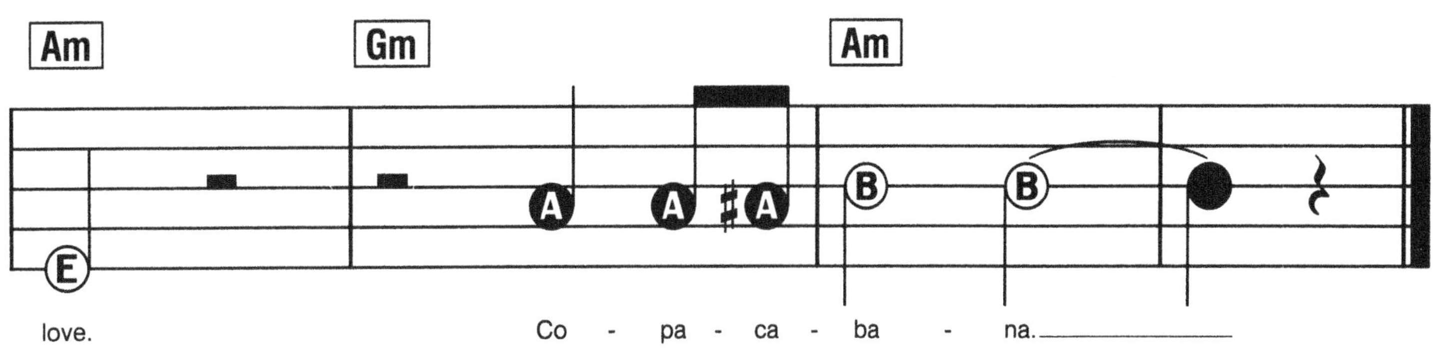
Am
Gm
Am
love.
Co - pa - ca - ba - na.

Could It Be Magic

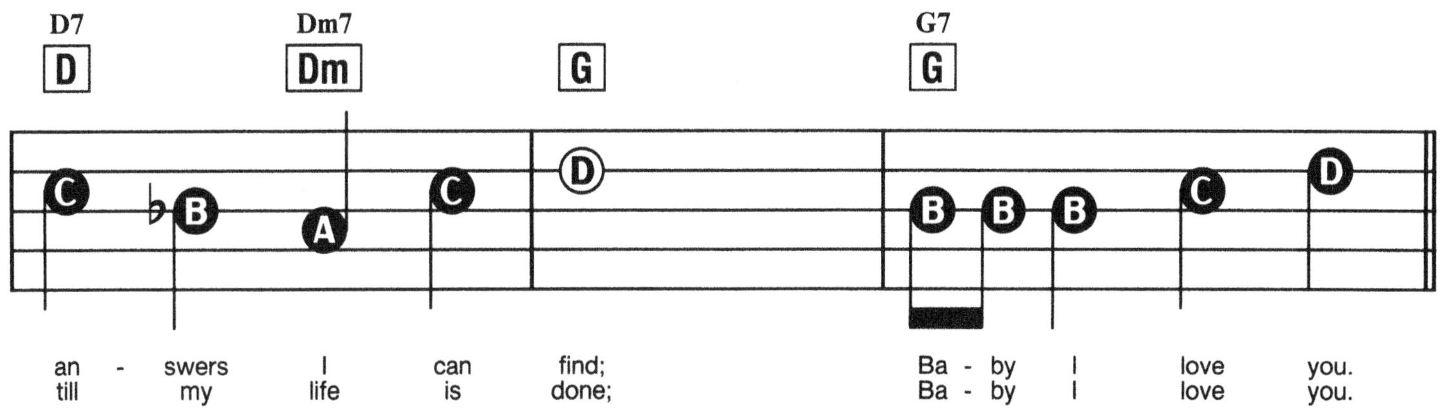
D7
D
Dm7
Dm
G
G7
G
an - swers I can find;
till my life is done;
Ba - by I love you.
Ba - by I love you.

Cm
Ab
G
Come,
Now,
come,
now,
come in - to my
now and hold on

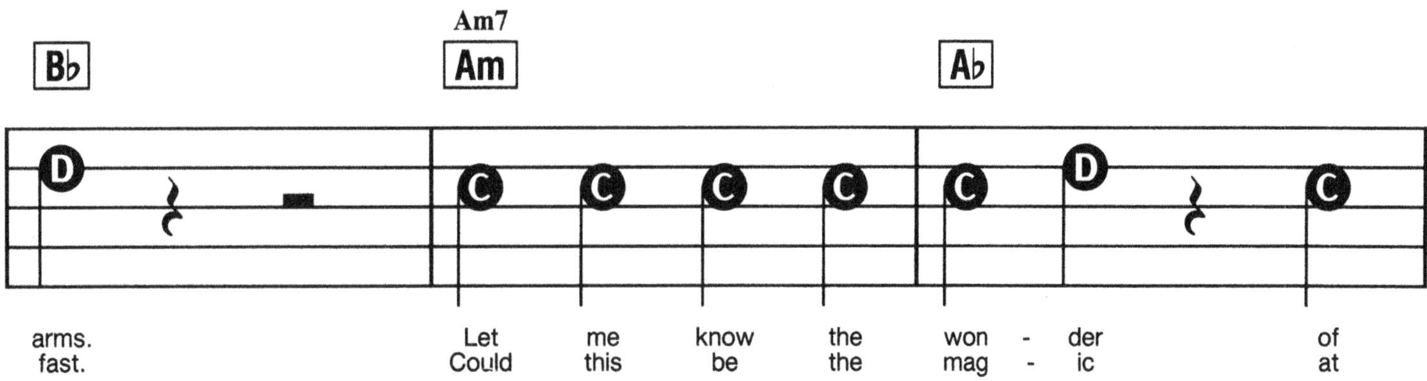
Bb
Am7
Am
Ab
arms.
fast.
Let me know the won - der of
Could this be the mag - ic at

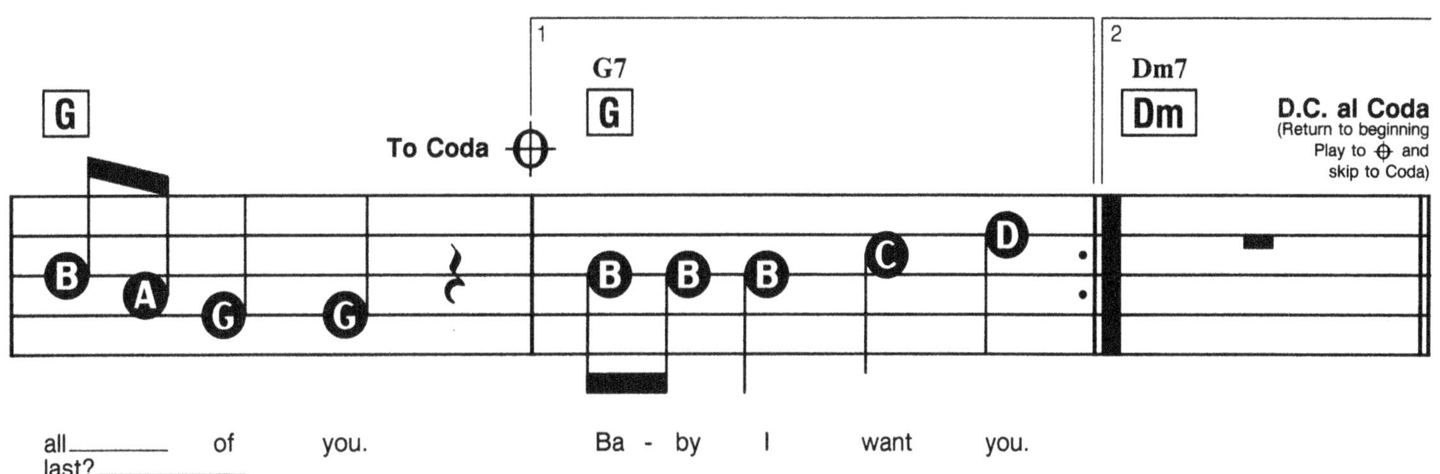
G
To Coda
1
G7
G
2
Dm7
Dm
D.C. al Coda
(Return to beginning
Play to ⊕ and
skip to Coda)
all of you.
last?
Ba - by I want you.

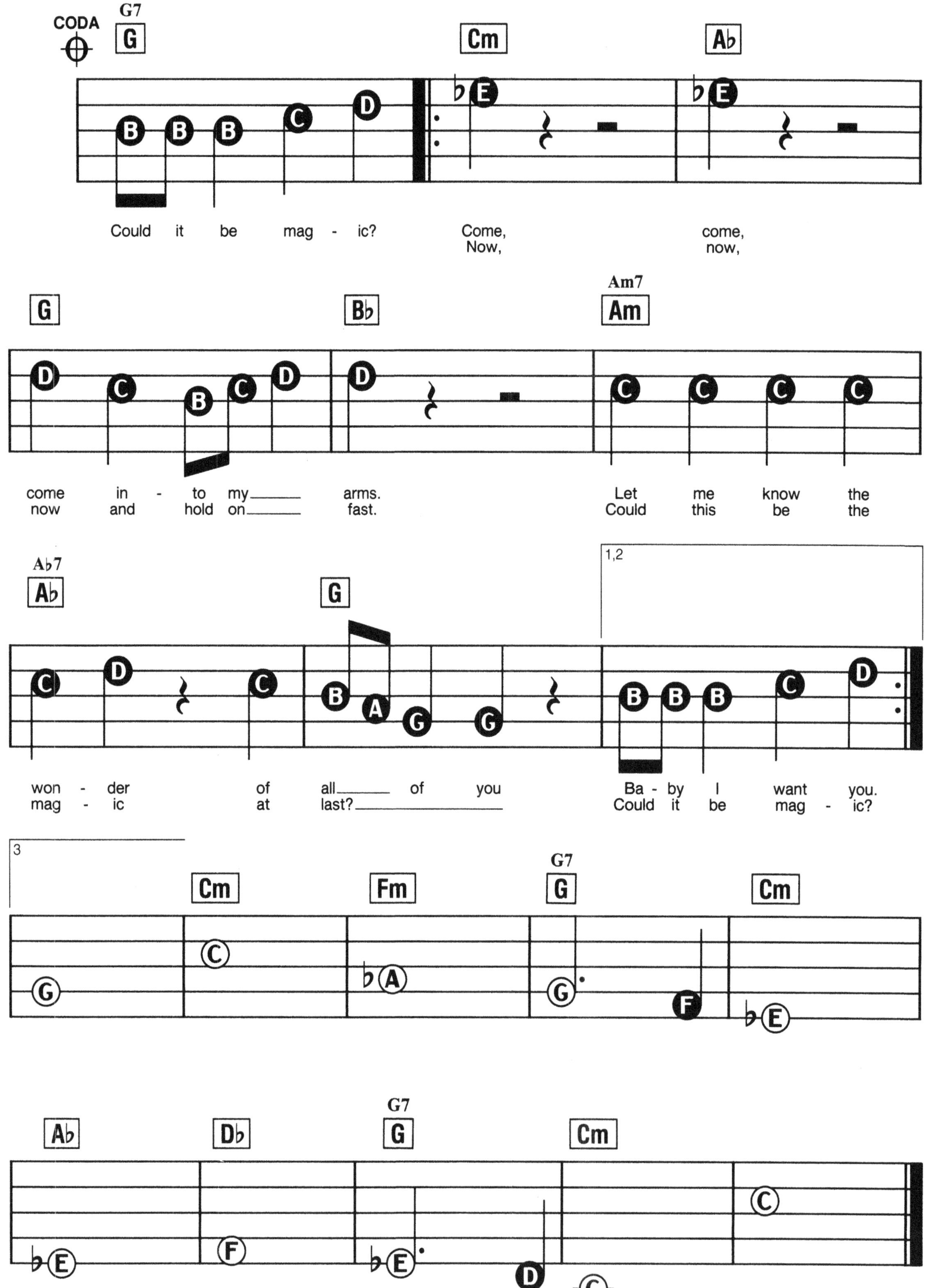
CODA
G7
G
B B B C D
Could it be mag - ic?
Cm
E
Come,
Now,
Ab
E
come,
now,
G
D C B C D
come in - to my
now and hold on
Bb
D
arms.
fast.
Am7
Am
C C C C
Let me know the
Could this be the
Ab7
Ab
C D C
won - der of
mag - ic at
G
B A G G
all of you
last?
1,2
B B B C D
Ba - by I want you.
Could it be mag - ic?
3
G
Cm
C
Fm
A
G7
G
G F
Cm
E
Ab
E
Db
F
G7
G
E D
Cm
C C

I Made It Through The Rain

Registration 3
Rhythm: Ballad

Music by Gerard Kenny
Lyrics by Drey Shepperd, Barry Manilow,
Jack Feldman and Bruce Sussman

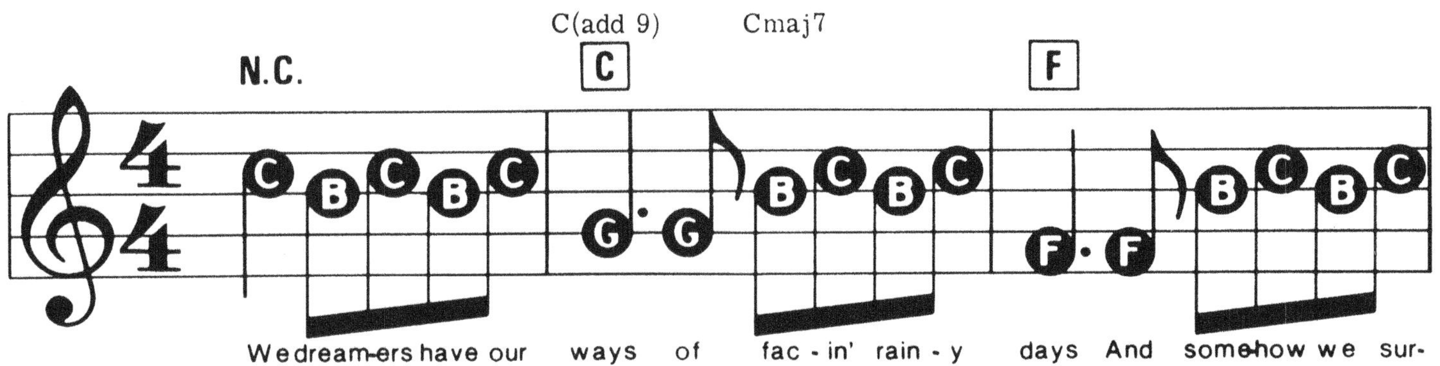

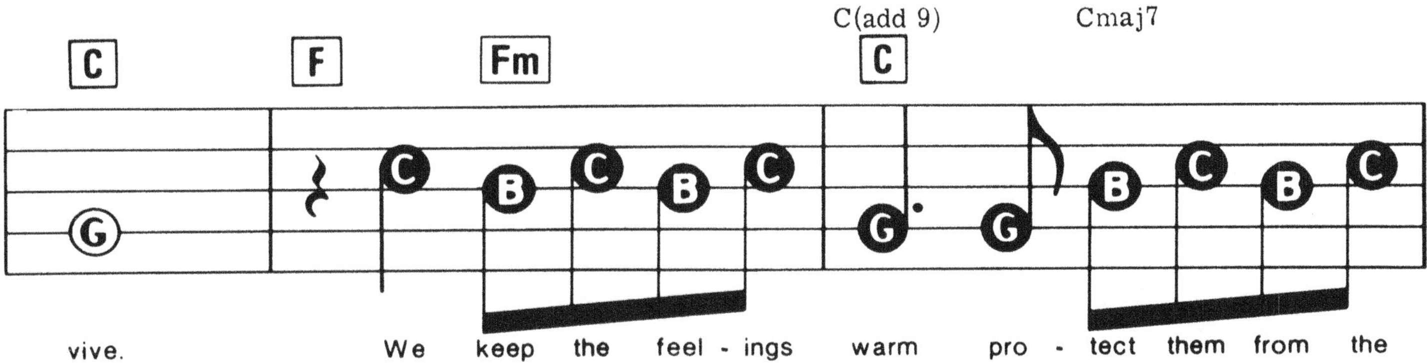

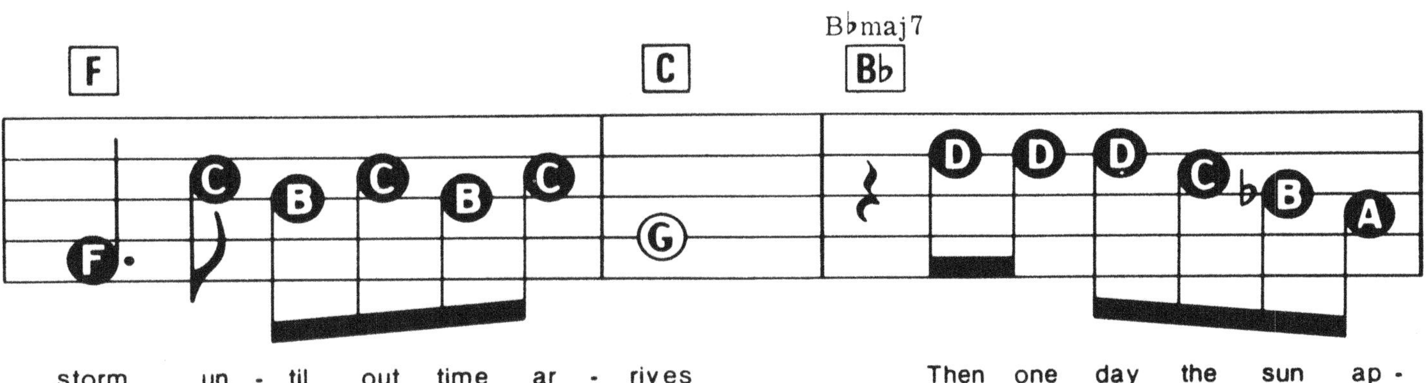

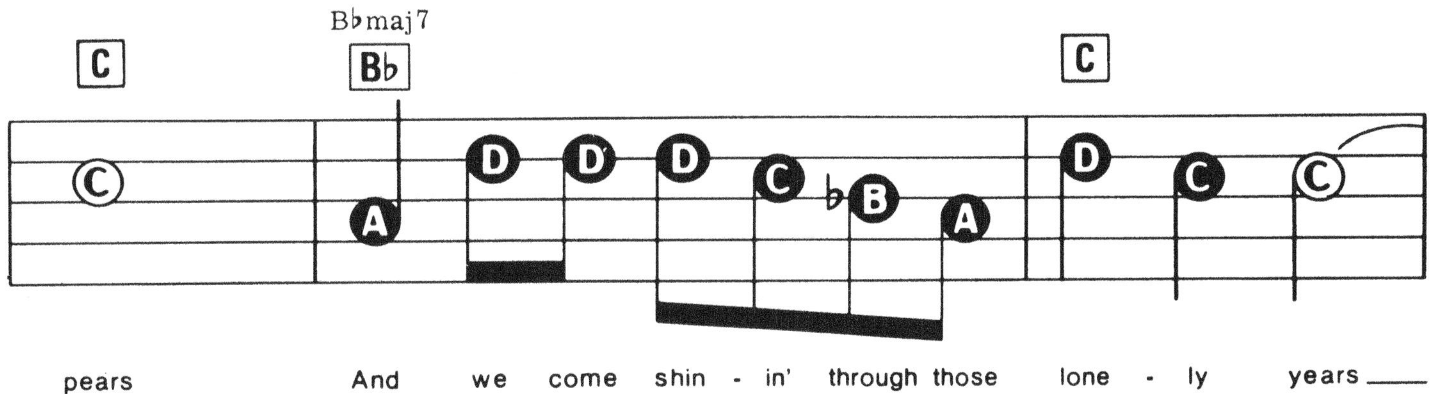

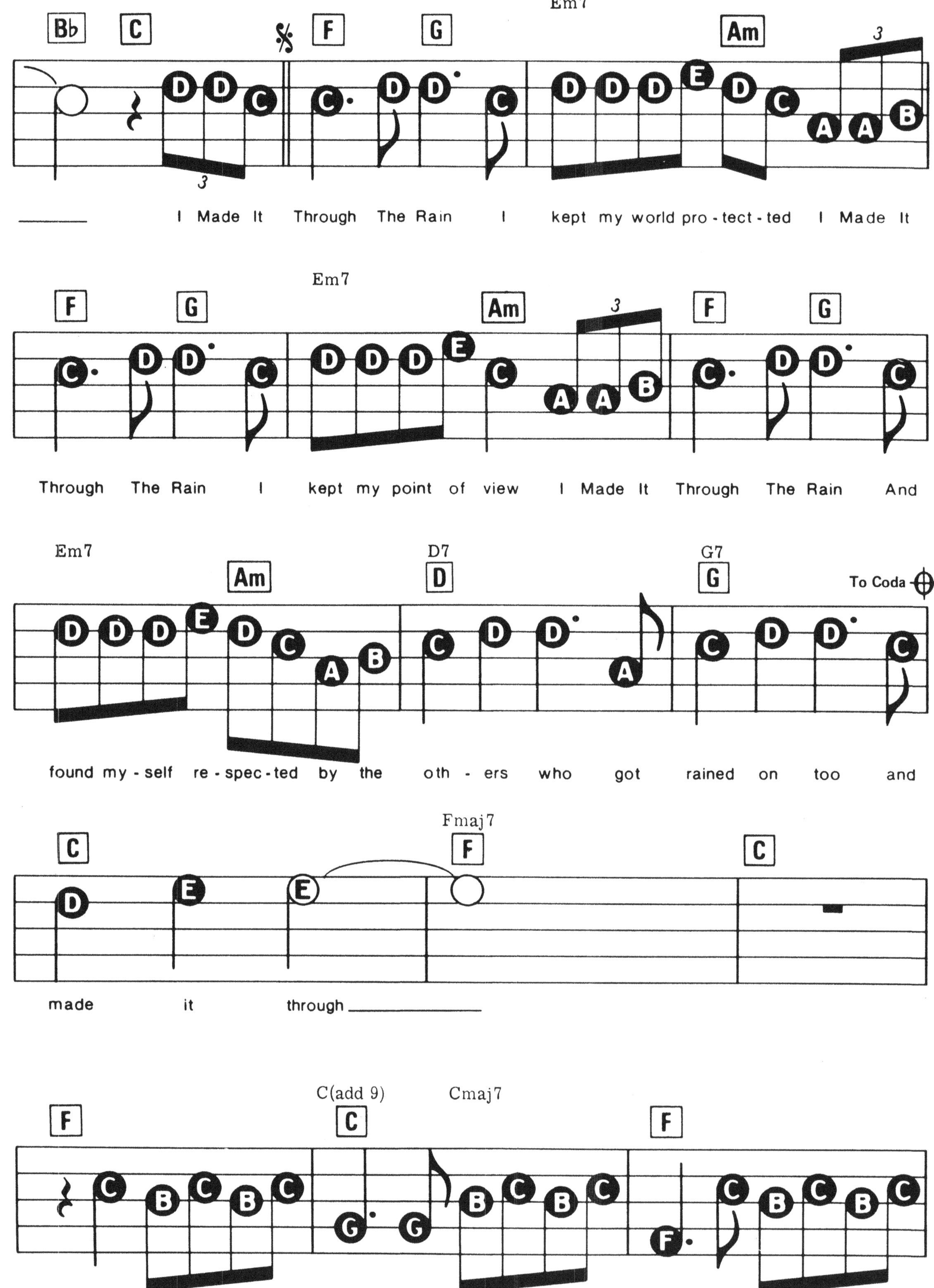
Bb C F G Em7 Am
I Made It Through The Rain I kept my world pro - tect - ted I Made It
F G Em7 Am F G
Through The Rain I kept my point of view I Made It Through The Rain And
Em7 Am D7 D G7 G
To Coda
found my - self re - spec - ted by the oth - ers who got rained on too and
C Fmaj7 F C
made it through
F C(add 9) C Cmaj7 F
When friends are hard to find And life seems so un - kind some-times you feel a -

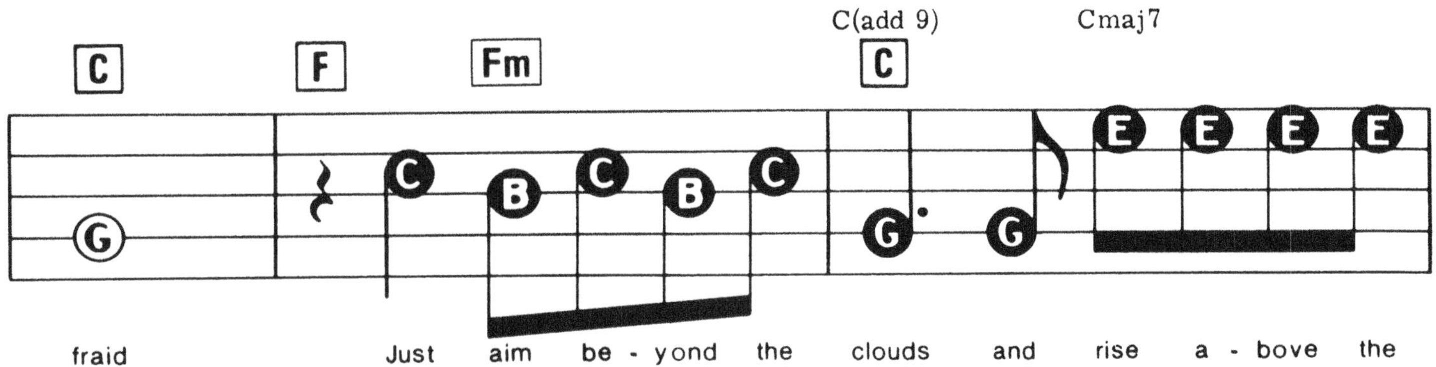
C(add 9)
Cmaj7
C
F
Fm
C
G
C B C B C
G G E E E E
fraid
Just aim be - yond the clouds and rise a - bove the

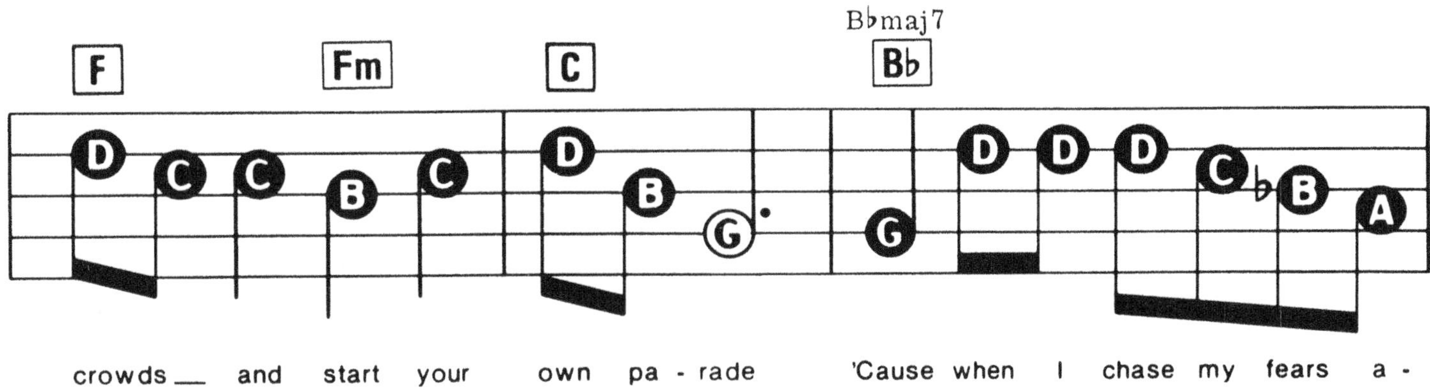
B♭maj7
F
Fm
C
B♭
D C C B C
D B G
G D D D C ♭B A
crowds ___ and start your own pa - rade 'Cause when I chase my fears a -

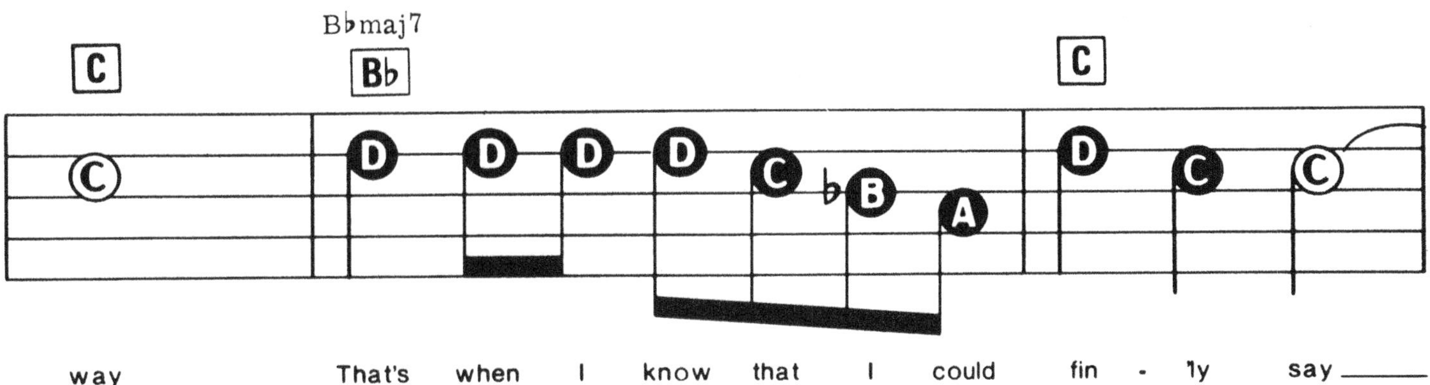
B♭maj7
C
B♭
C
C
D D D D C ♭B A
D C C
way That's when I know that I could fin - 'ly say ______

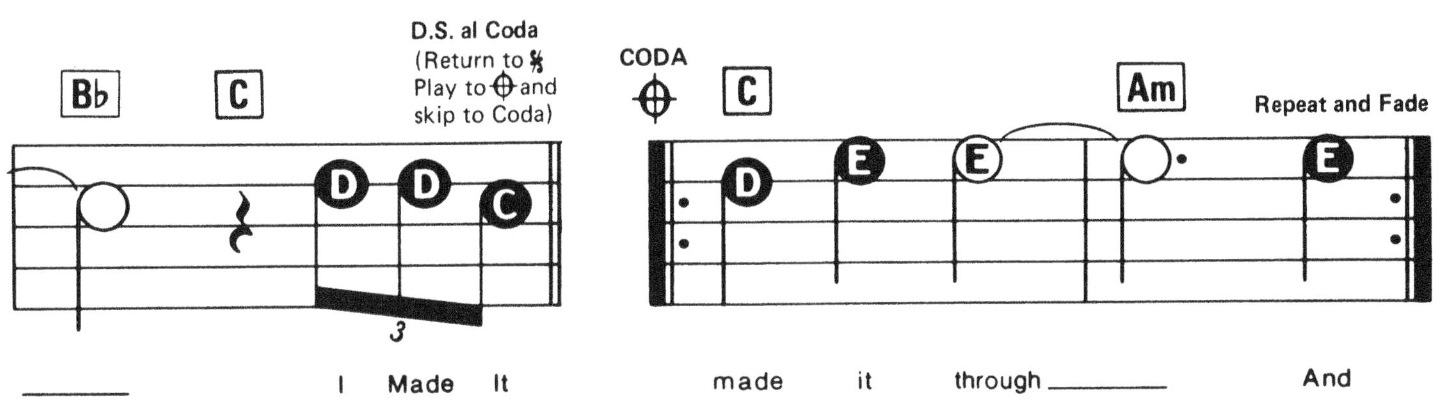
D.S. al Coda
(Return to 𝄋
Play to ⊕ and
skip to Coda)
CODA
B♭
C
C
Am
Repeat and Fade
D D C
3
D E E E
______ I Made It
made it through ________ And

Daybreak

Registration: 5
Rhythm: Fox Trot or Swing

Words by Adrienne Anderson
Music by Barry Manilow

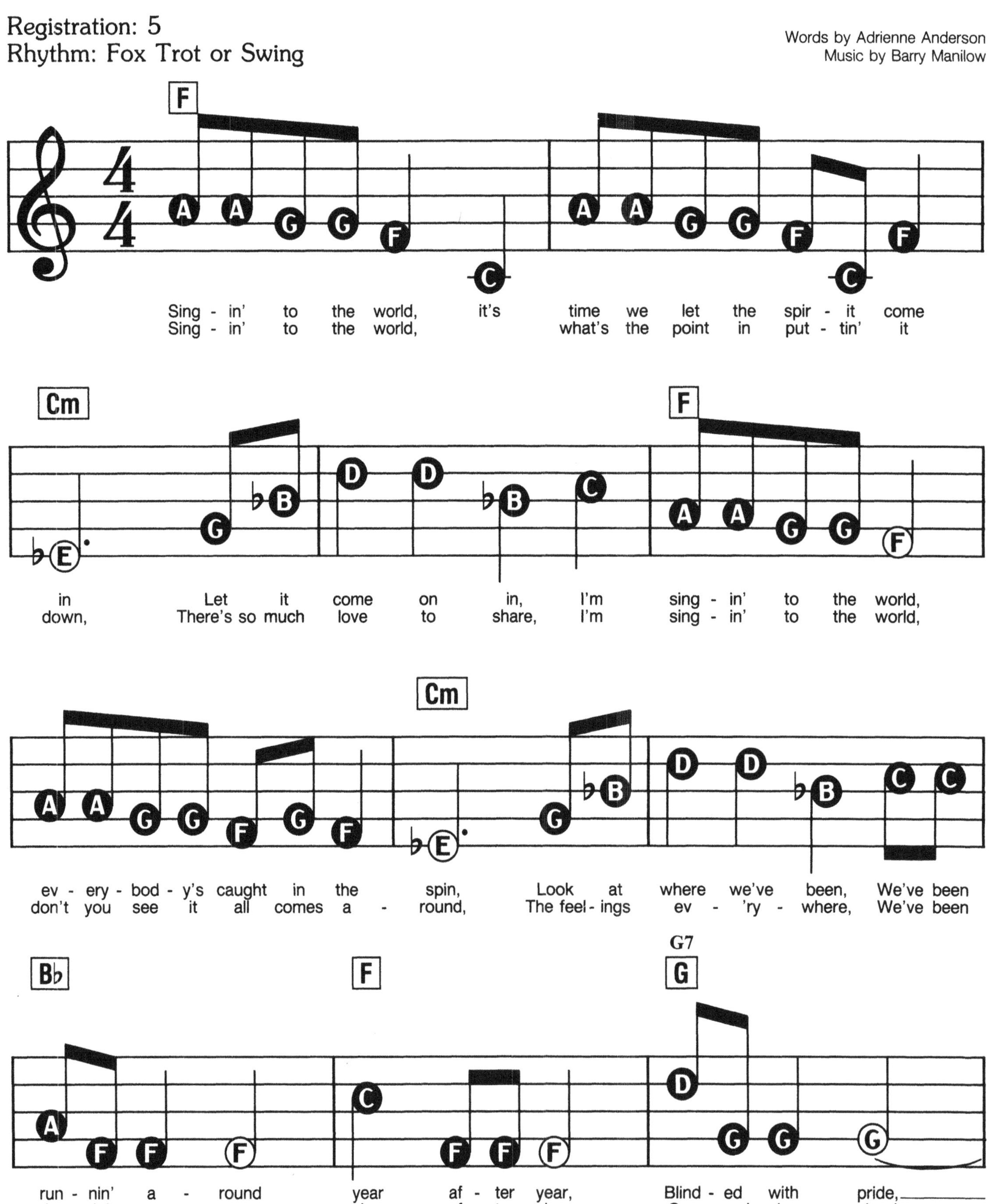

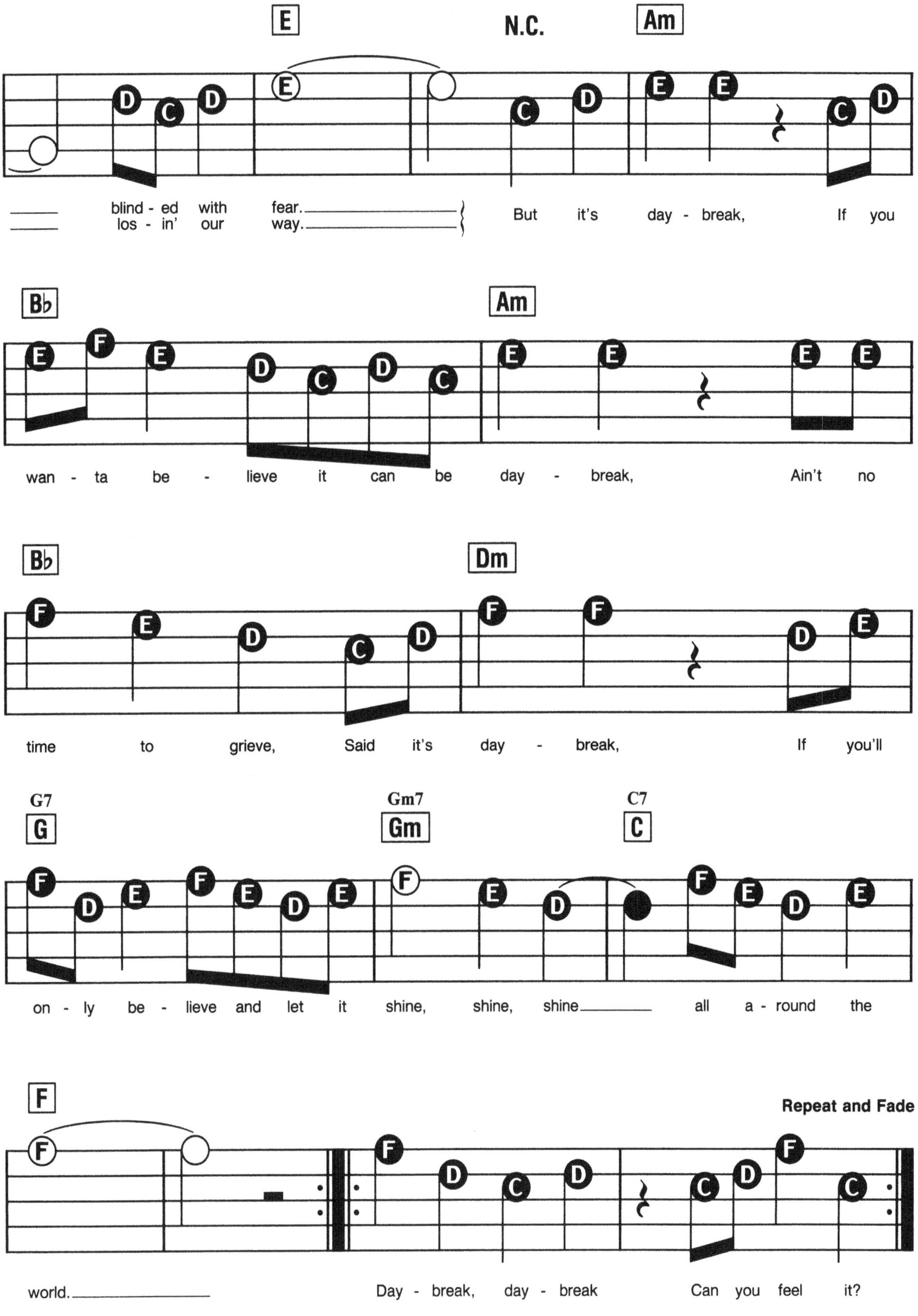

E N.C. Am

blind - ed with fear. But it's day - break, If you
los - in' our way.

Bb Am

wan - ta be - lieve it can be day - break, Ain't no

Bb Dm

time to grieve, Said it's day - break, If you'll

G7 Gm7 C7
G Gm C

on - ly be - lieve and let it shine, shine, shine all a - round the

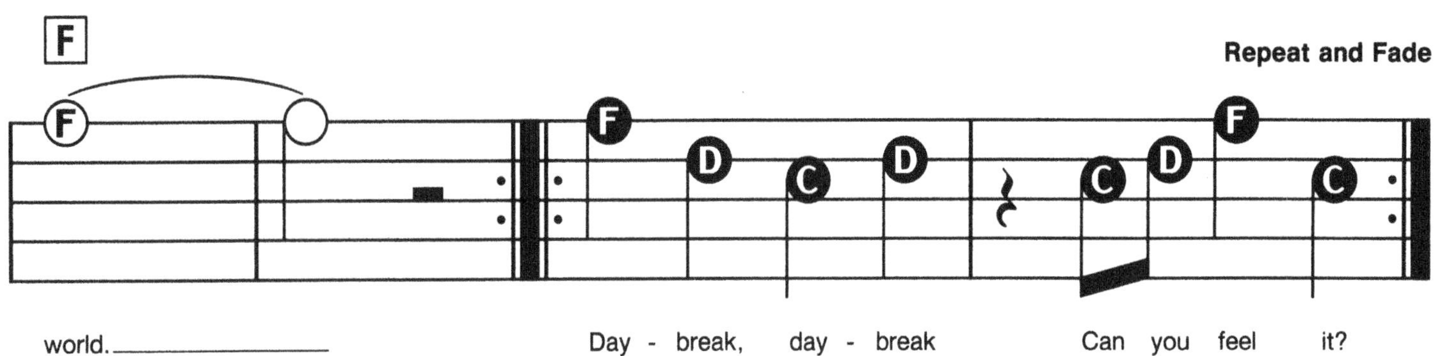

Even Now

Registration: 5
Rhythm: Rock

Words by Marty Panzer
Music by Barry Manilow

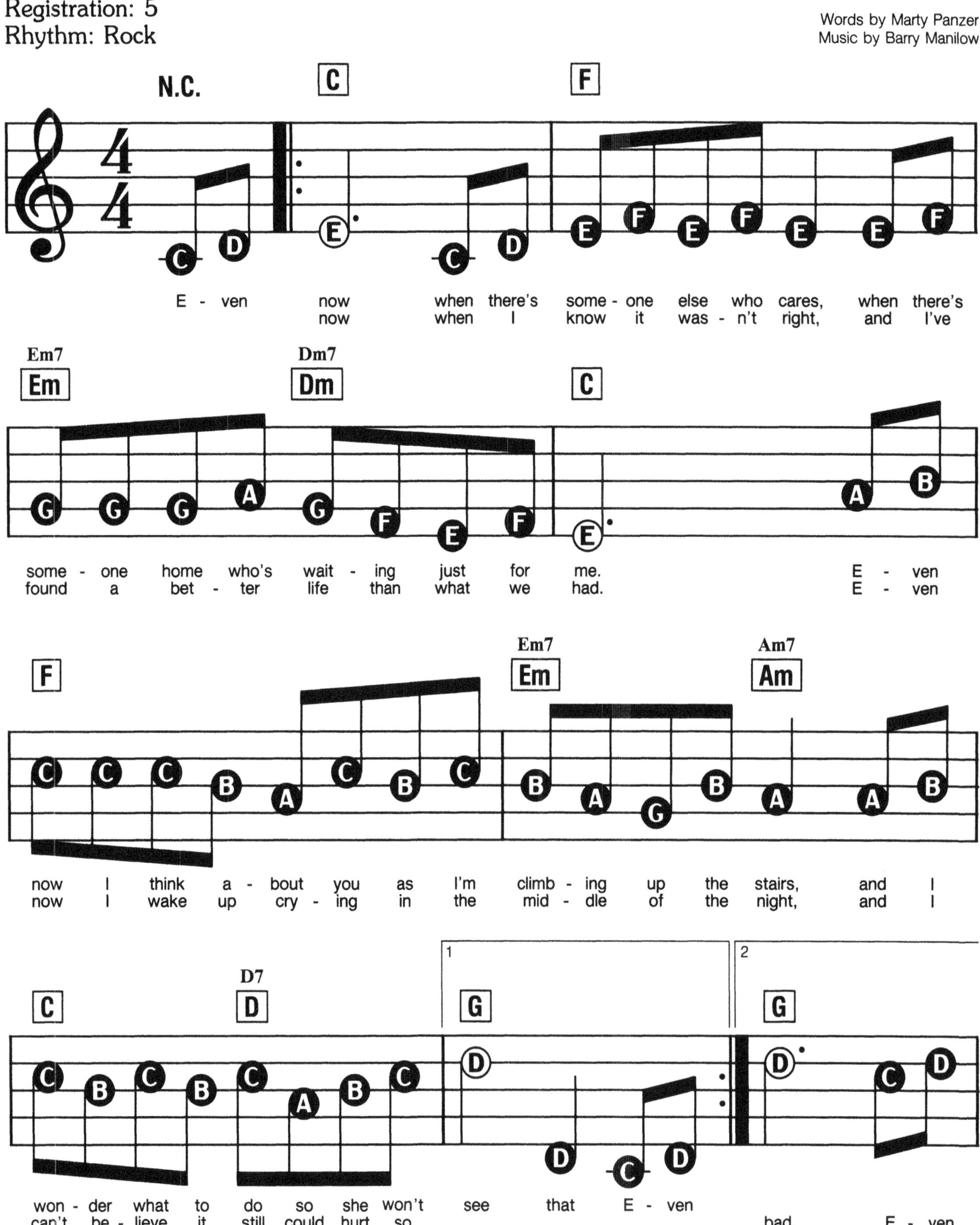

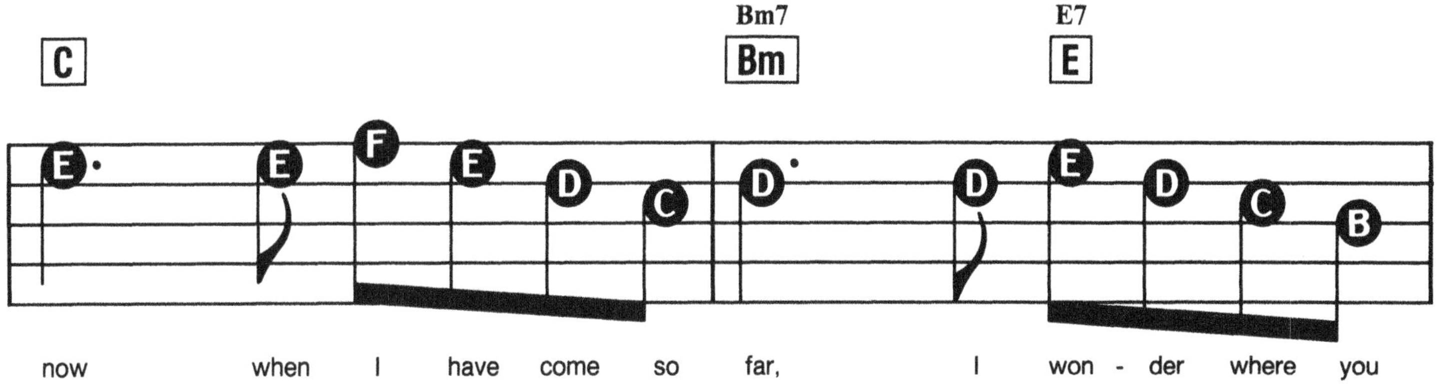
Bm7
E7
C
Bm
E
E
E
F
E
D
C
D
D
E
D
C
B
now when I have come so far, I won - der where you

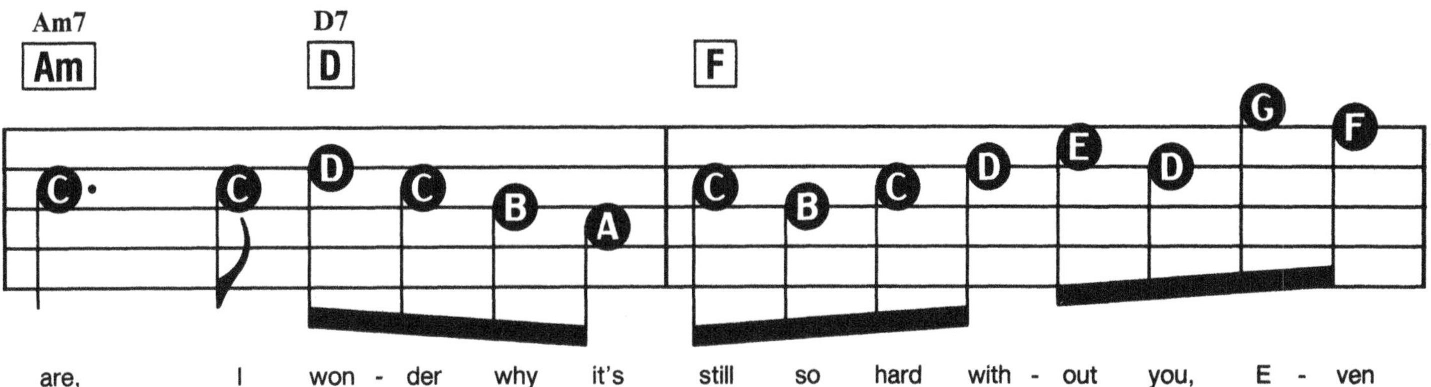
Am7
D7
Am
D
F
C
C
D
C
B
A
C
B
C
D
E
D
G
F
are, I won - der why it's still so hard with - out you, E - ven

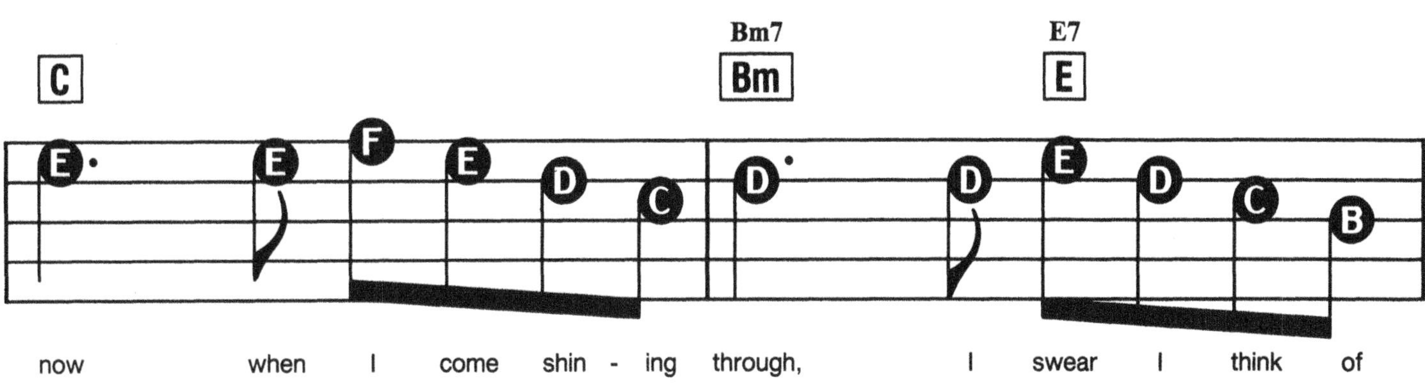
Bm7
E7
C
Bm
E
E
E
F
E
D
C
D
D
E
D
C
B
now when I come shin - ing through, I swear I think of

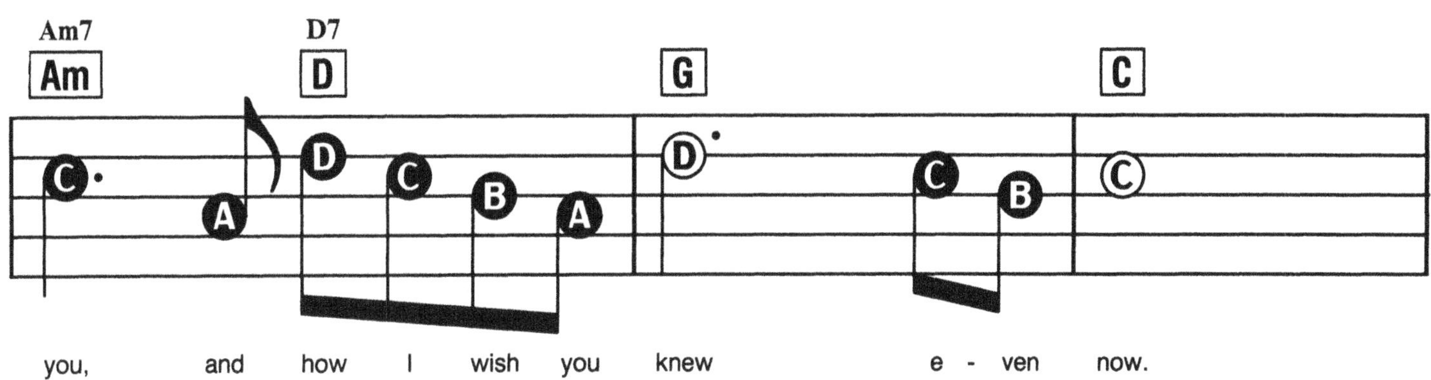
Am7
D7
Am
D
G
C
C
A
D
C
B
A
D
C
B
C
you, and how I wish you knew e - ven now.

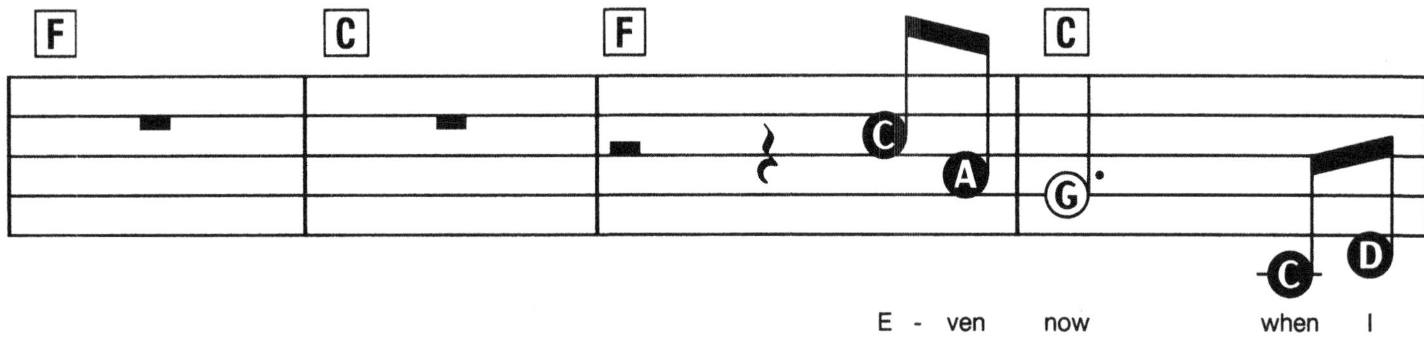
F
C
F
C
C
A
G
C
D
E - ven now when I

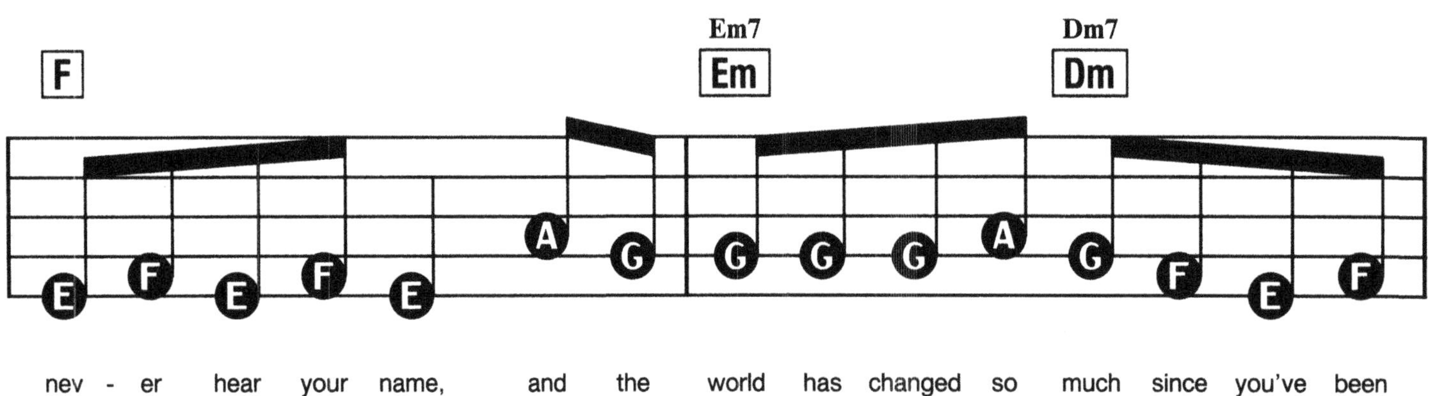
F
Em7
Em
Dm7
Dm
E F E F E A G G G G A G F E F
nev - er hear your name, and the world has changed so much since you've been

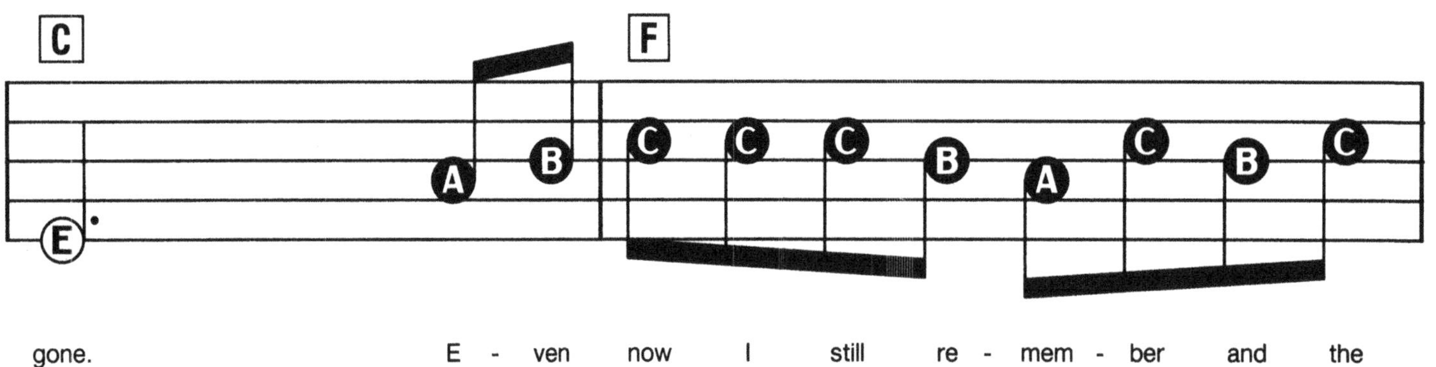
C
F
E A B C C C B A C B C
gone. E - ven now I still re - mem - ber and the

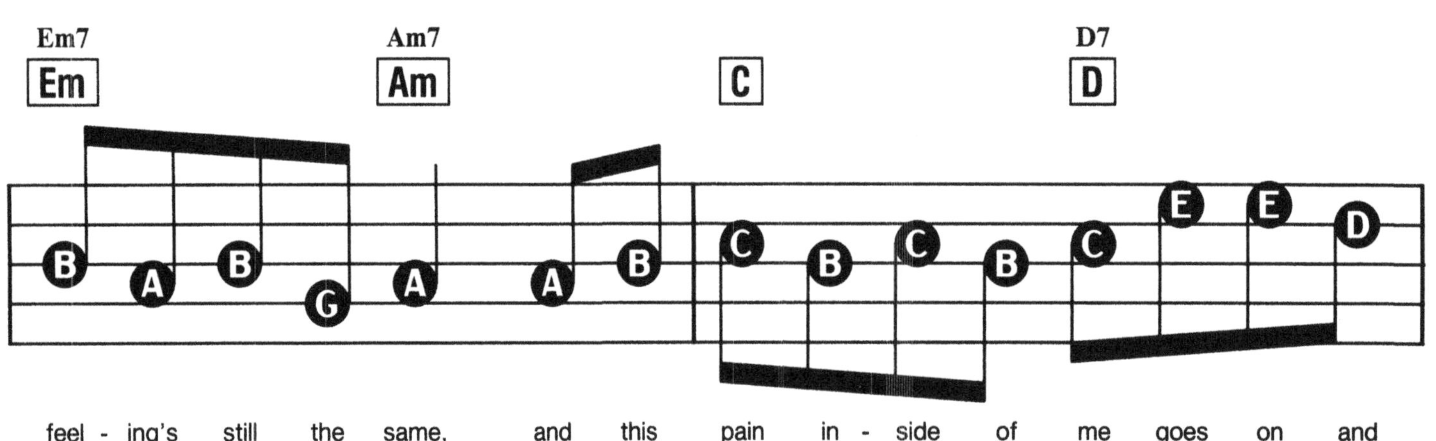
Em7
Em
Am7
Am
C
D7
D
B A B G A A B C B C B C E E D
feel - ing's still the same, and this pain in - side of me goes on and

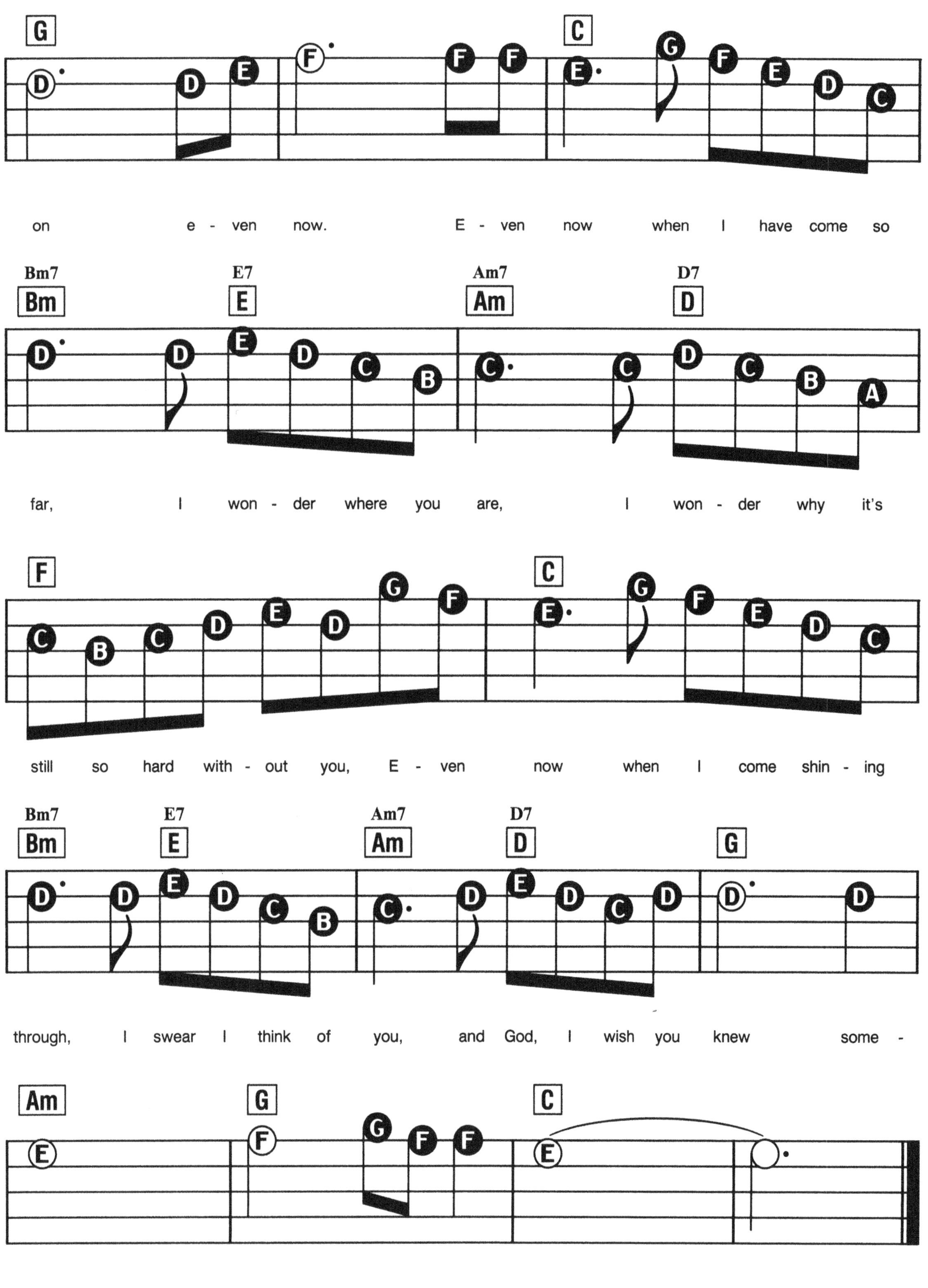
G
C
on e - ven now. E - ven now when I have come so
Bm7
E7
Am7
D7
far, I won - der where you are, I won - der why it's
F
C
still so hard with - out you, E - ven now when I come shin - ing
Bm7
E7
Am7
D7
G
through, I swear I think of you, and God, I wish you knew some -
Am
G
C
how e - ven now.

I Write The Songs

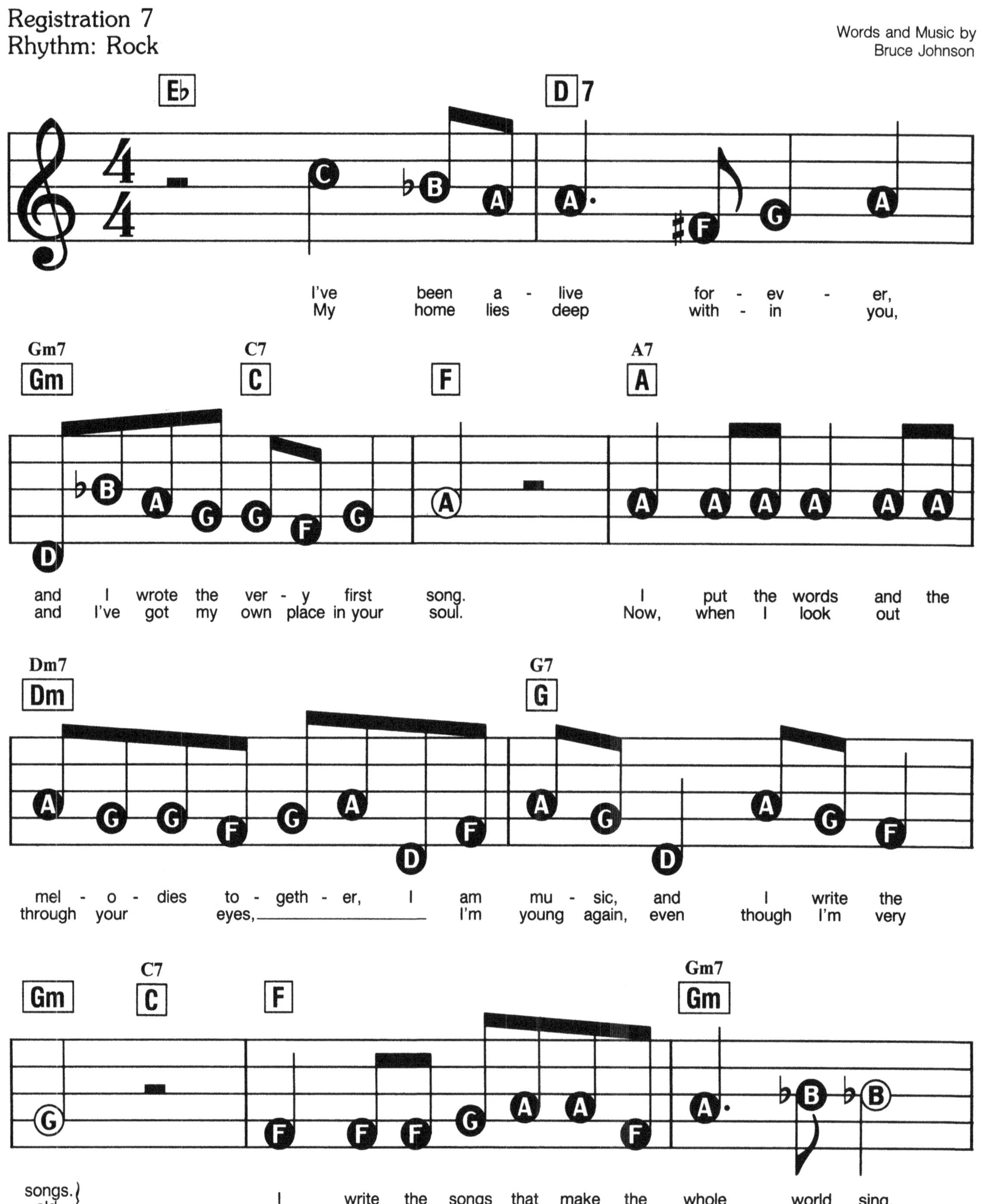

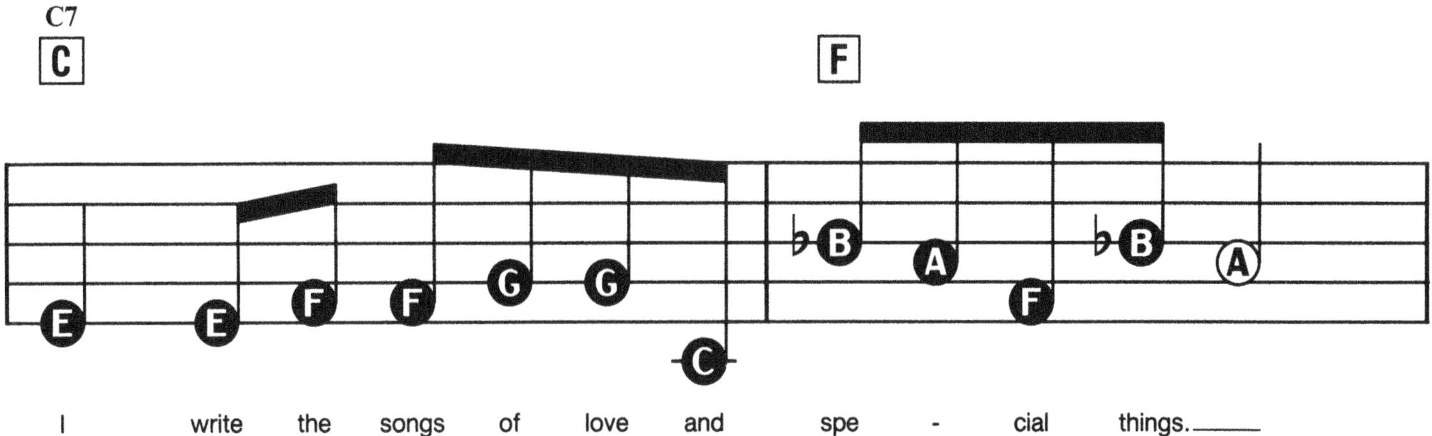
C7
C
F
E E F F G G C
♭B A F ♭B A
I write the songs of love and spe - cial things.

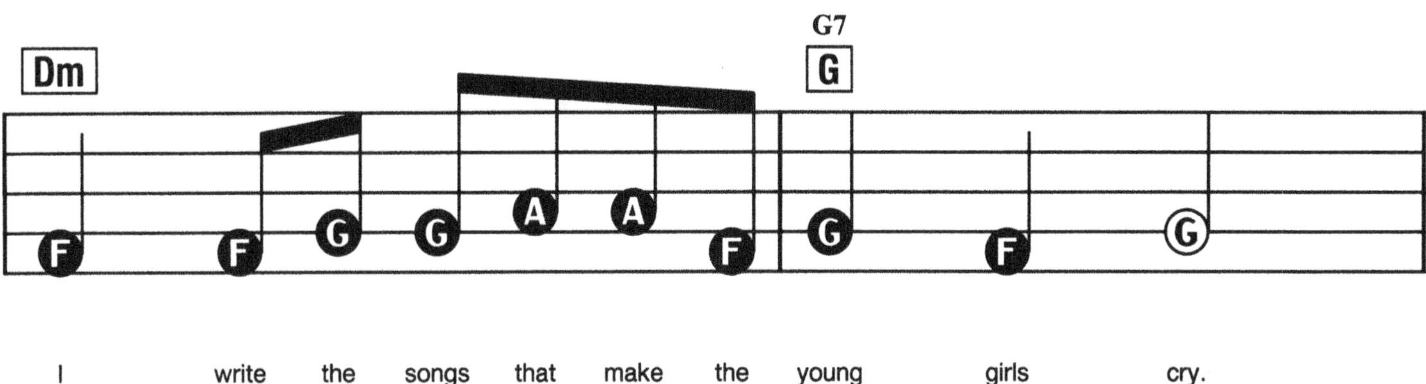
Dm
G7
G
F F G G A A F
G F G
I write the songs that make the young girls cry.

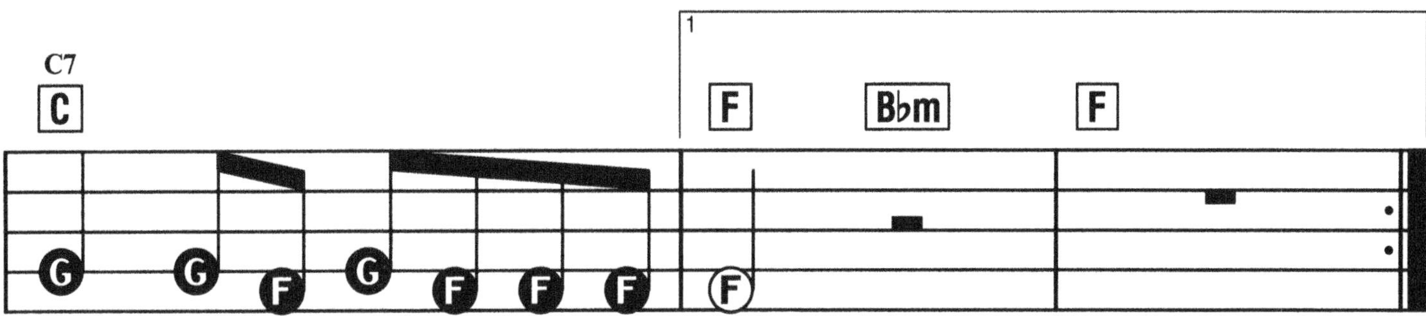
C7
C
1
F
B♭m
F
G G F G F F F
F
I write the songs, I write the songs.

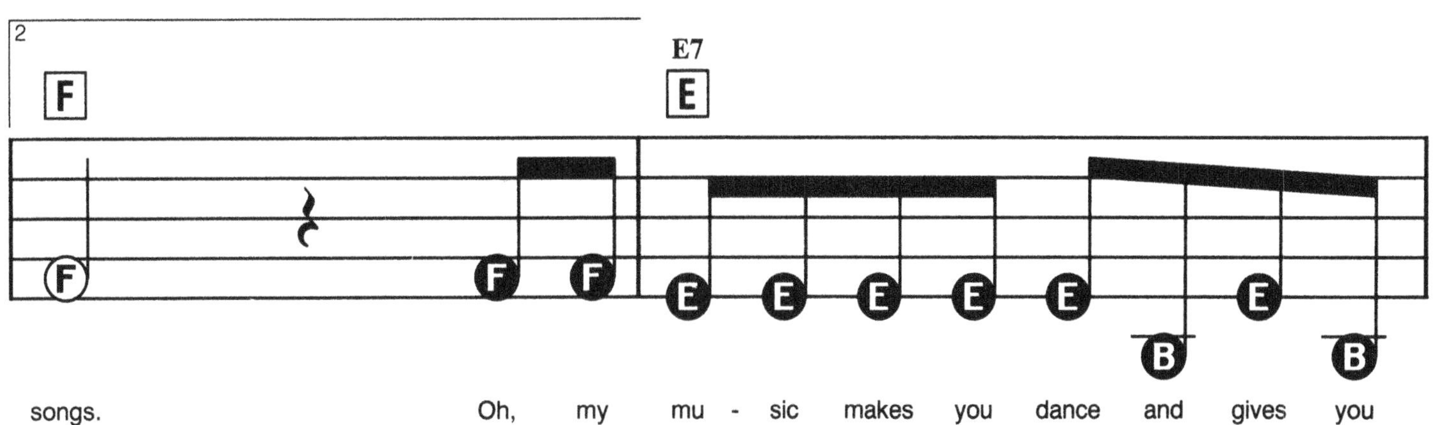
2
F
E7
E
F F F
E E E E E B E B
songs. Oh, my mu - sic makes you dance and gives you

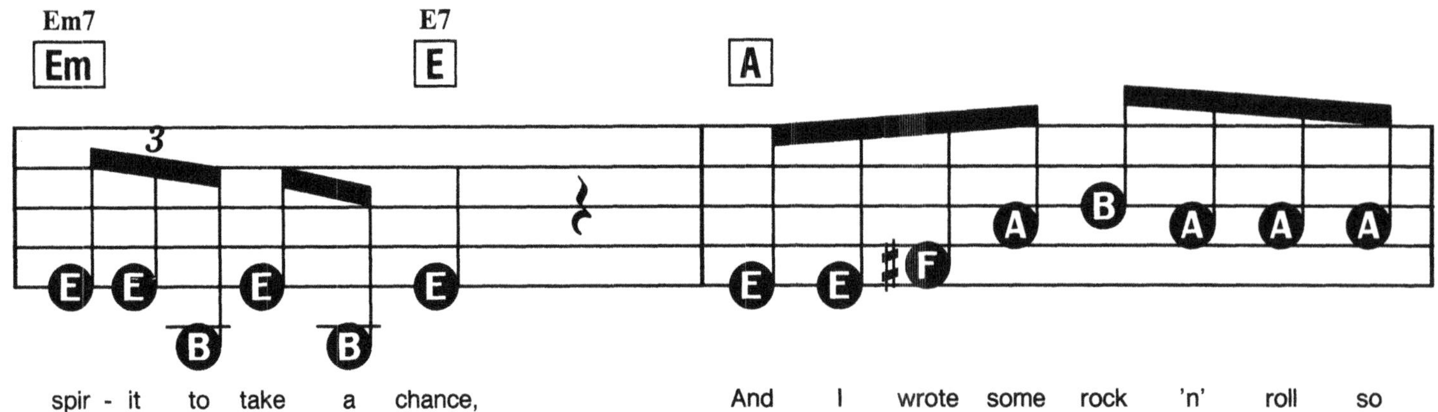
Em7
Em
E7
E
A
3
E E B E B E
E E F A B A A A
spir - it to take a chance,
And I wrote some rock 'n' roll so

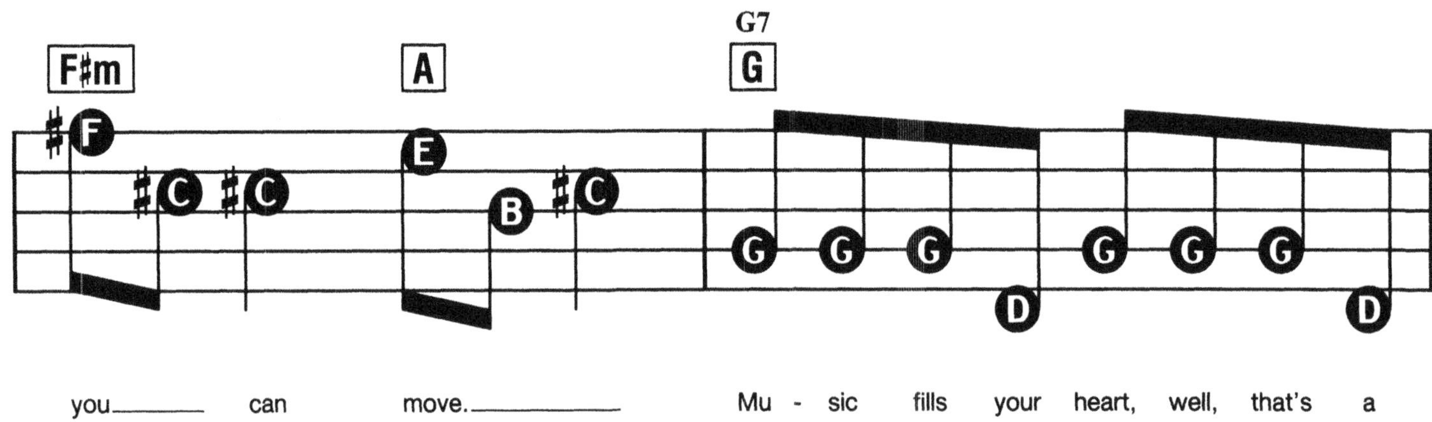
F♯m
A
G7
G
F C C E B C
G G G D G G G D
you can move.
Mu - sic fills your heart, well, that's a

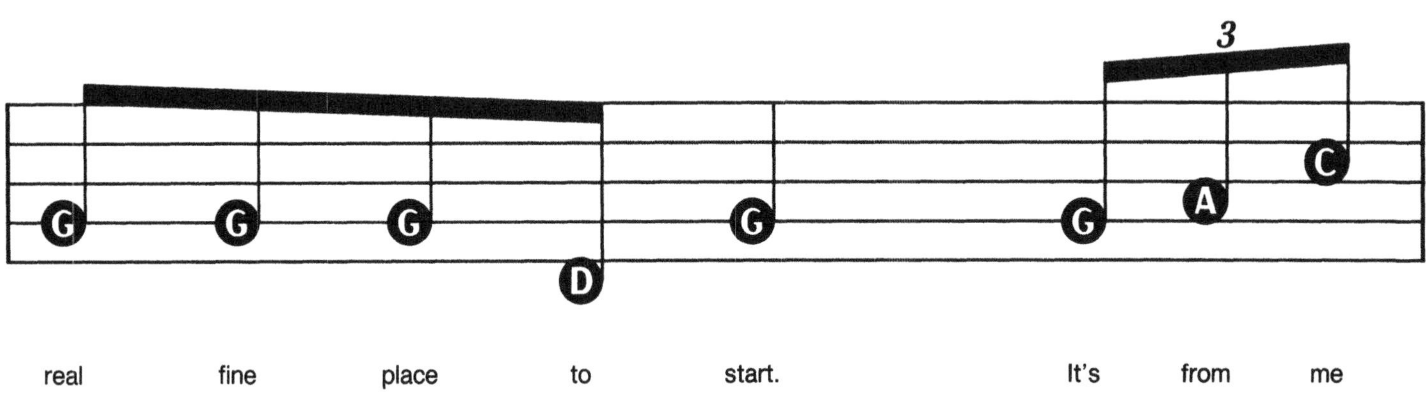
3
G G G D G G A C
real fine place to start. It's from me

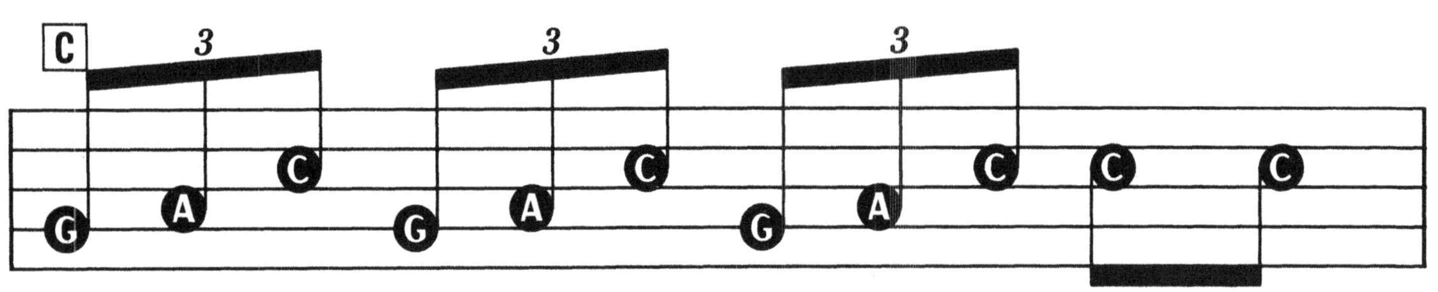
C
3
3
3
G A C G A C G A C C C
it's for you, it's from you, it's for me, it's a

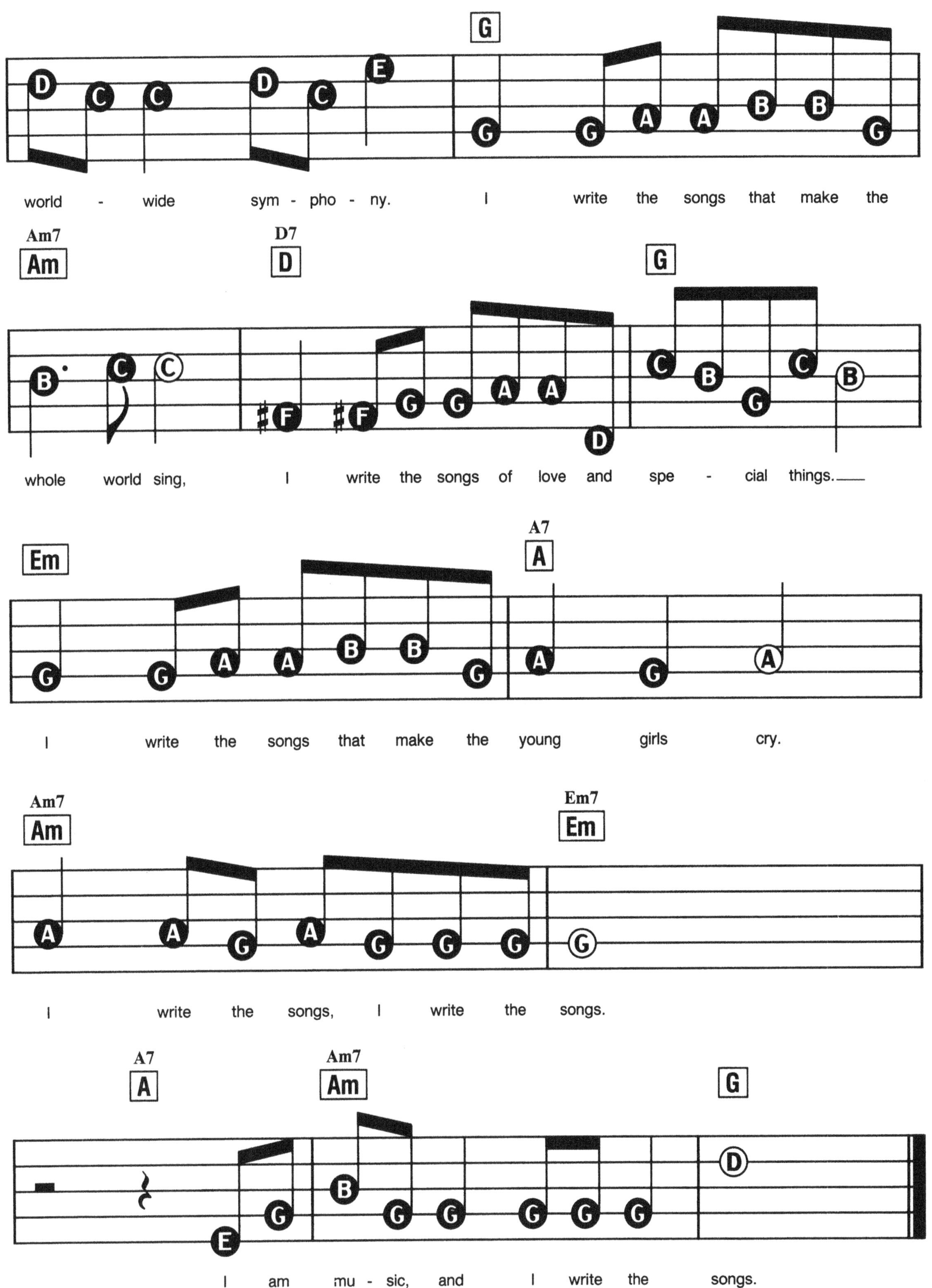
G
D
C
C
D
C
E
G
G
A
A
B
B
G
world - wide sym - pho - ny. I write the songs that make the
Am7
Am
D7
D
G
B
C
C
F
F
G
G
A
A
D
C
B
G
C
B
whole world sing, I write the songs of love and spe - cial things.
Em
A7
A
G
G
A
A
B
B
G
A
G
A
I write the songs that make the young girls cry.
Am7
Am
Em7
Em
A
A
G
A
G
G
G
G
I write the songs, I write the songs.
A7
A
Am7
Am
G
E
G
B
G
G
G
G
G
D
I am mu - sic, and I write the songs.

If I Should Love Again

Registration 1
Rhythm: Ballad or Rock

Words and Music by
Barry Manilow

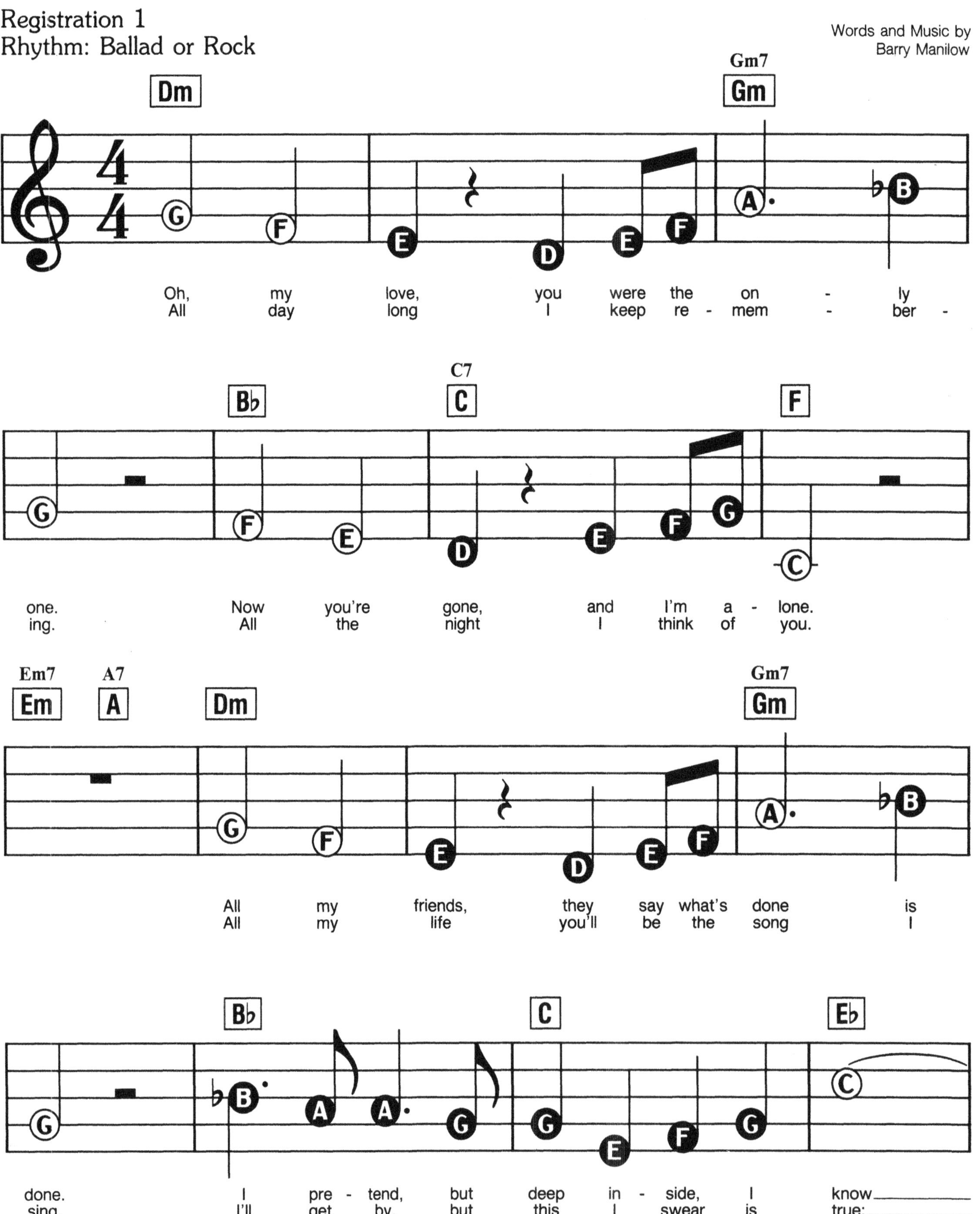

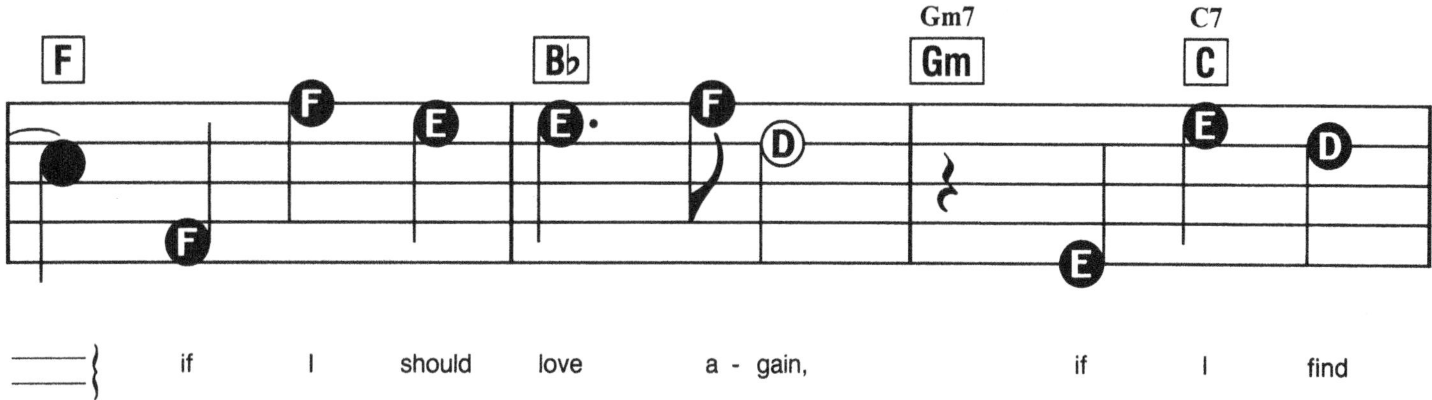
F
B♭
Gm7
Gm
C7
C
if I should love a - gain, if I find

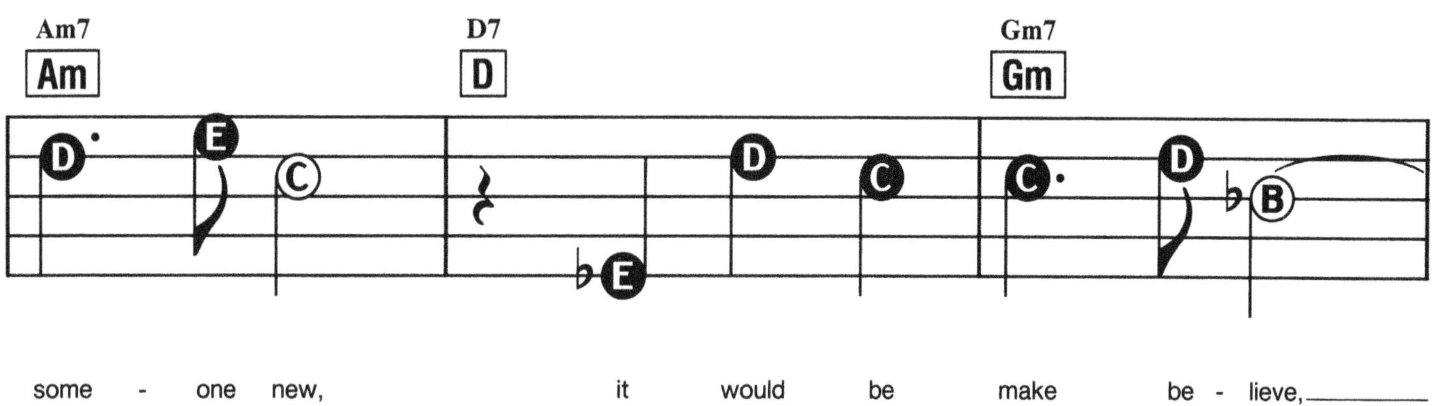
Am7
Am
D7
D
Gm7
Gm
some - one new, it would be make be - lieve,

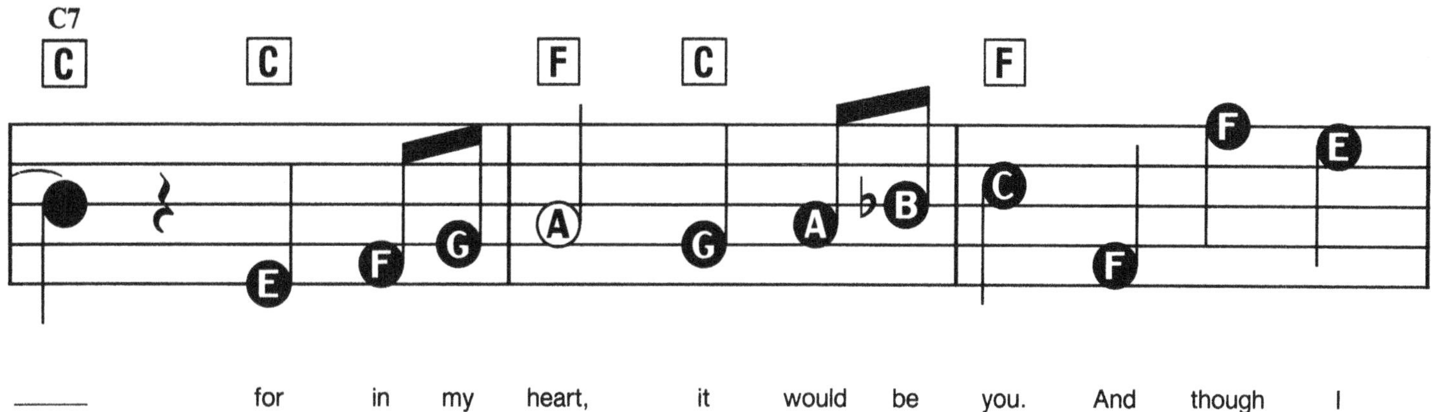
C7
C
C
F
C
F
for in my heart, it would be you. And though I

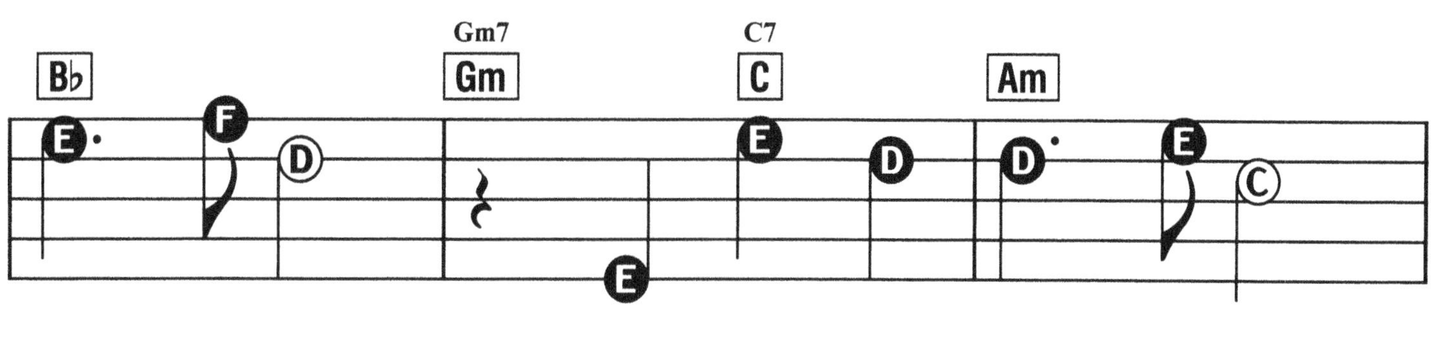
B♭
Gm7
Gm
C7
C
Am
hold her close and want her now and then,

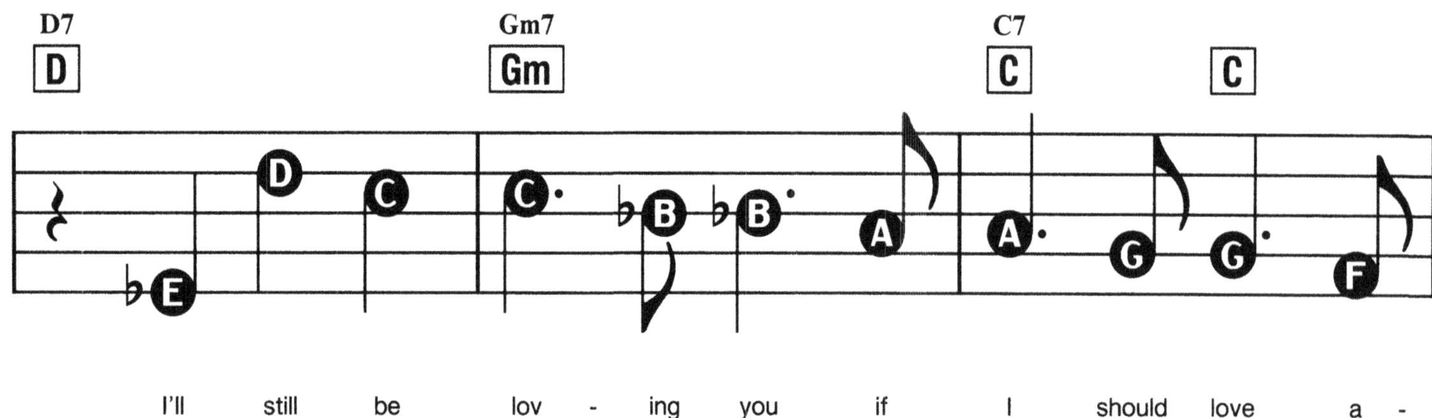
D7
D
Gm7
Gm
C7
C
C
E D C C B B A A G G F
I'll still be lov - ing you if I should love a -

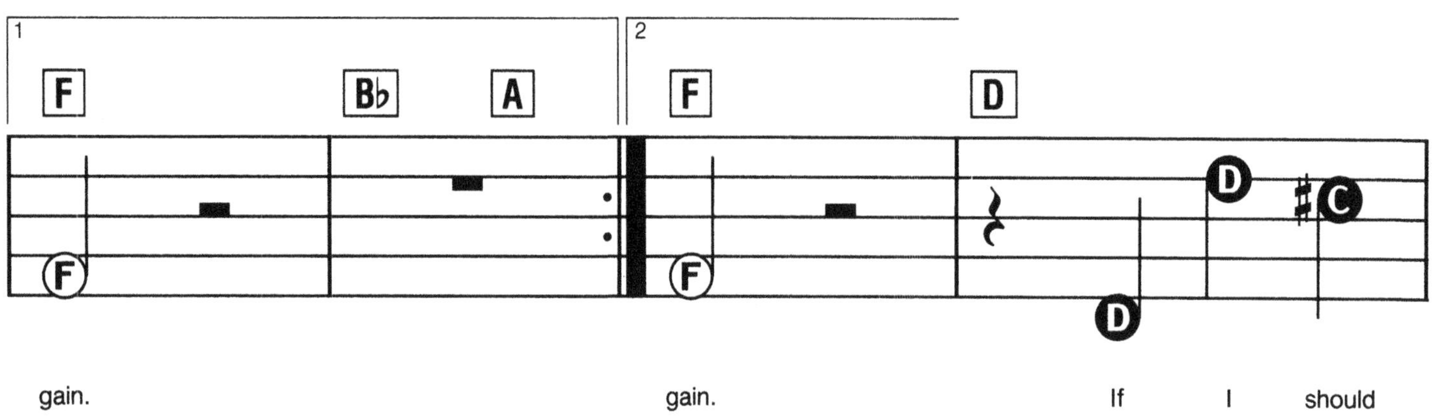
1
F
B♭
A
2
F
D
F F D D C
gain. gain. If I should

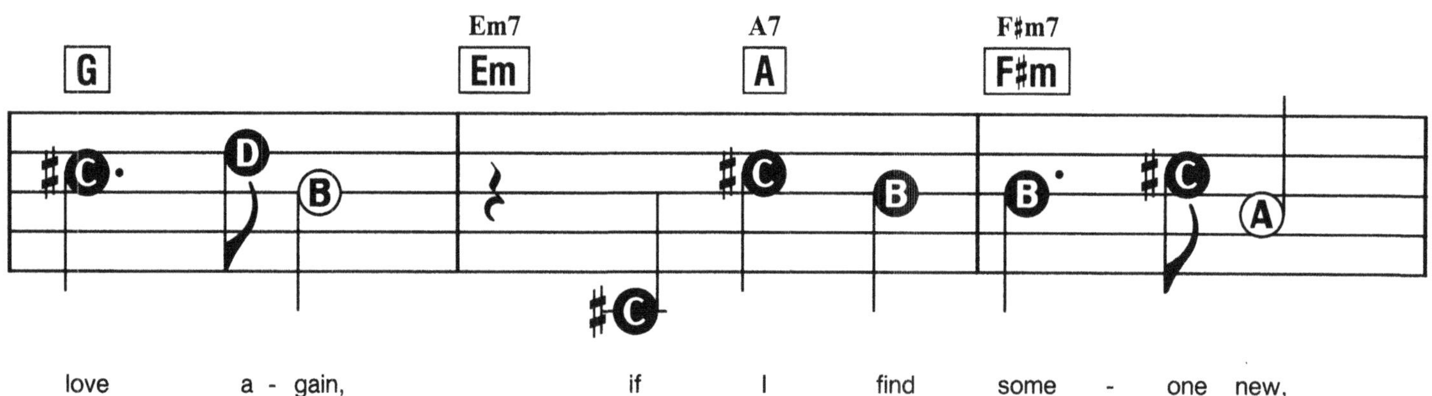
G
Em7
Em
A7
A
F♯m7
F♯m
C D B C C B B C A
love a - gain, if I find some - one new,

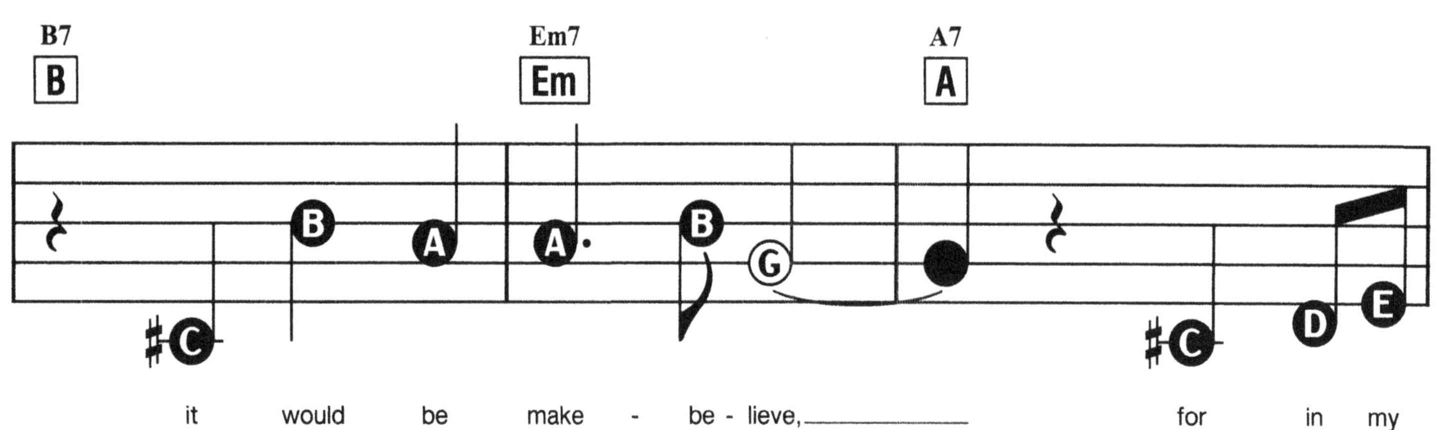
B7
B
Em7
Em
A7
A
C B A A B G C D E
it would be make - be - lieve, for in my

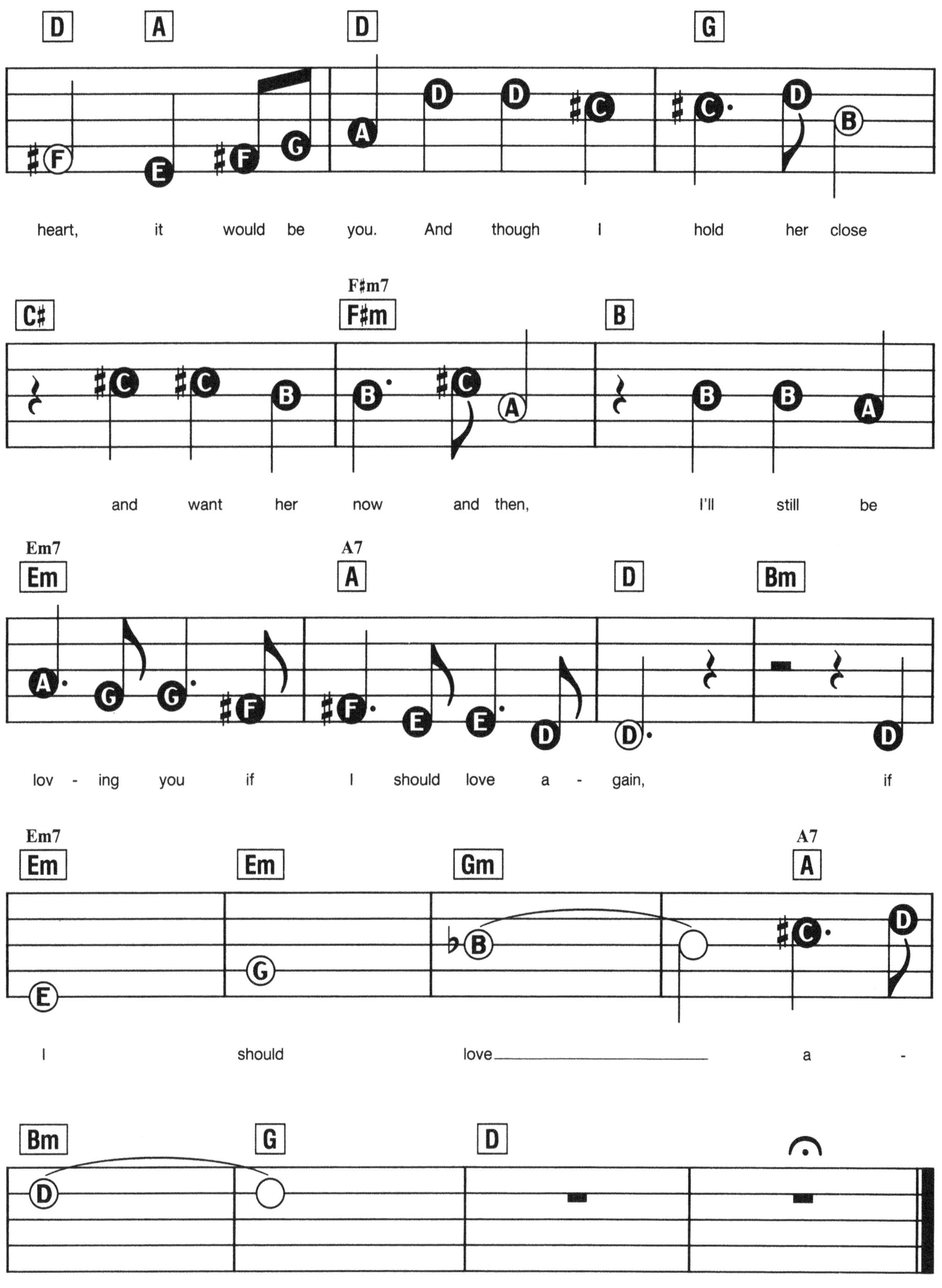
D
A
D
G
heart, it would be you. And though I hold her close
C♯
F♯m7
F♯m
B
and want her now and then, I'll still be
Em7
Em
A7
A
D
Bm
lov - ing you if I should love a - gain, if
Em7
Em
Em
Gm
A7
A
I should love a -
Bm
G
D
gain.

If You Were Here With Me Tonight

Registration 5
Rhythm: Ballad or Rock

Music by Eric Borenstein and Barry Manilow
Lyric by Eric Borenstein and Lisa Sennett Thomas

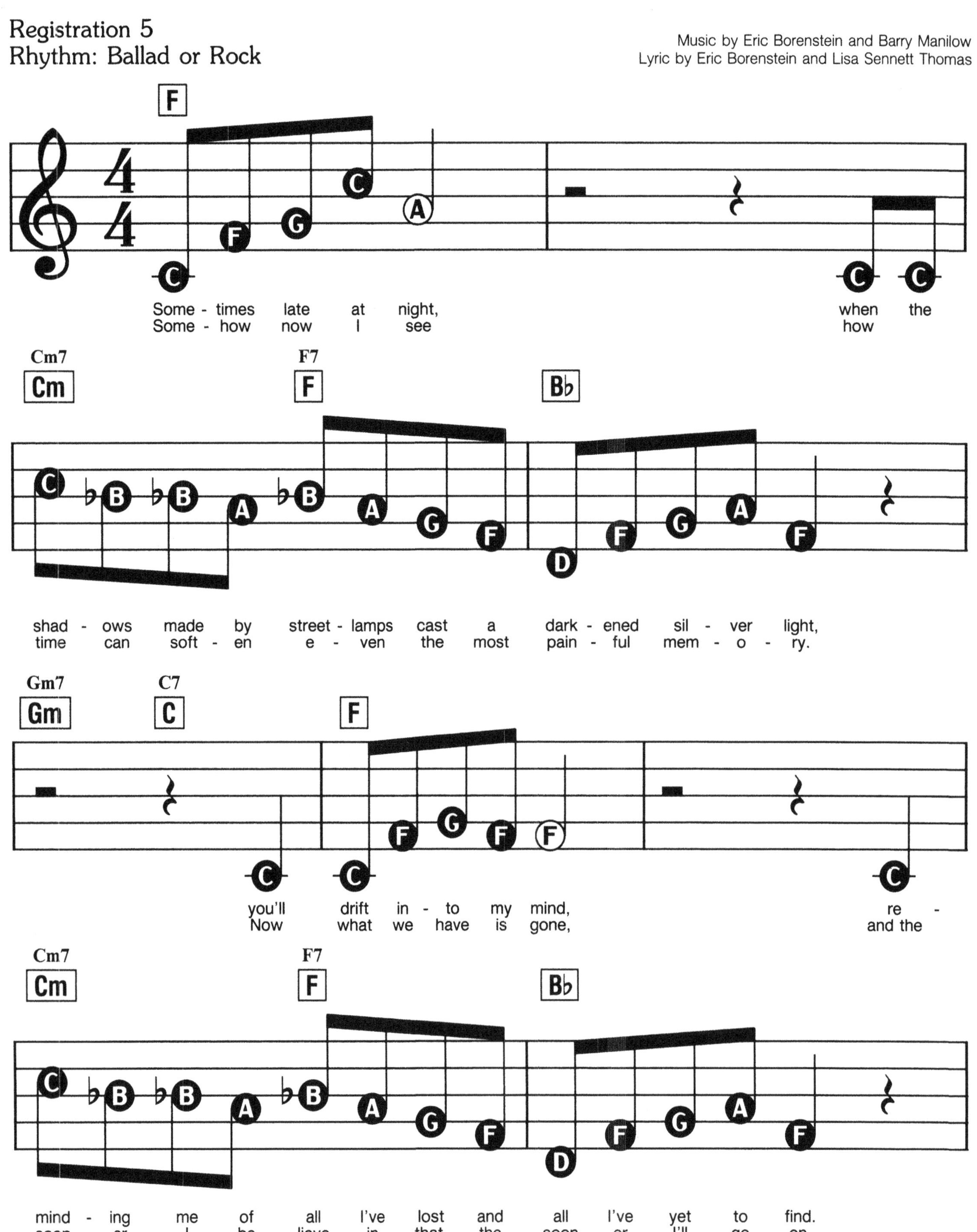

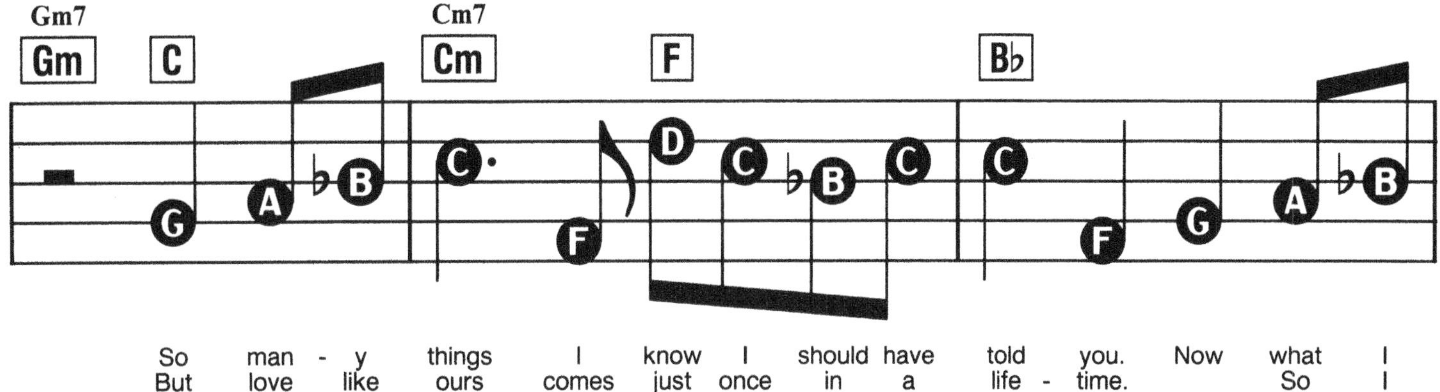
Gm7
Gm
C
Cm7
Cm
F
B♭
G
A
B
C
F
D
C
B
C
C
F
G
A
B
So man - y things I know I should have told you. Now what I
But love like ours comes just once in a life - time. So I

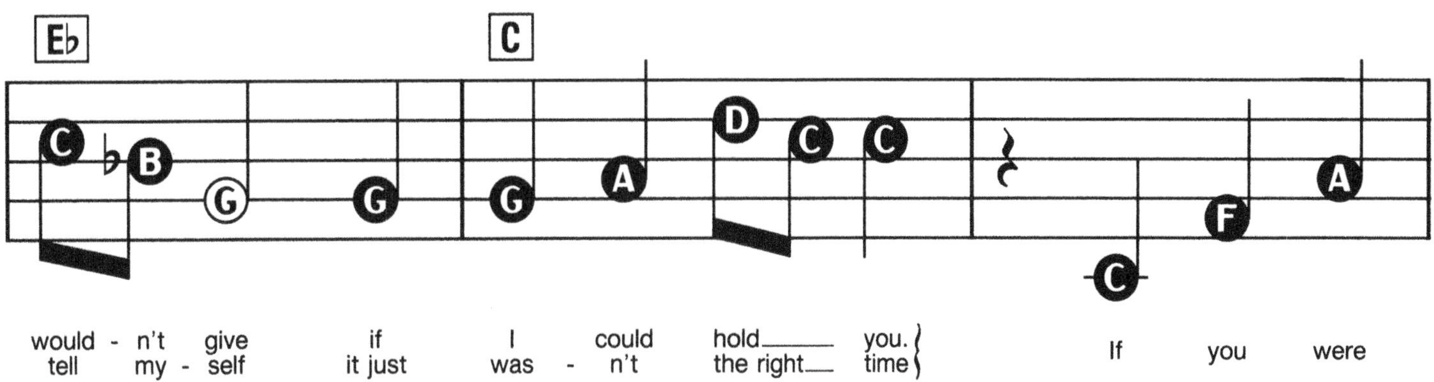
E♭
C
C
B
G
G
G
A
D
C
C
C
F
A
would - n't give if I could hold you.
tell my - self it just was - n't the right time
If you were

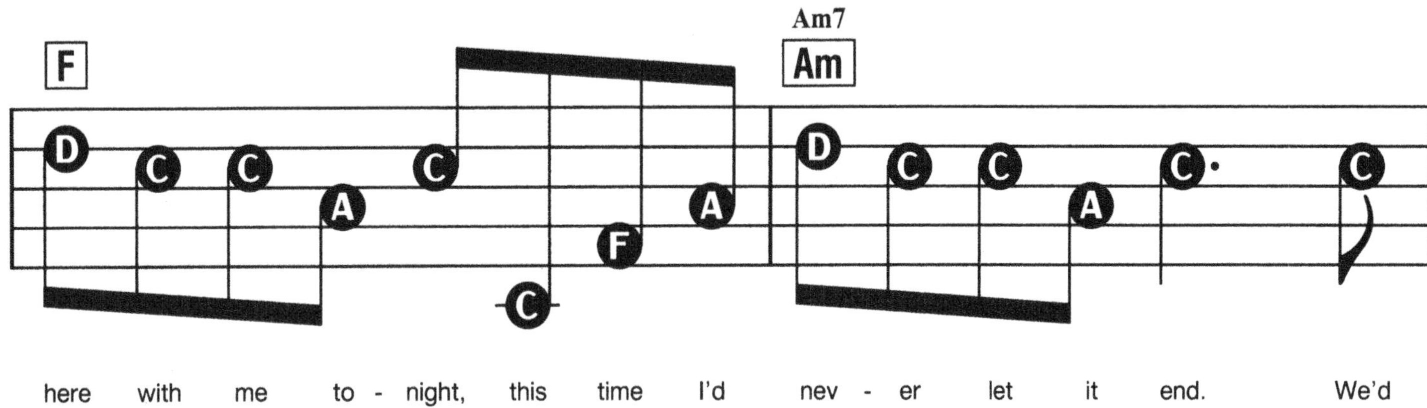
F
Am7
Am
D
C
C
A
C
C
F
A
D
C
C
A
C
C
here with me to - night, this time I'd nev - er let it end. We'd

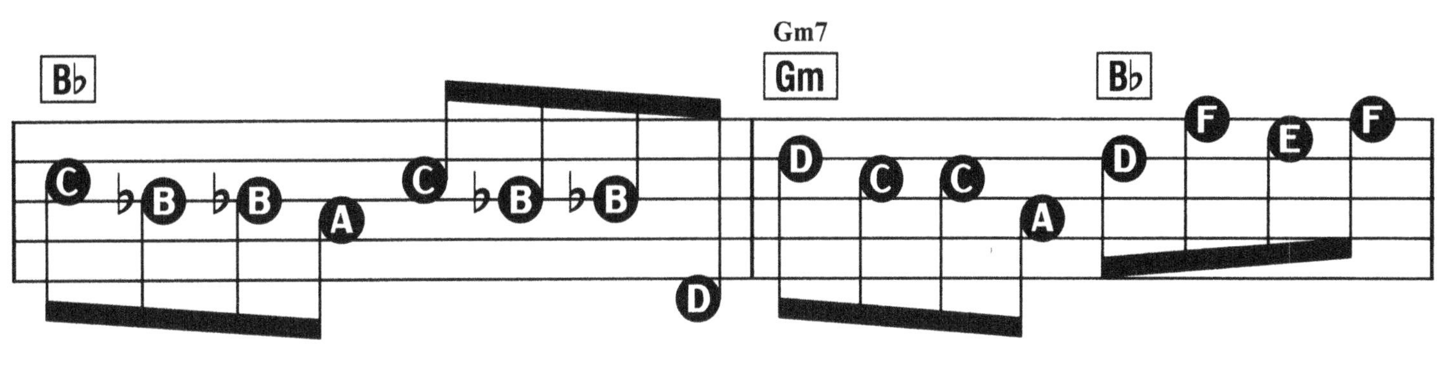
B♭
Gm7
Gm
B♭
C
B
B
A
C
B
B
D
D
C
C
A
D
F
E
F
find those feel - ings we once had and feel them all a - gain. We'd make love

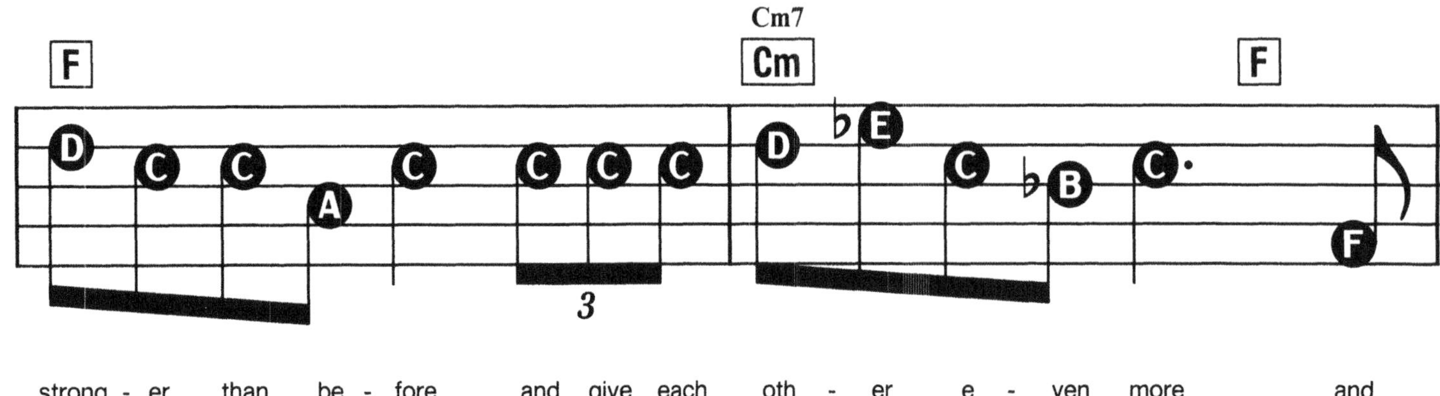
Cm7
F
Cm
F
D C C A C C C C D E C B C F
3
strong - er than be - fore and give each oth - er e - ven more and

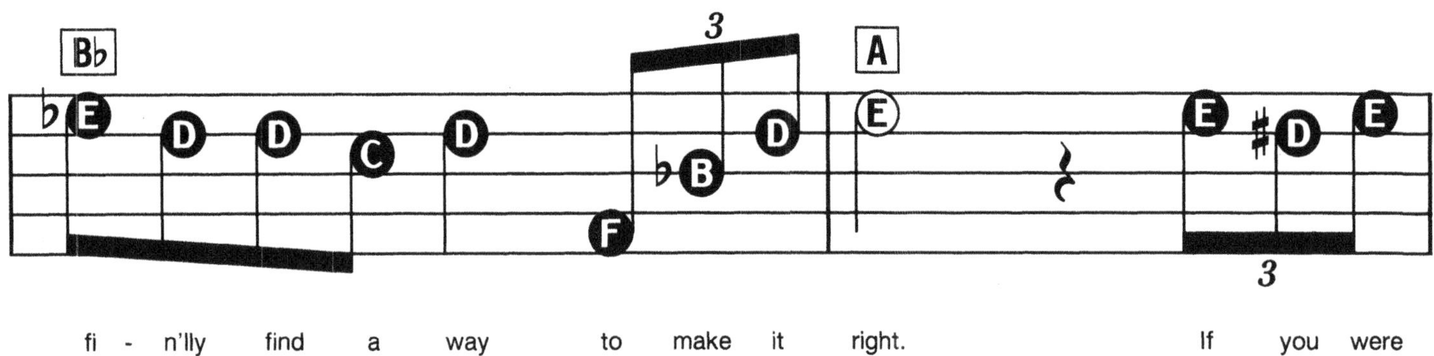
B♭
A
E D D C D F B D E E D E
3
3
fi - n'lly find a way to make it right. If you were

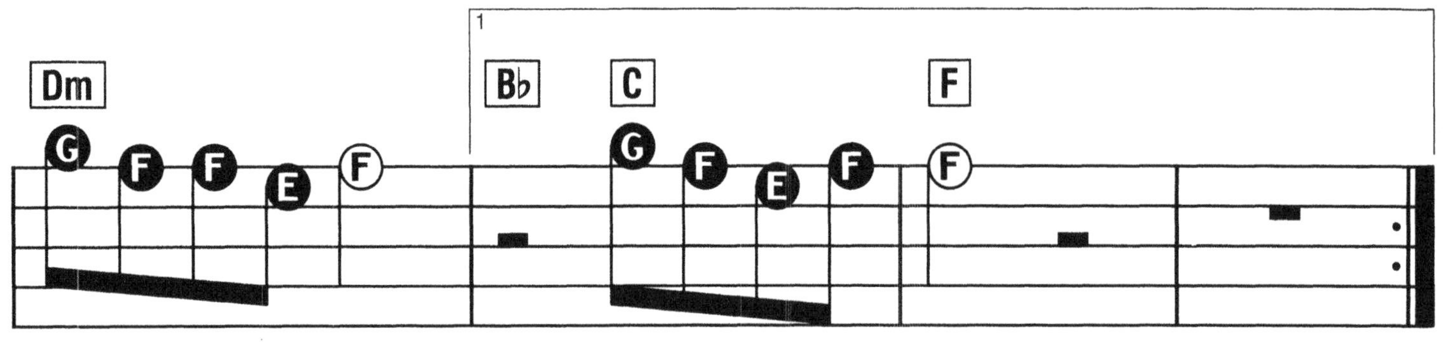
1
Dm
B♭
C
F
G F F E F G F E F F
here with me to - night, here with me to - night.

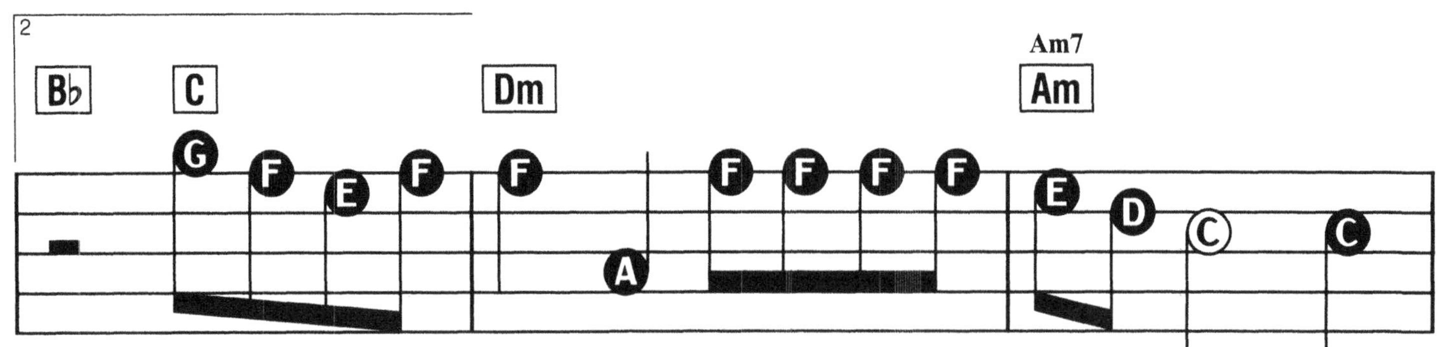
2
Am7
B♭
C
Dm
Am
G F E F F A F F F F E D C C
here with me to - night the min - utes seem like hours. How

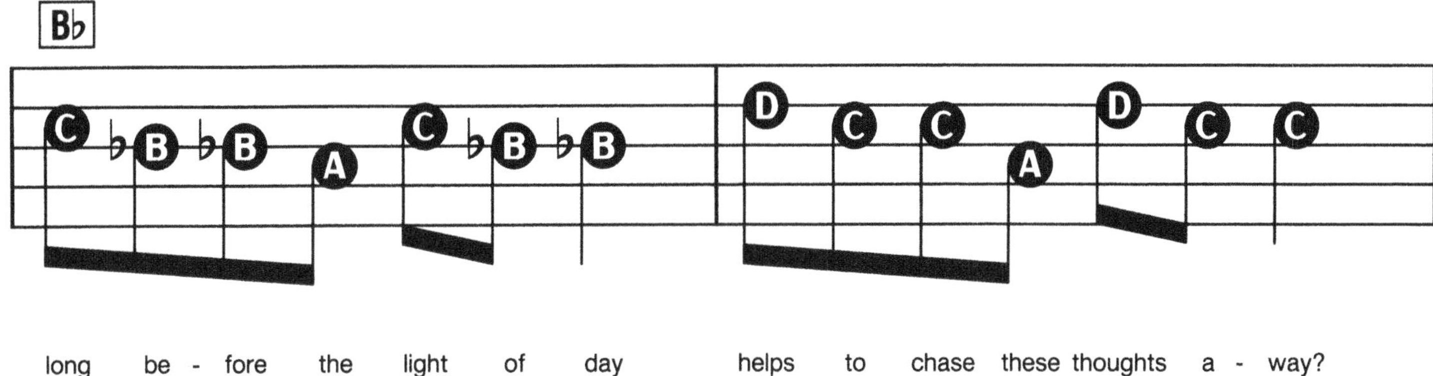

long be - fore the light of day helps to chase these thoughts a - way?

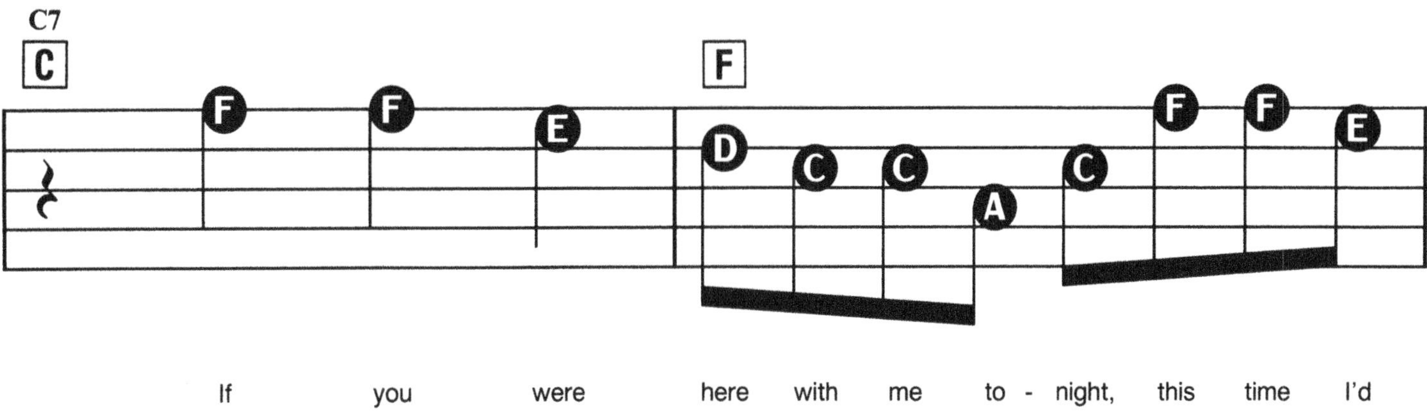

If you were here with me to - night, this time I'd

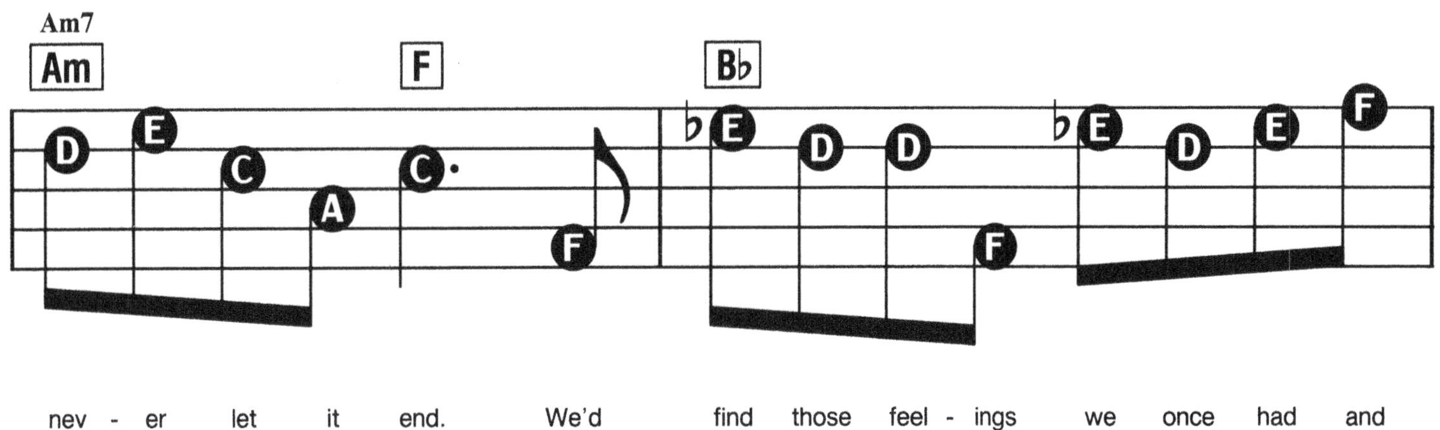

nev - er let it end. We'd find those feel - ings we once had and

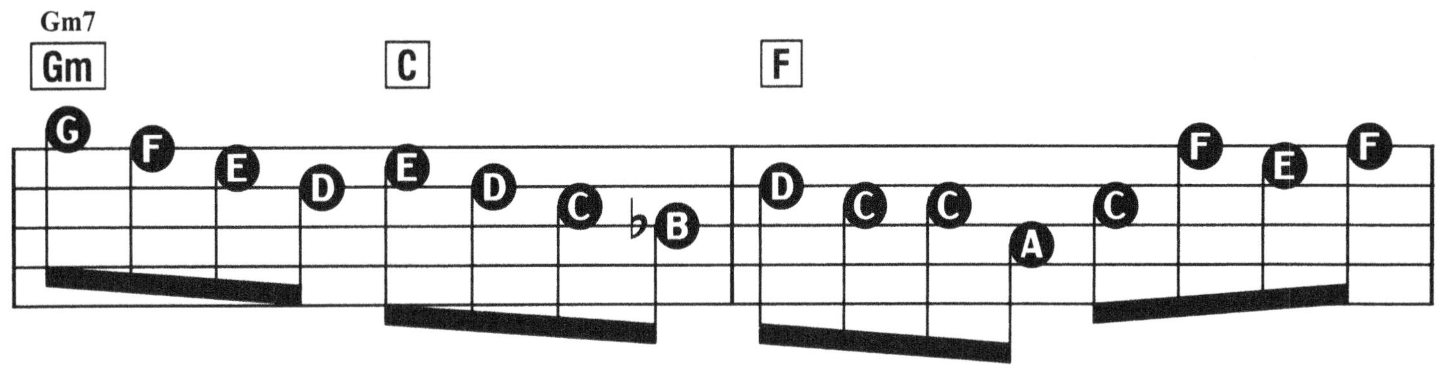

feel them once a - gain. We'd make love strong - er than be - fore and give each

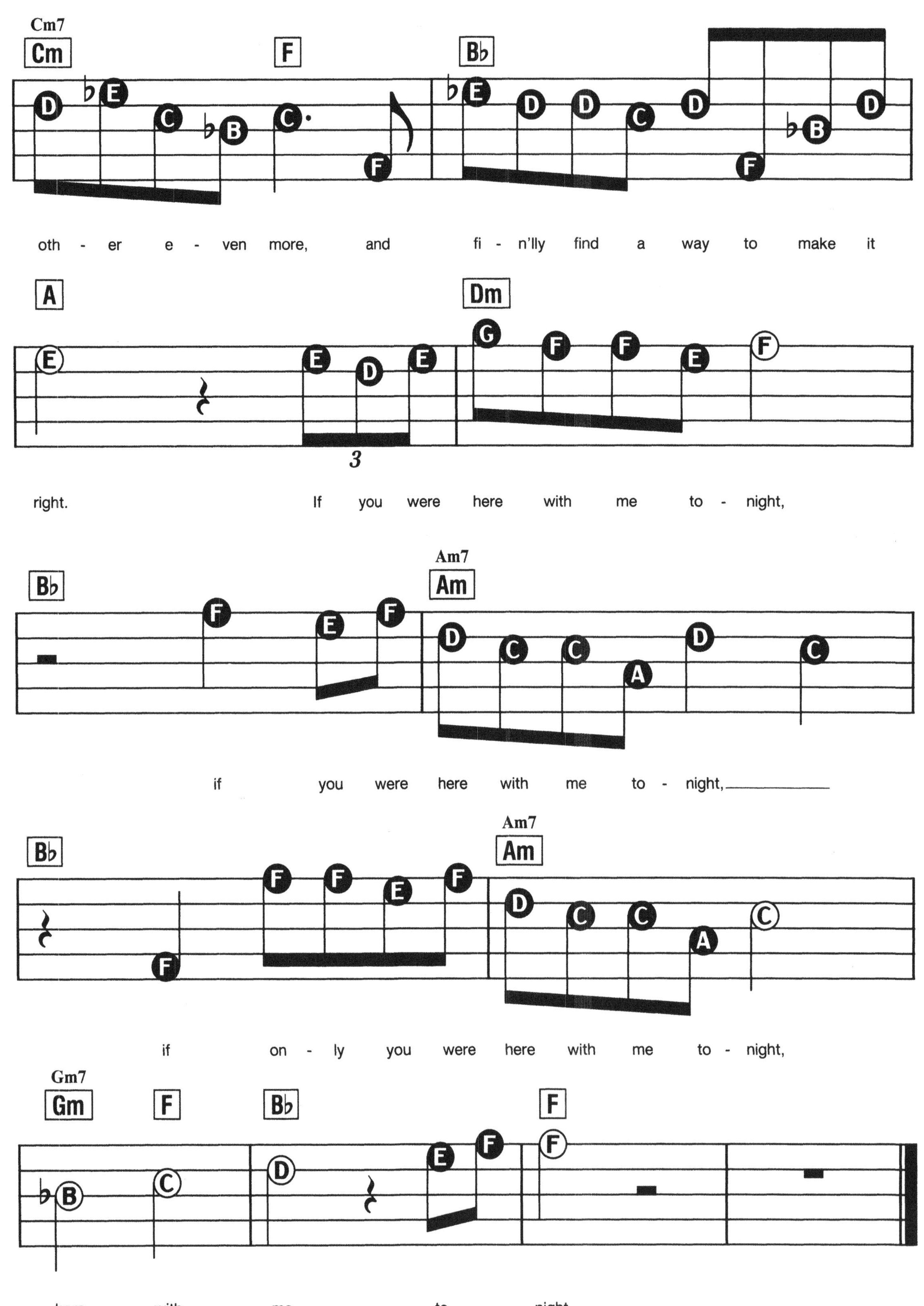
Cm7
Cm
F
B♭
D E C B C F E D D C D F B D
oth - er e - ven more, and fi - n'lly find a way to make it
A
Dm
E E D E G F F E F
3
right. If you were here with me to - night,
B♭
Am7
Am
F E F D C C A D C
if you were here with me to - night,
B♭
Am7
Am
F F F E F D C C A C
if on - ly you were here with me to - night,
Gm7
Gm
F
B♭
F
B C D E F F
here with me to - night.

It's A Miracle

Registration 1
Rhythm: Rock or Disco

Words by Barry Manilow and Marty Panzer
Music by Barry Manilow

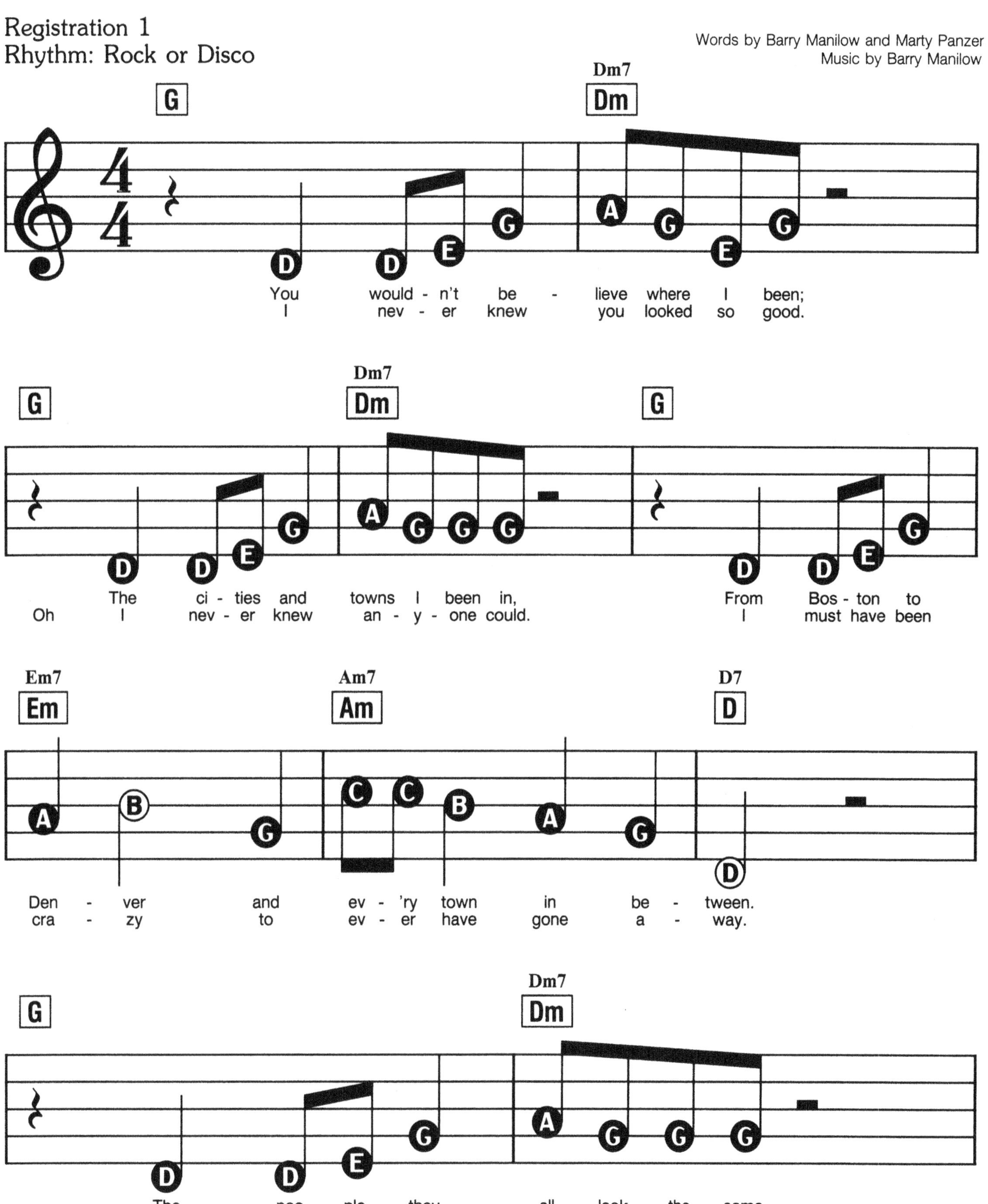

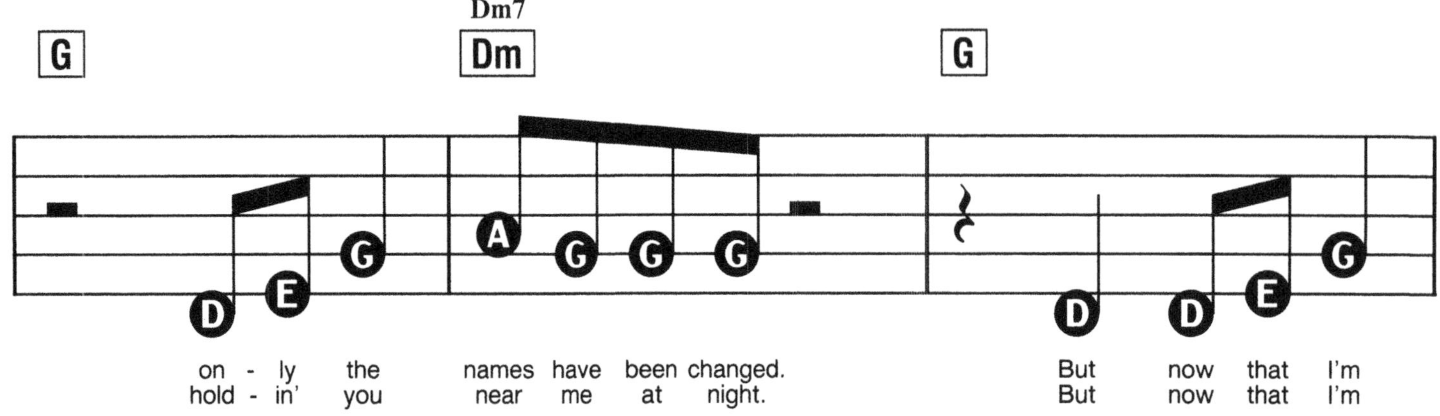
G
Dm7
Dm
G
on - ly the names have been changed. But now that I'm
hold - in' you near me at night. But now that I'm

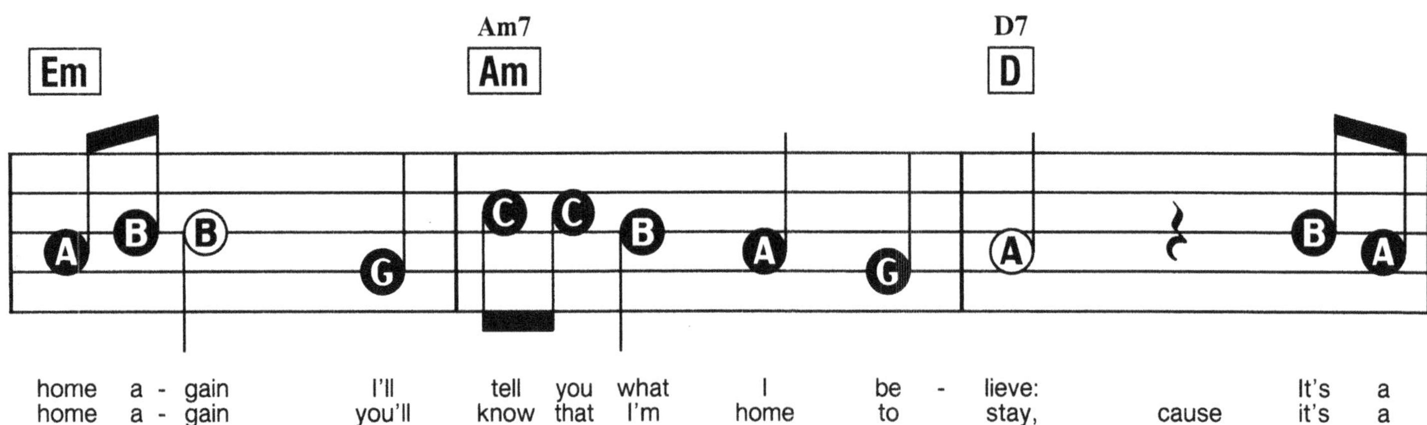
Em
Am7
Am
D7
D
home a - gain I'll tell you what I be - lieve: It's a
home a - gain you'll know that I'm home to stay, cause it's a

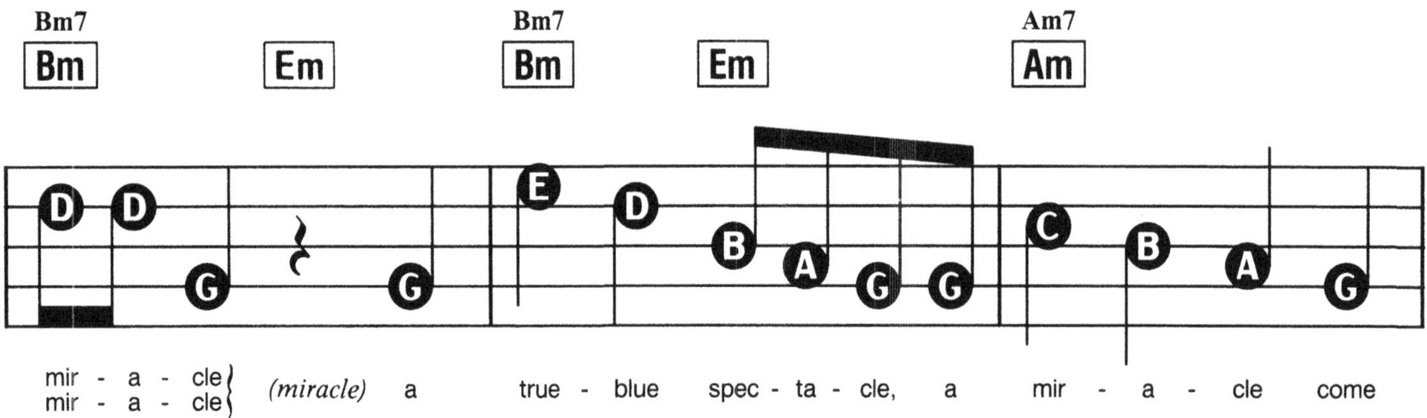
Bm7
Bm
Em
Bm7
Bm
Em
Am7
Am
mir - a - cle
mir - a - cle
(miracle) a true - blue spec - ta - cle, a mir - a - cle come

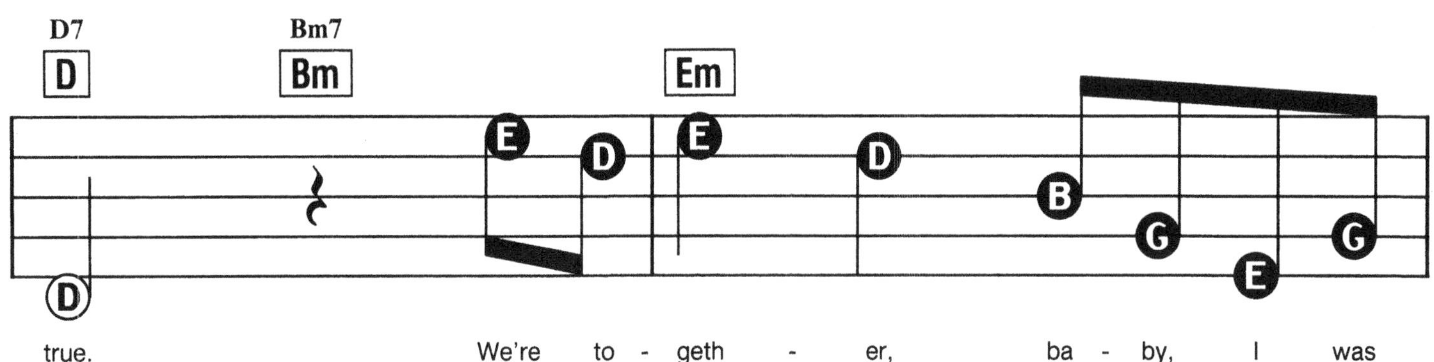
D7
D
Bm7
Bm
Em
true. We're to - geth - er, ba - by, I was

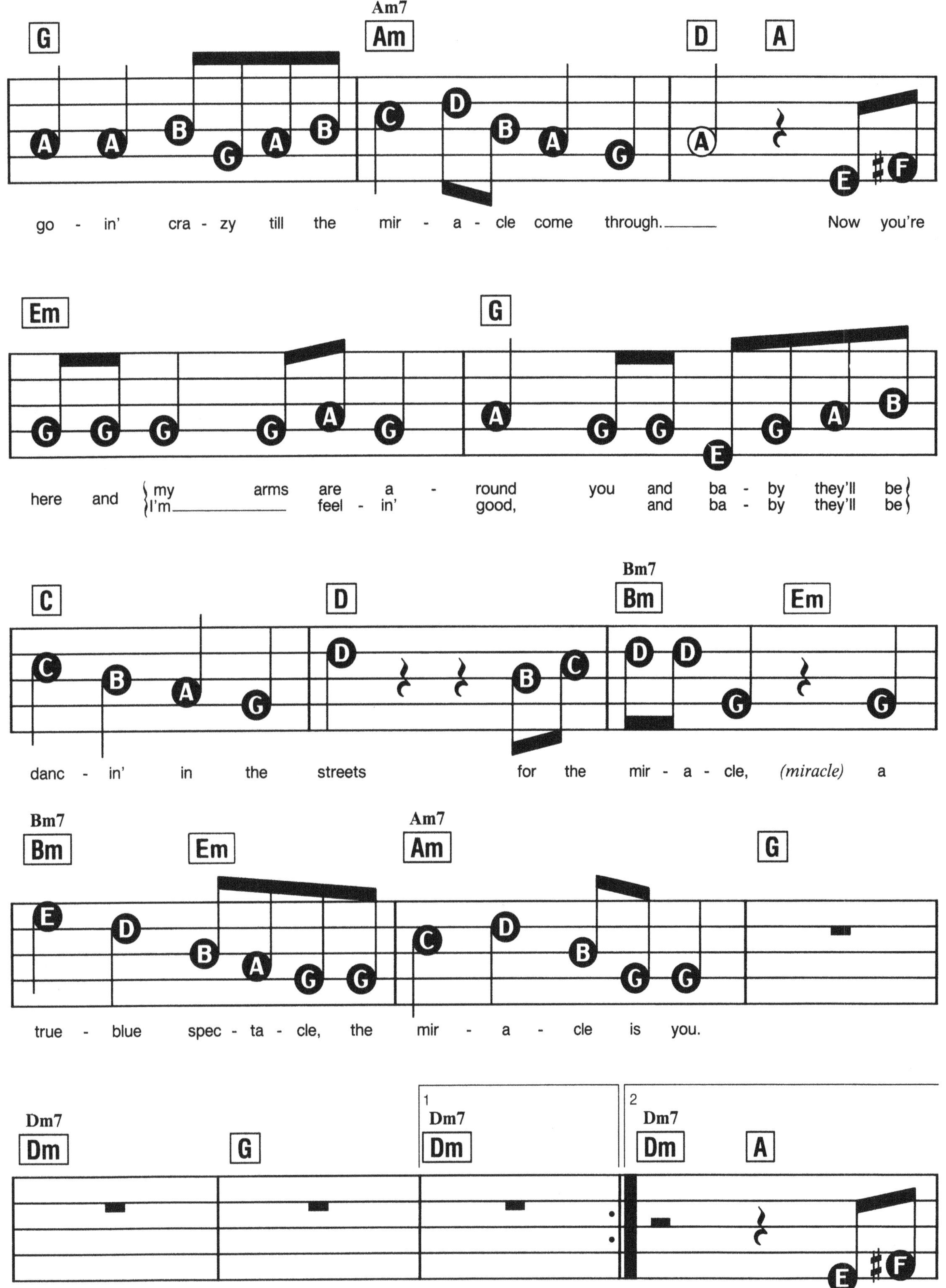
G Am7 Am D A
go - in' cra - zy till the mir - a - cle come through. Now you're
Em G
here and my arms are a - round you and ba - by they'll be
I'm feel - in' good, and ba - by they'll be
C D Bm7 Bm Em
danc - in' in the streets for the mir - a - cle, (miracle) a
Bm7 Bm Em Am7 Am G
true - blue spec - ta - cle, the mir - a - cle is you.
Dm7 Dm G 1 Dm7 Dm 2 Dm7 Dm A
Now you're

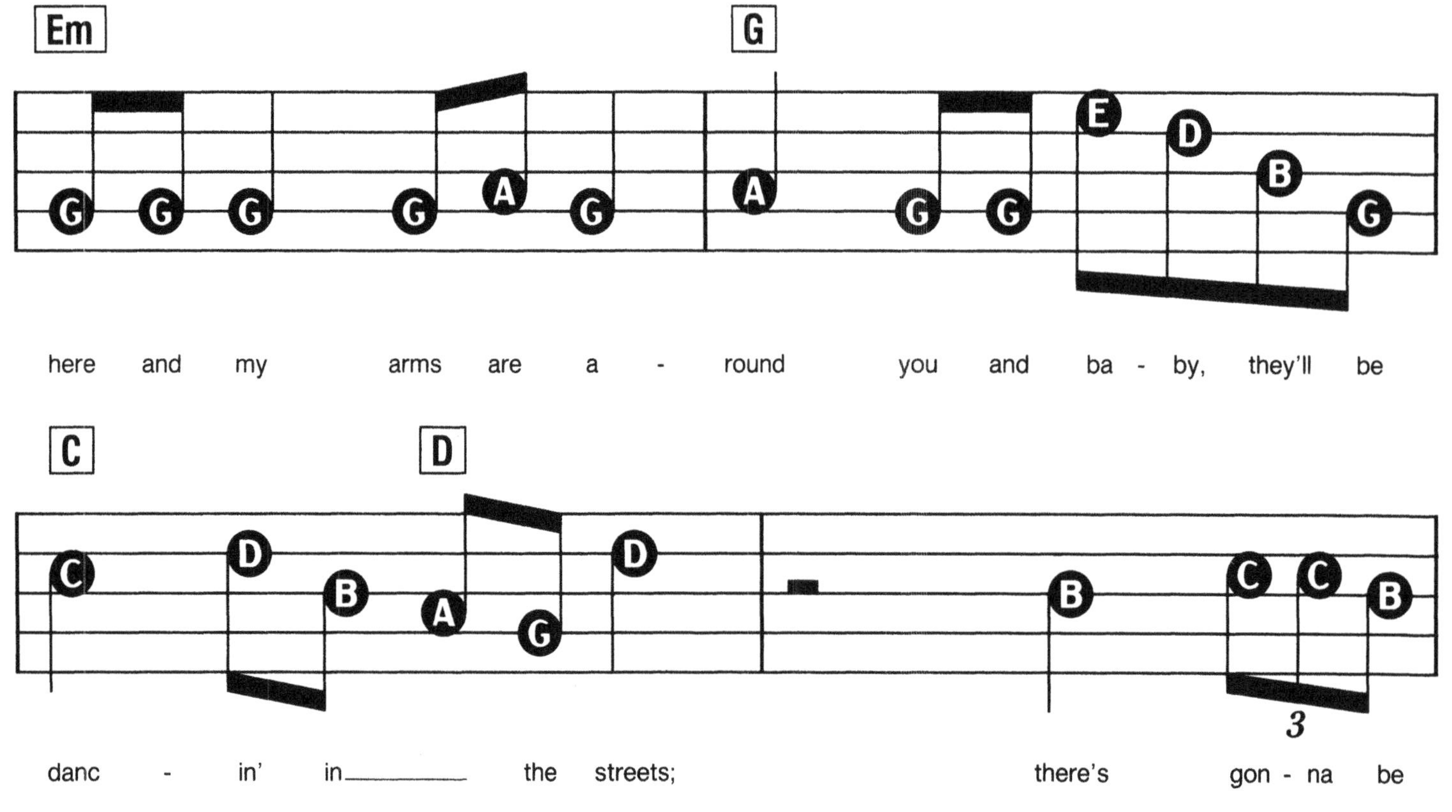
Em
G
here and my arms are a - round you and ba - by, they'll be
C
D
danc - in' in ___ the streets; there's gon - na be
3

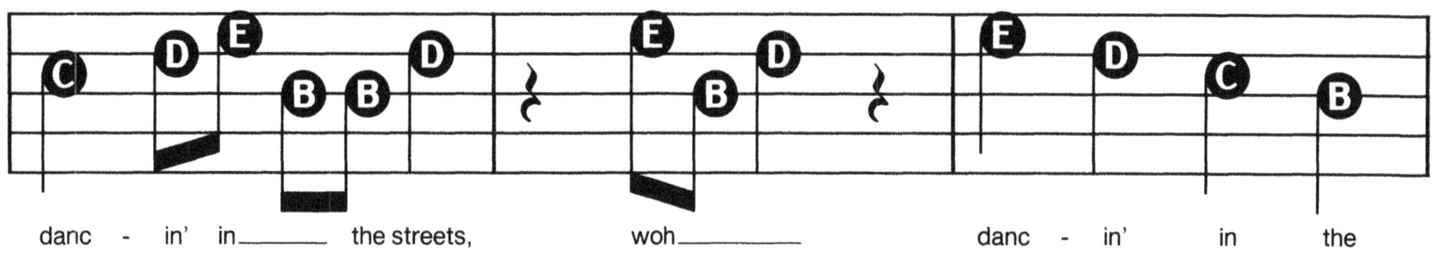
danc - in' in ___ the streets, woh ___ danc - in' in the

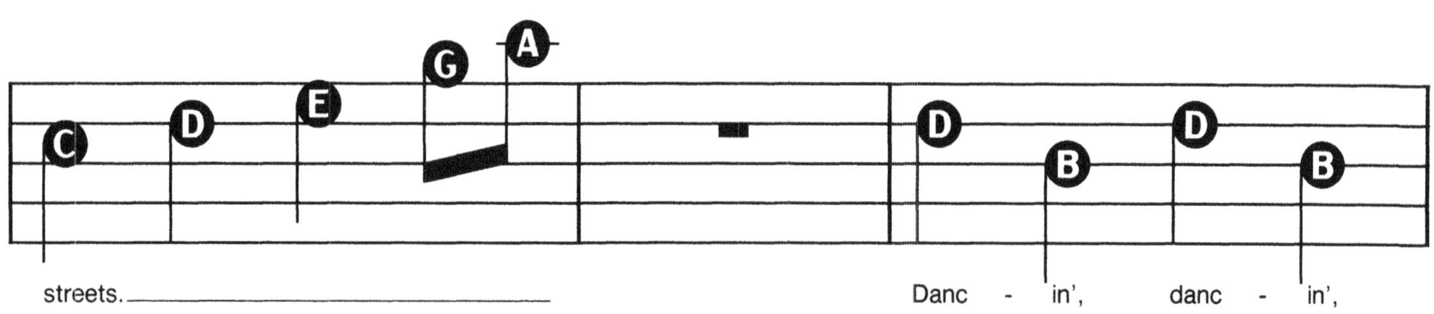
streets. ___ Danc - in', danc - in',

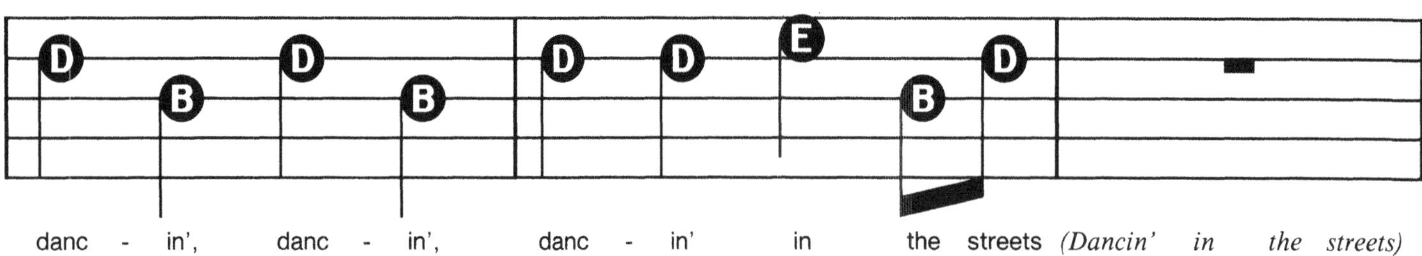
danc - in', danc - in', danc - in' in the streets (Dancin' in the streets)

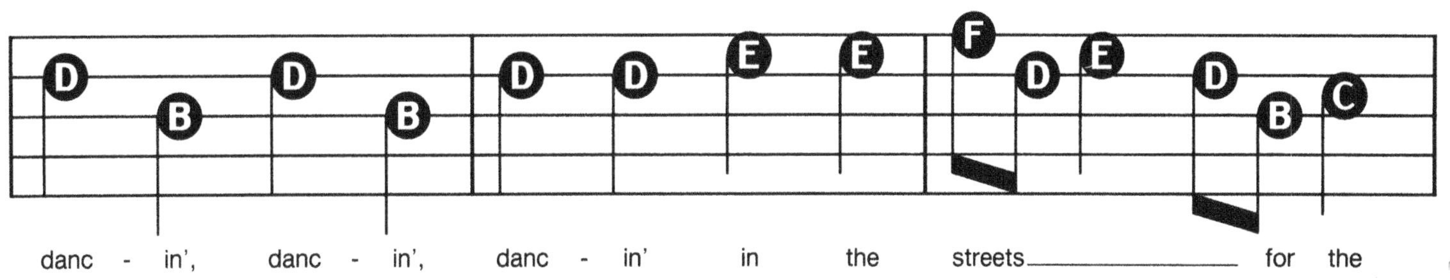
danc - in', danc - in', danc - in' in the streets ___ for the

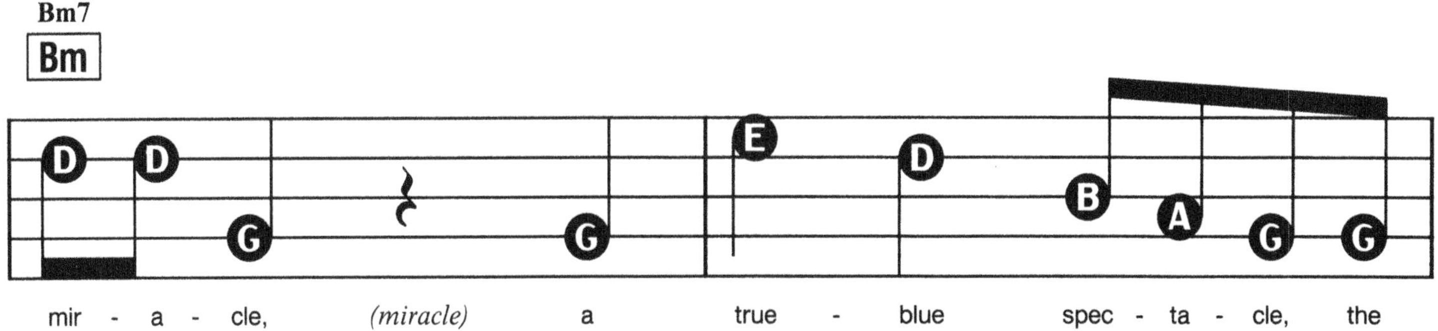
Bm7
Bm
mir - a - cle, (miracle) a true - blue spec - ta - cle, the

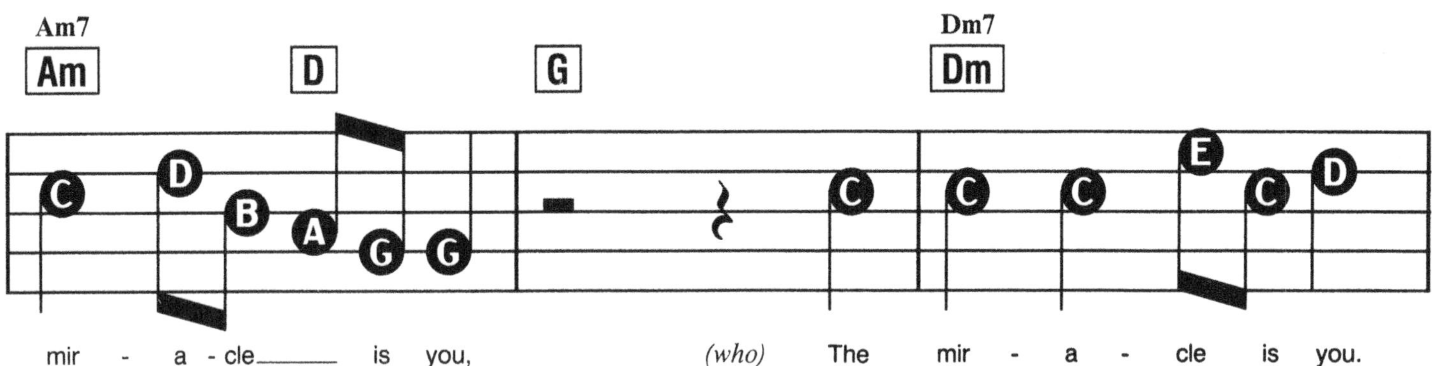
Am7
Am
D
G
Dm7
Dm
mir - a - cle ___ is you, (who) The mir - a - cle is you.

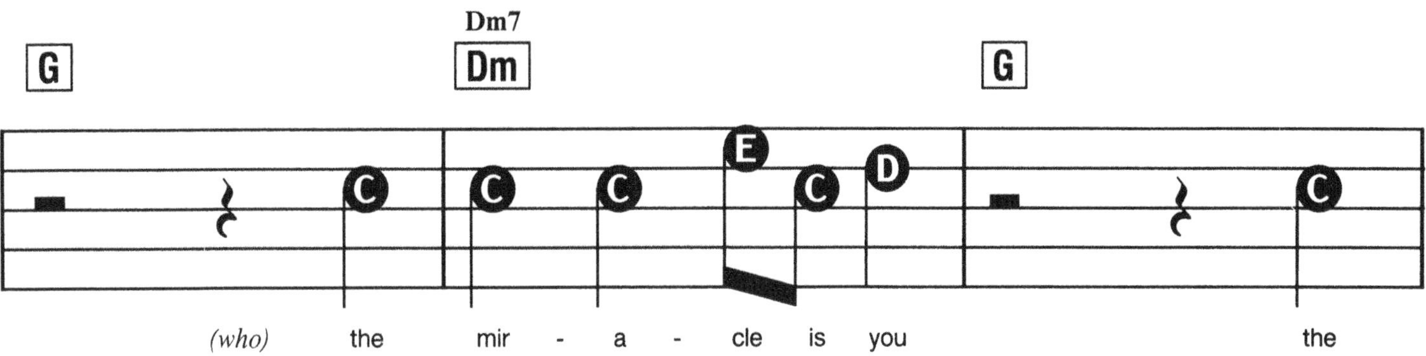
G
Dm7
Dm
G
(who) the mir - a - cle is you the

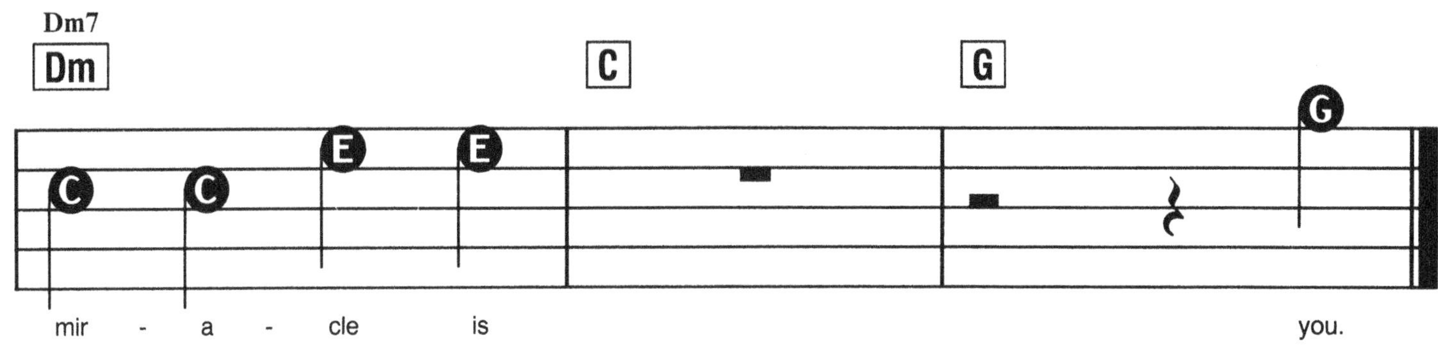
Dm7
Dm
C
G
mir - a - cle is you.

Looks Like We Made It

Registration 4
Rhythm: Rock

Words by Will Jennings
Music by Richard Kerr

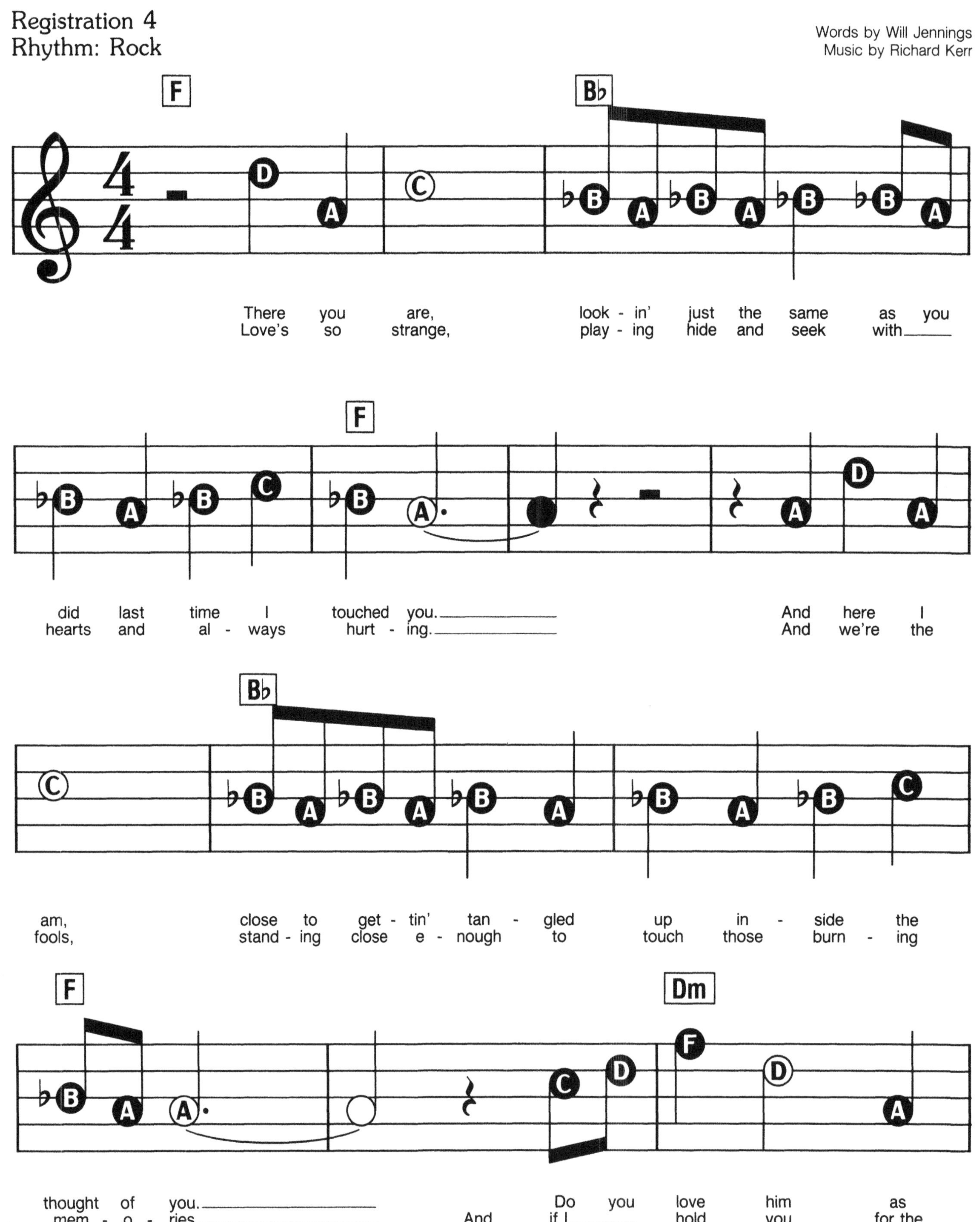

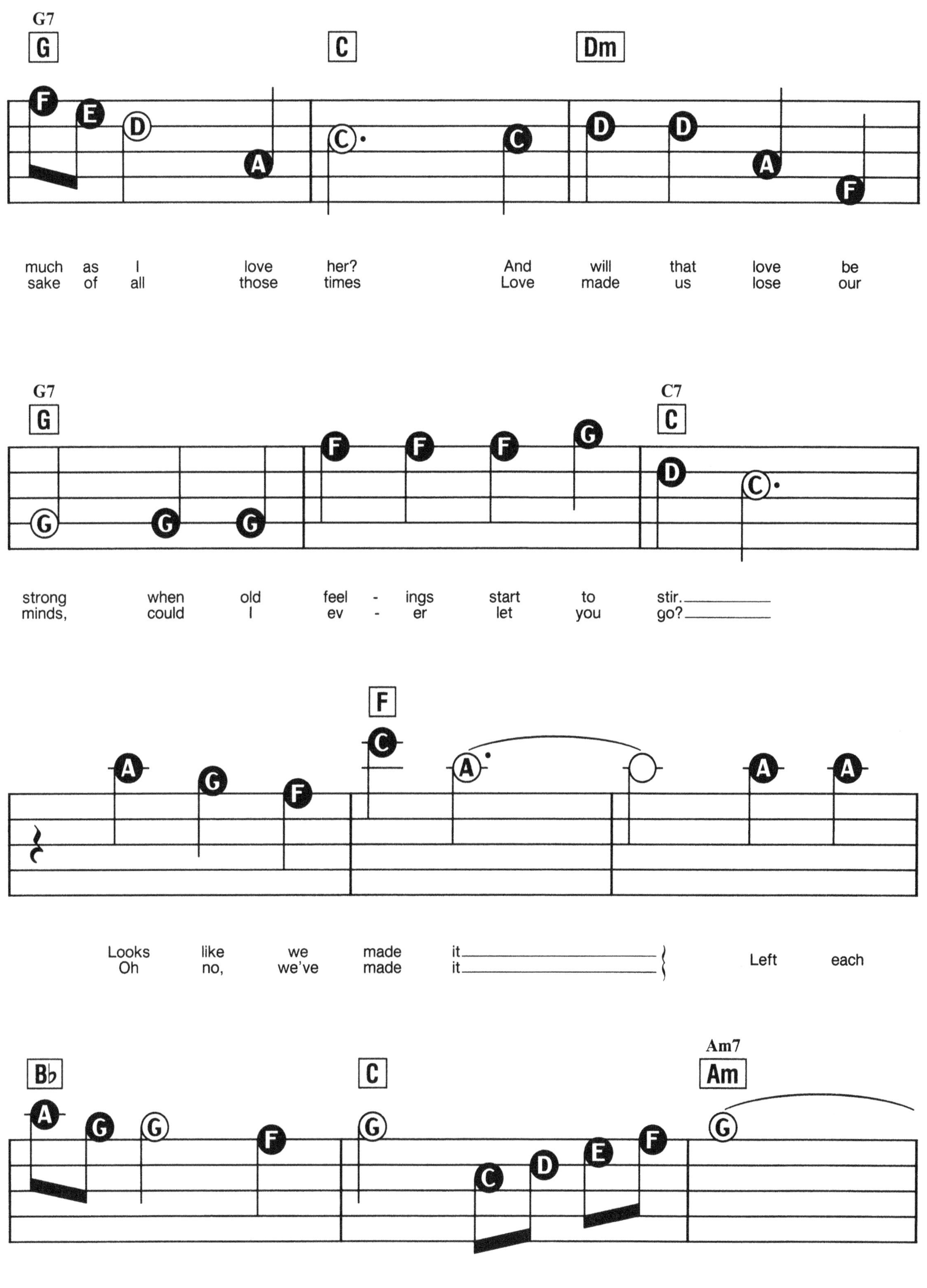
G7
G
C
Dm
F
E
D
A
C
C
D
D
A
F
much as I love her? And will that love be
sake of all those times Love made us lose our
G7
G
C7
C
G
G
G
F
F
F
G
D
C
strong when old feel - ings start to stir.
minds, could I ev - er let you go?
F
A
G
F
C
A
A
A
Looks like we made it
Oh no, we've made it
Left each
B♭
C
Am7
Am
A
G
G
F
G
C
D
E
F
G
oth - er on the way to an - oth - er love

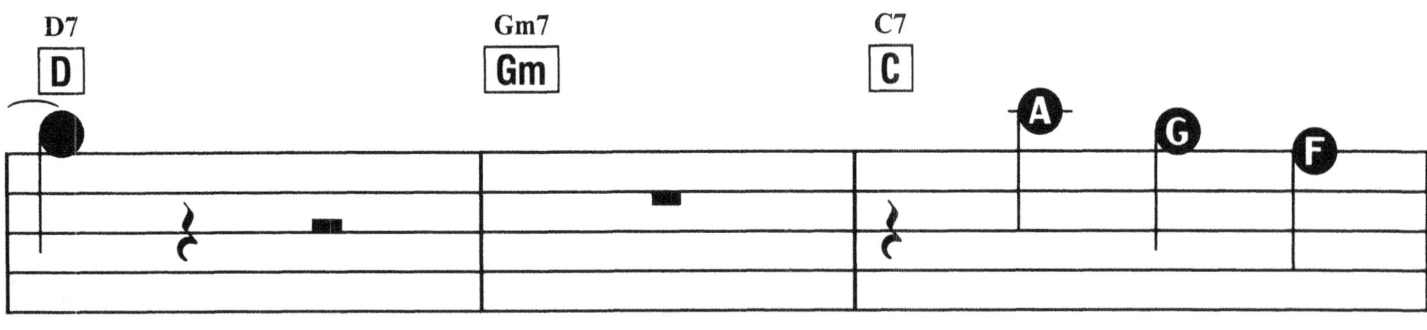
D7
D
Gm7
Gm
C7
C
A
G
F
Looks like we

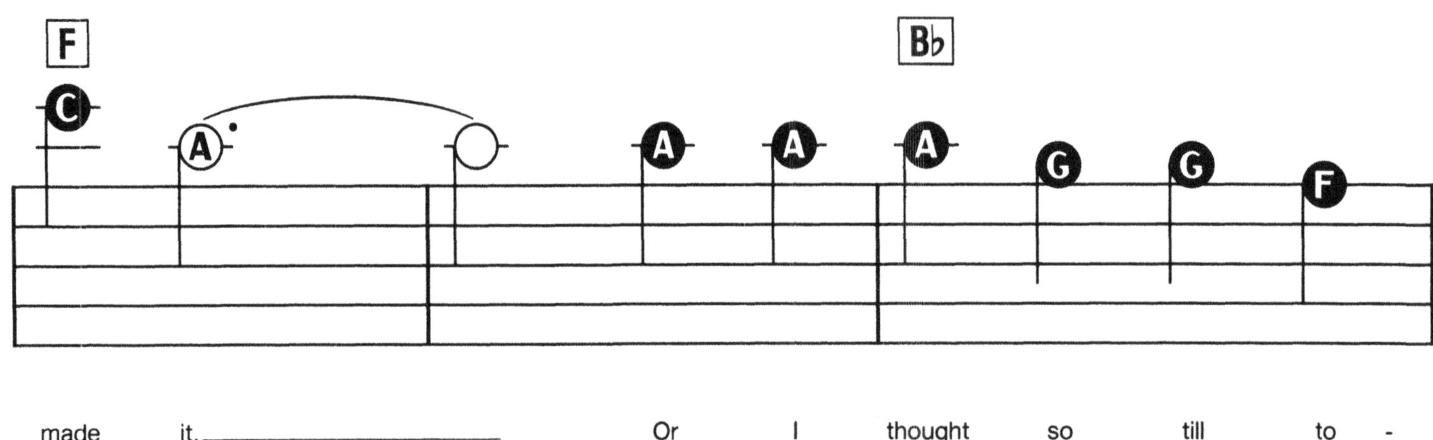
F
C
A
Bb
A
A
A
G
G
F
made it,
Or I thought so till to -

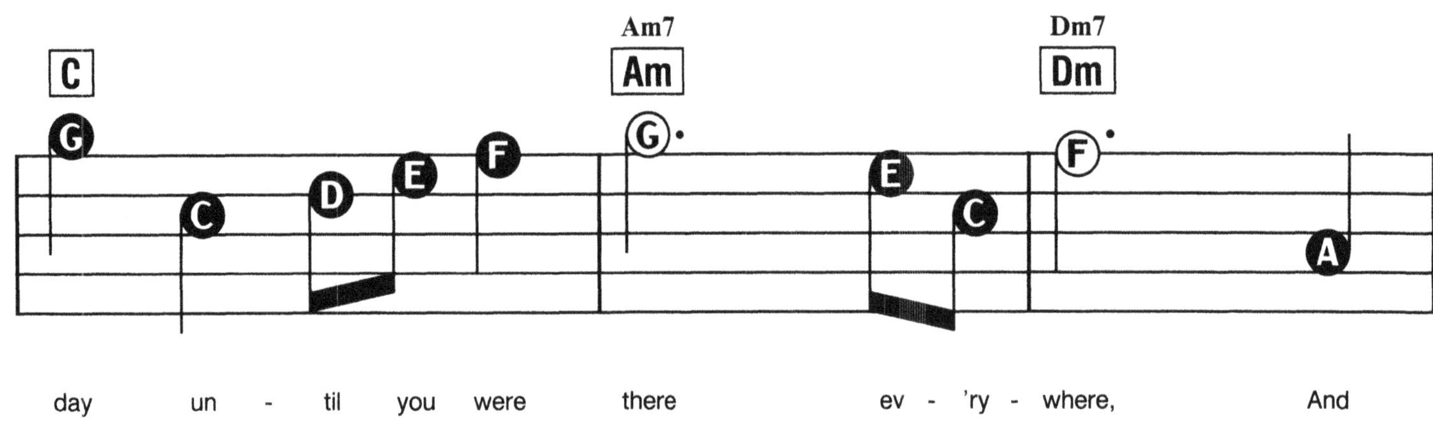
C
Am7
Am
Dm7
Dm
G
C
D
E
F
G
E
C
F
A
day un - til you were there ev - 'ry - where, And

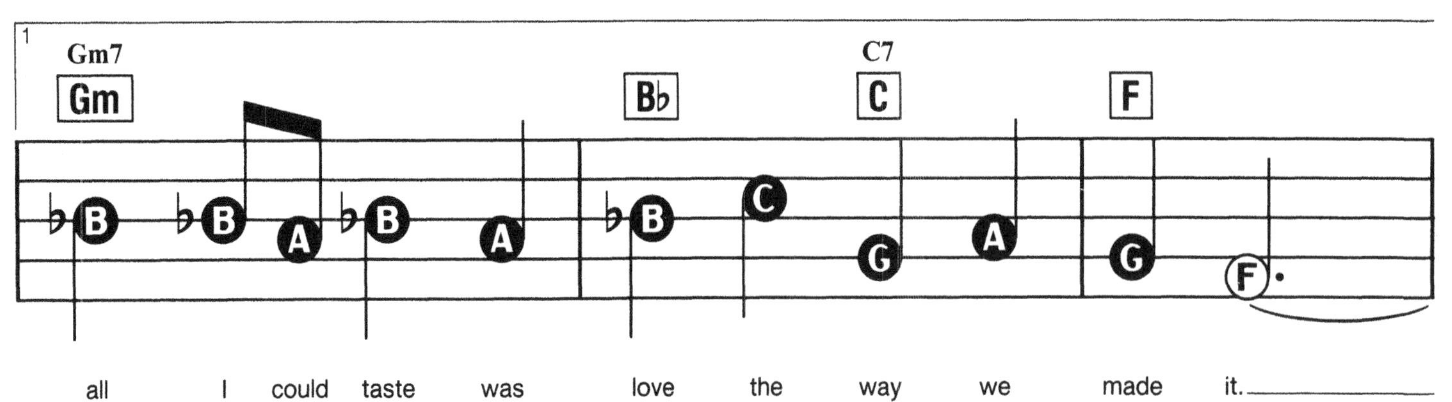
1
Gm7
Gm
Bb
C7
C
F
B
B
A
B
A
B
C
G
A
G
F
all I could taste was love the way we made it.

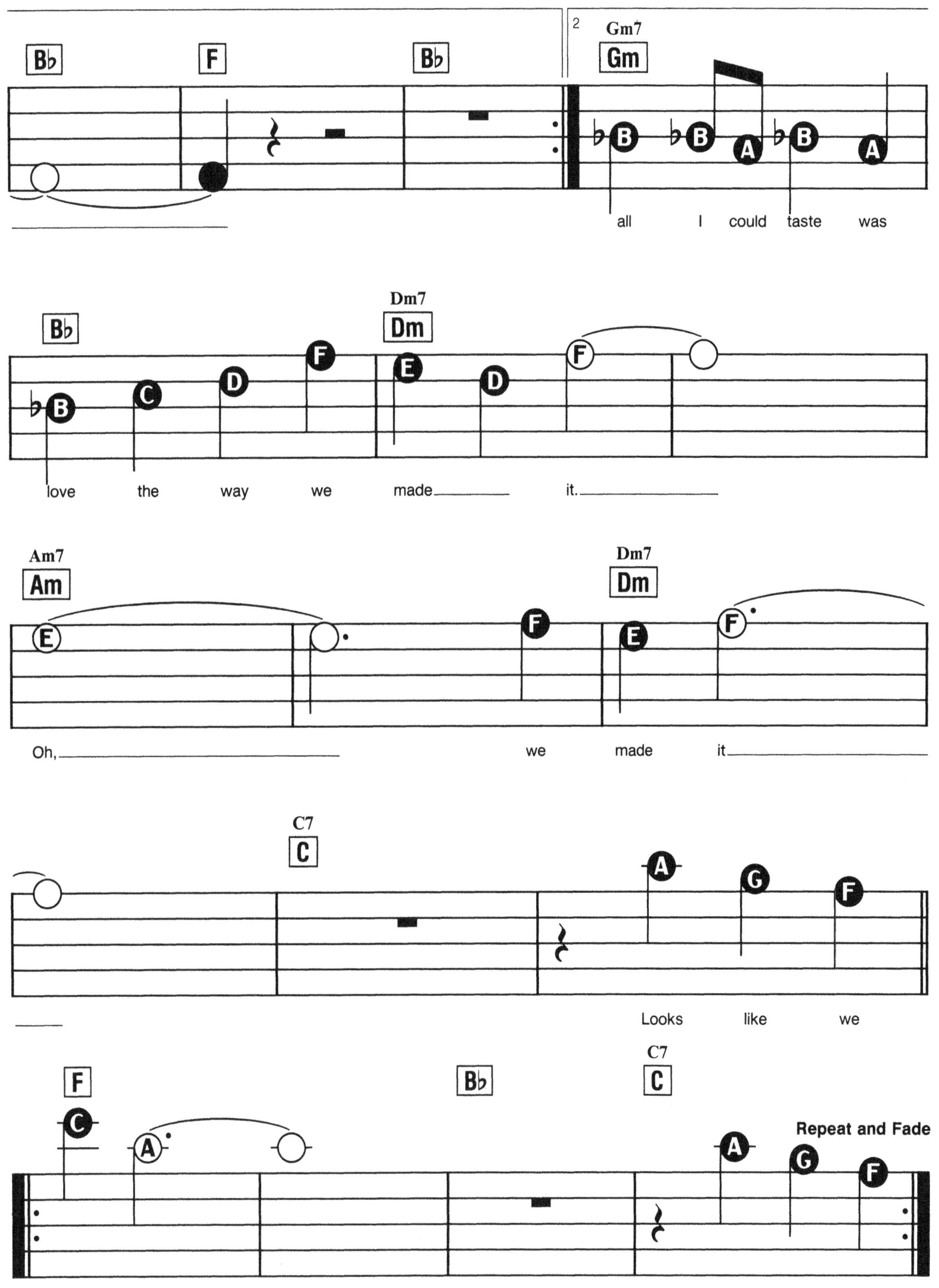
2
Gm7
Gm
B♭
F
B♭
all I could taste was
B♭
Dm7
Dm
love the way we made it.
Am7
Am
Dm7
Dm
Oh, we made it
C7
C
Looks like we
F
B♭
C7
C
Repeat and Fade
made it
Looks like we

Mandy

Registration 1
Rhythm: Rock

Words and Music by
Scott English and Richard Kerr

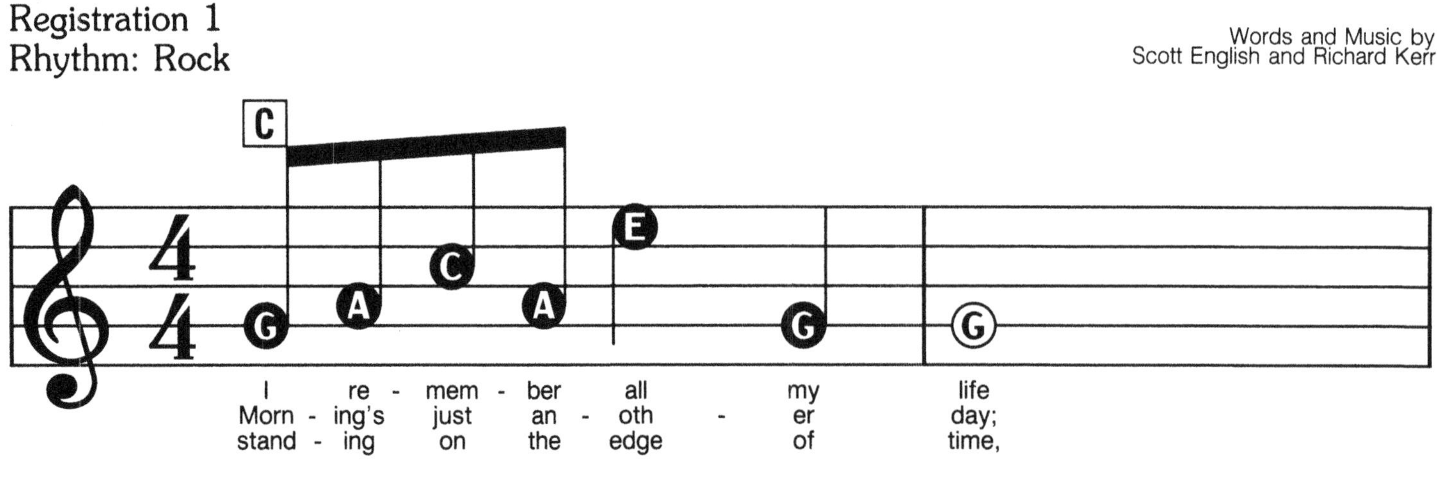

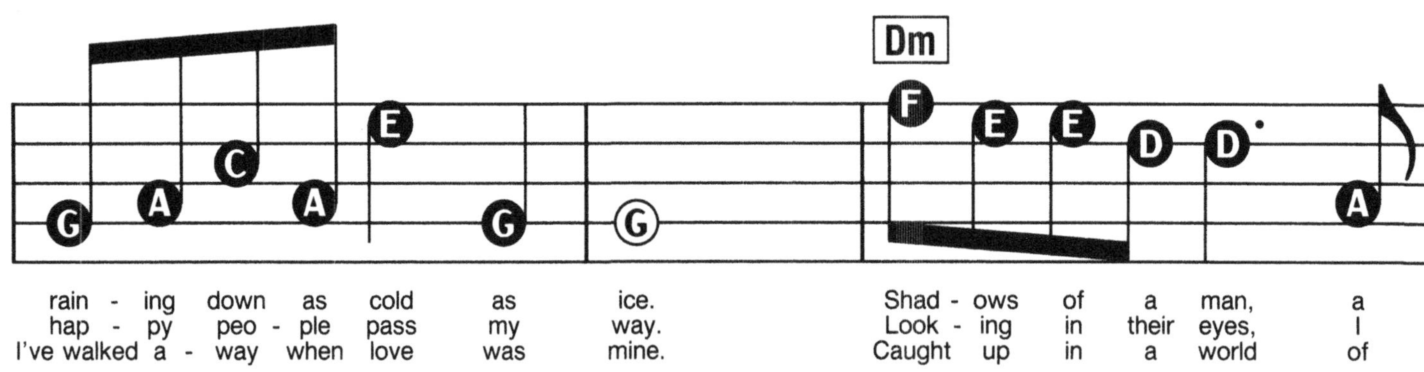

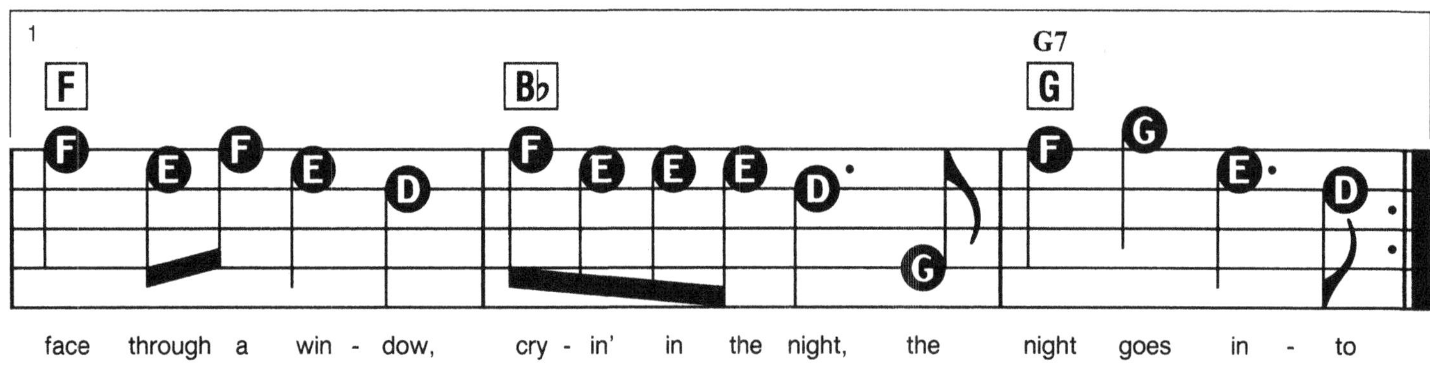

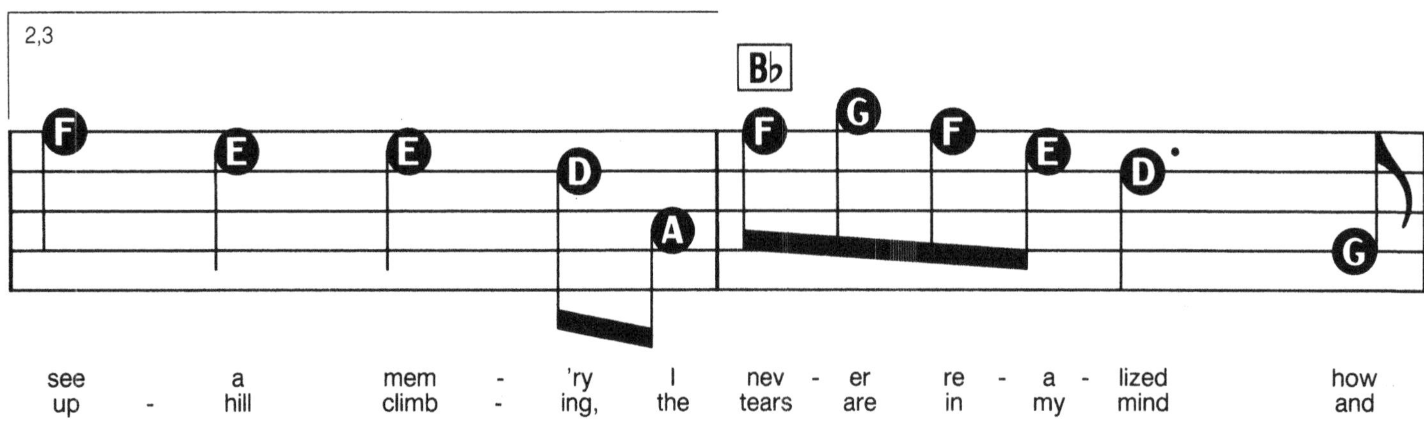

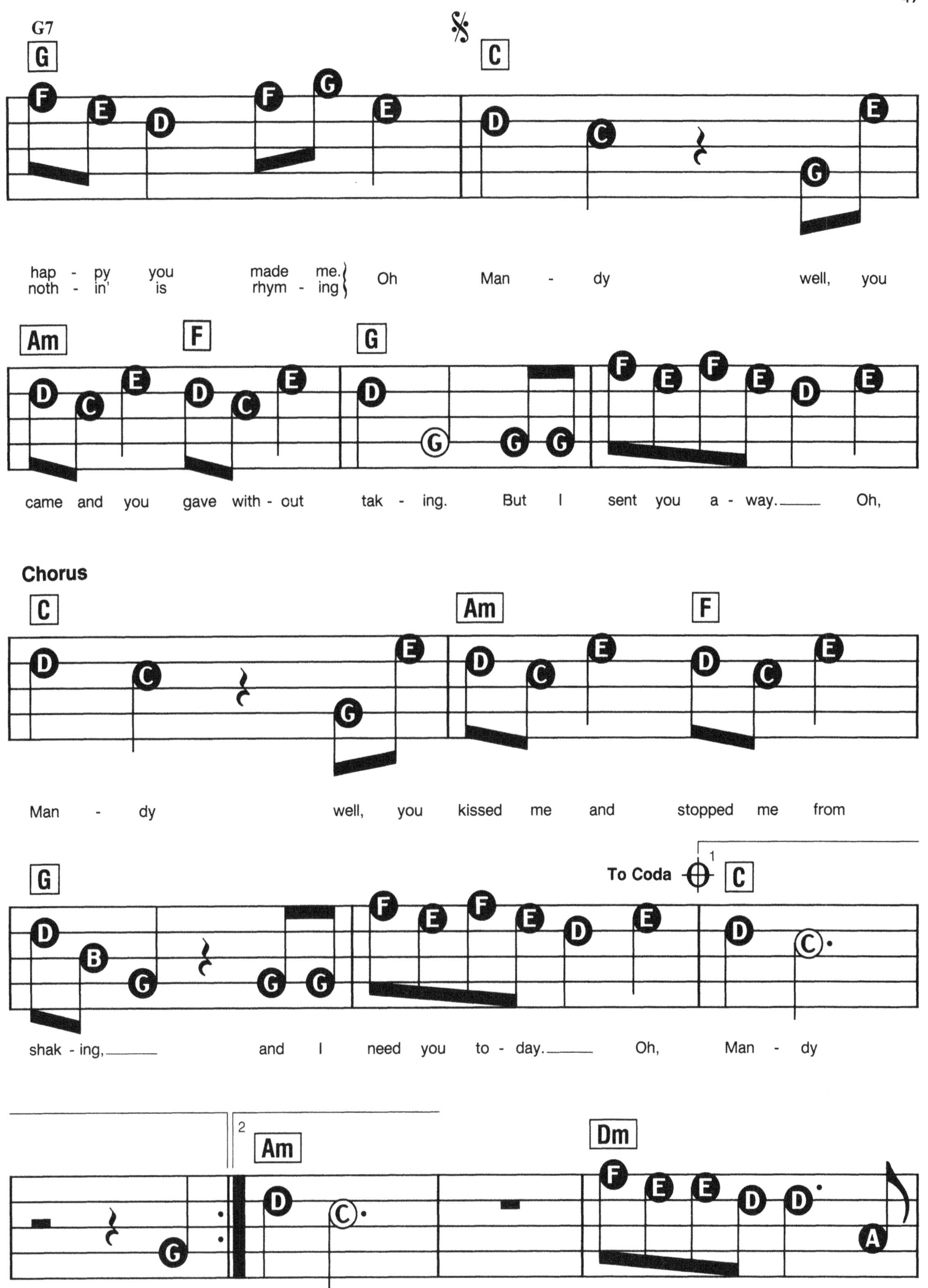
G7
G F E D F G E
C D C G E
hap - py you made me.
noth - in' is rhym - ing
Oh Man - dy well, you
Am D C E F D C E
G D G G G F E F E D E
came and you gave with - out tak - ing. But I sent you a - way. Oh,
Chorus
C D C G E
Am D C E F D C E
Man - dy well, you kissed me and stopped me from
G D B G G G F E F E D E
To Coda
1 C D C
shak - ing, and I need you to - day. Oh, Man - dy
G
2 Am D C
Dm F E E D D A
I'm Man - dy! Yes - ter - day's a dream, I

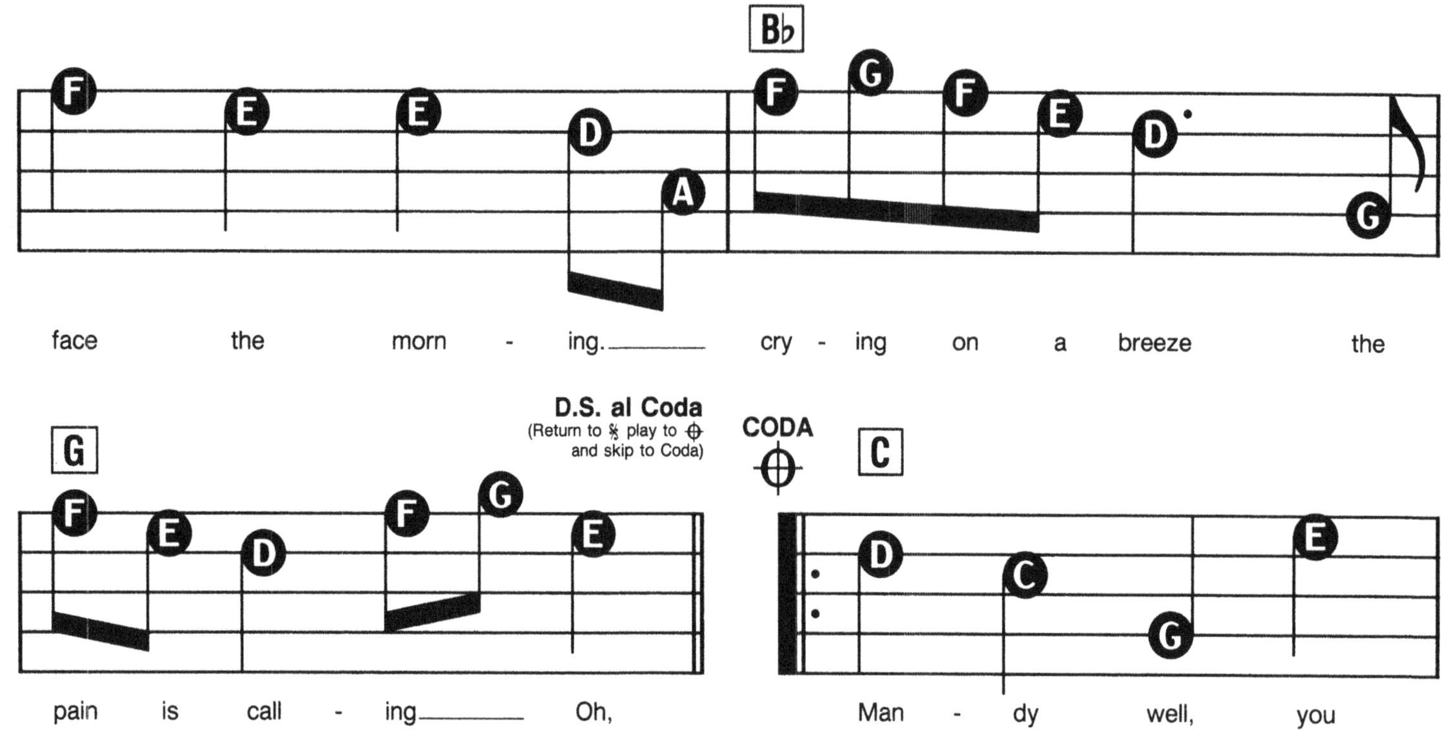
B♭
F E E D A F G F E D G
face the morn - ing. cry - ing on a breeze the
G
D.S. al Coda
(Return to 𝄋 play to ⊕ and skip to Coda)
F E D F G E
pain is call - ing Oh,
CODA
C
D C G E
Man - dy well, you

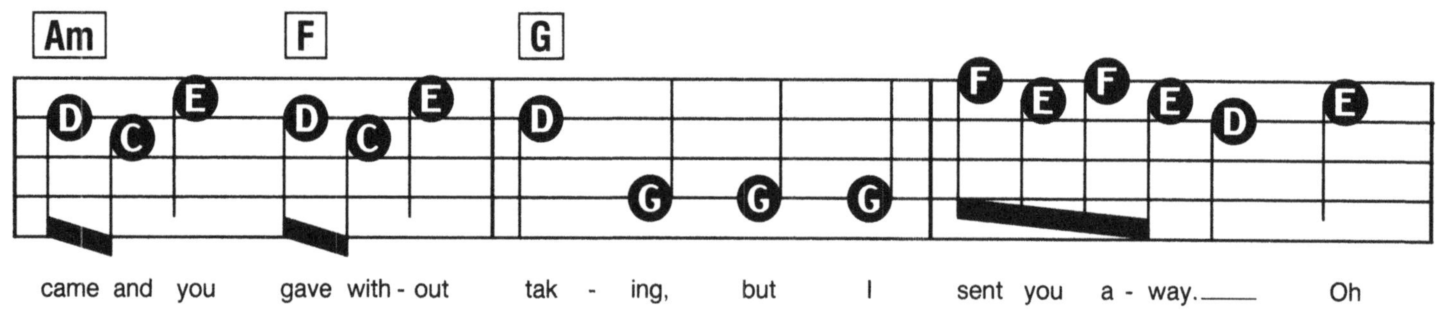
Am F G
D C E D C E D G G G F E F E D E
came and you gave with - out tak - ing, but I sent you a - way. Oh

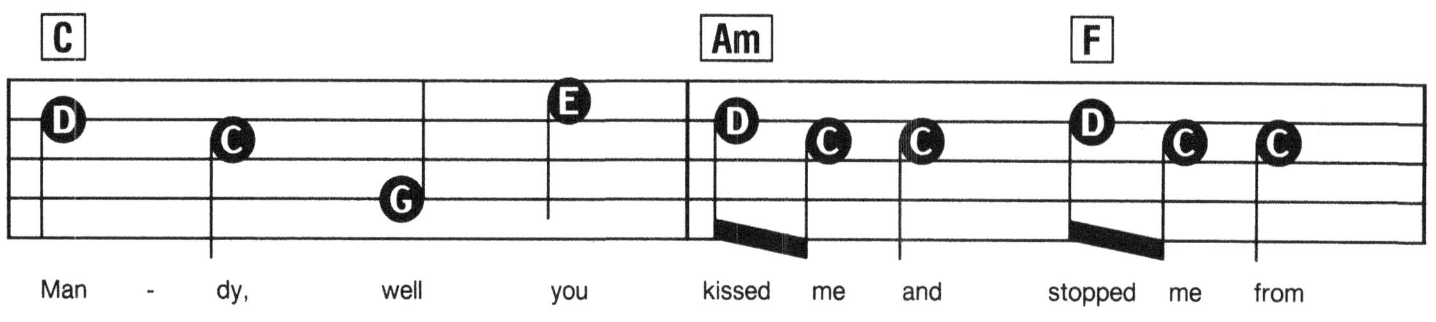
C Am F
D C G E D C C D C C
Man - dy, well you kissed me and stopped me from

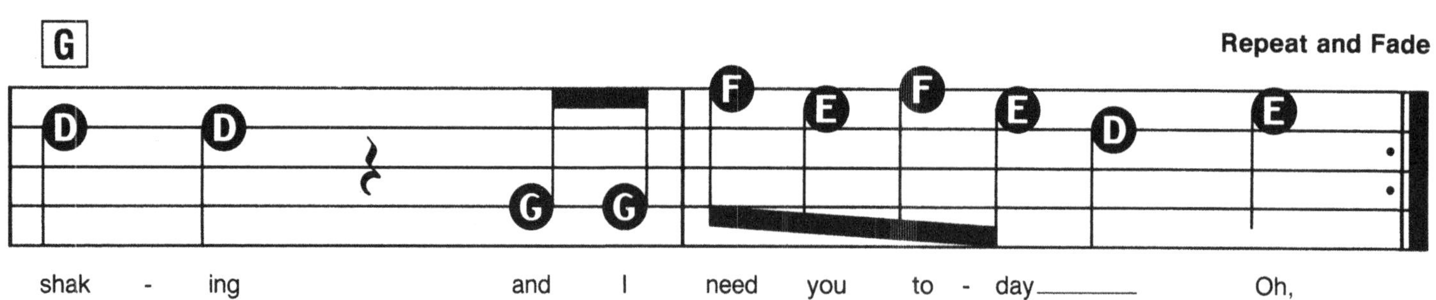
G
Repeat and Fade
D D G G F E F E D E
shak - ing and I need you to - day Oh,

The Old Songs

Registration 1
Rhythm: Ballad or Rock

Words and Music by
David Pomeranz and Buddy Kaye

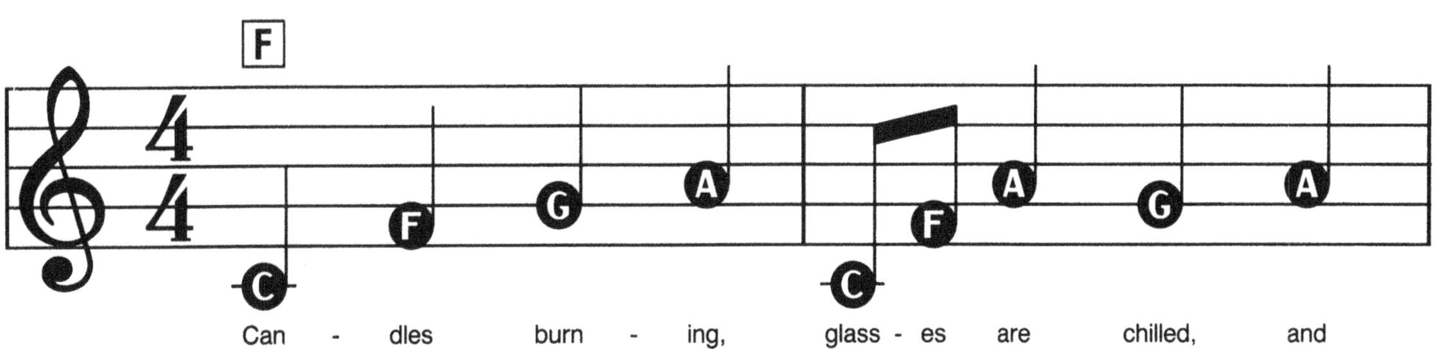

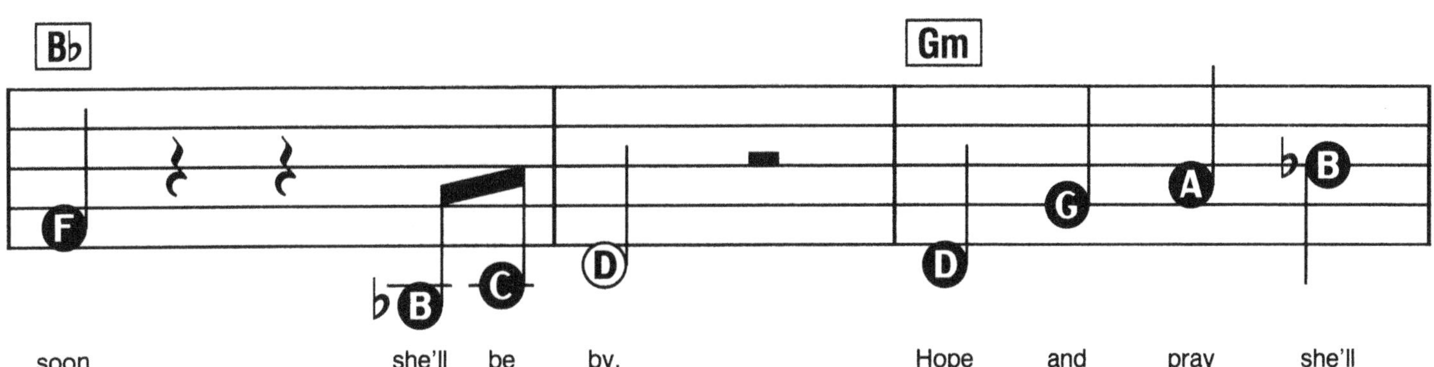

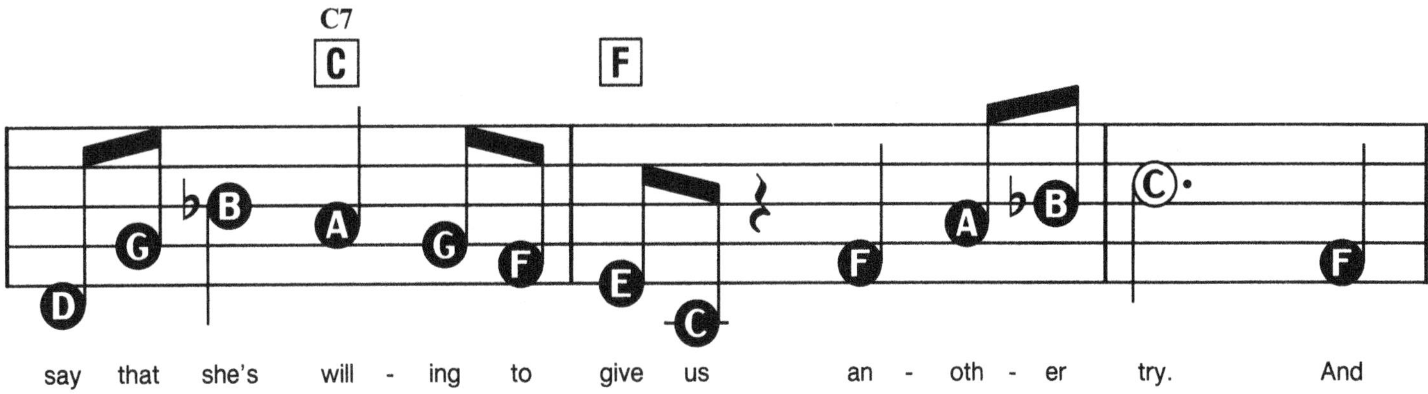

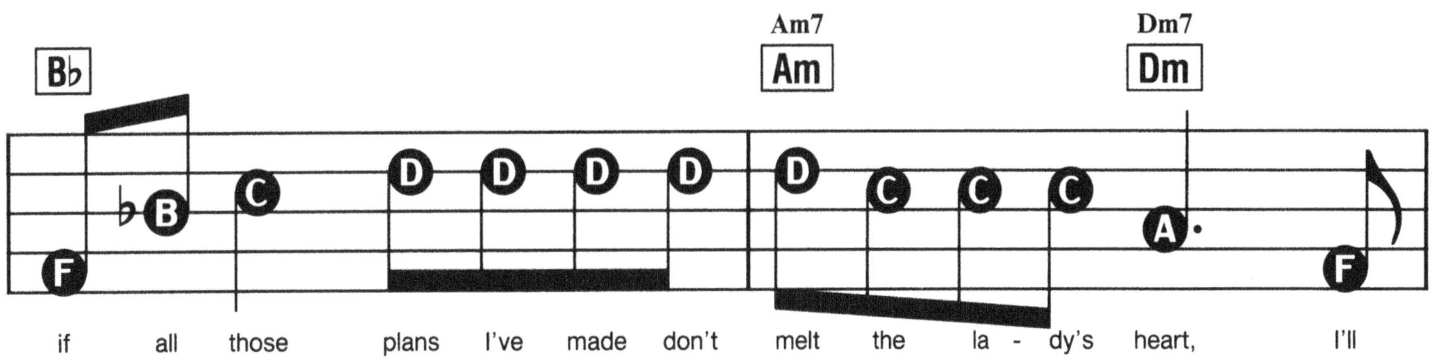

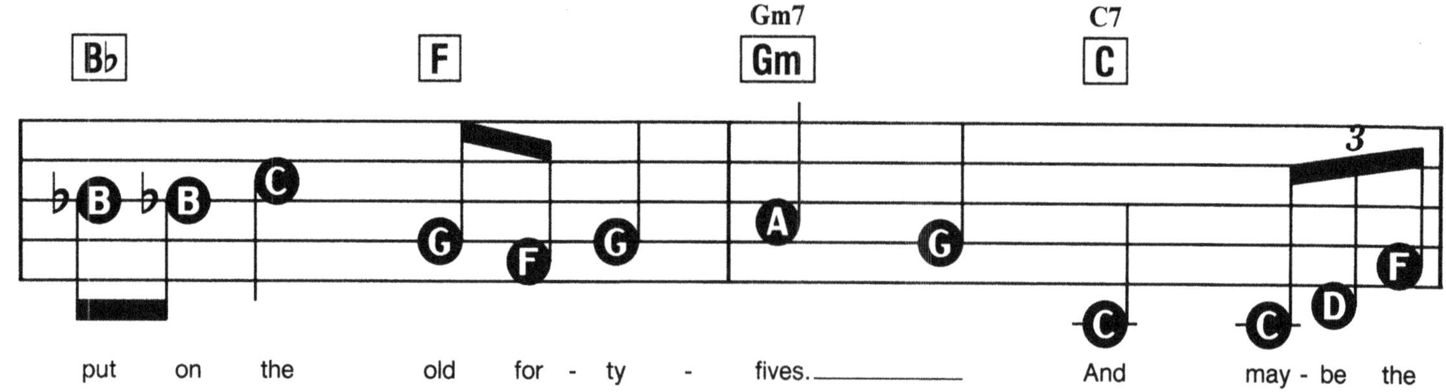
Gm7
C7
B♭
F
Gm
C
put on the old for - ty - fives.
And may - be the

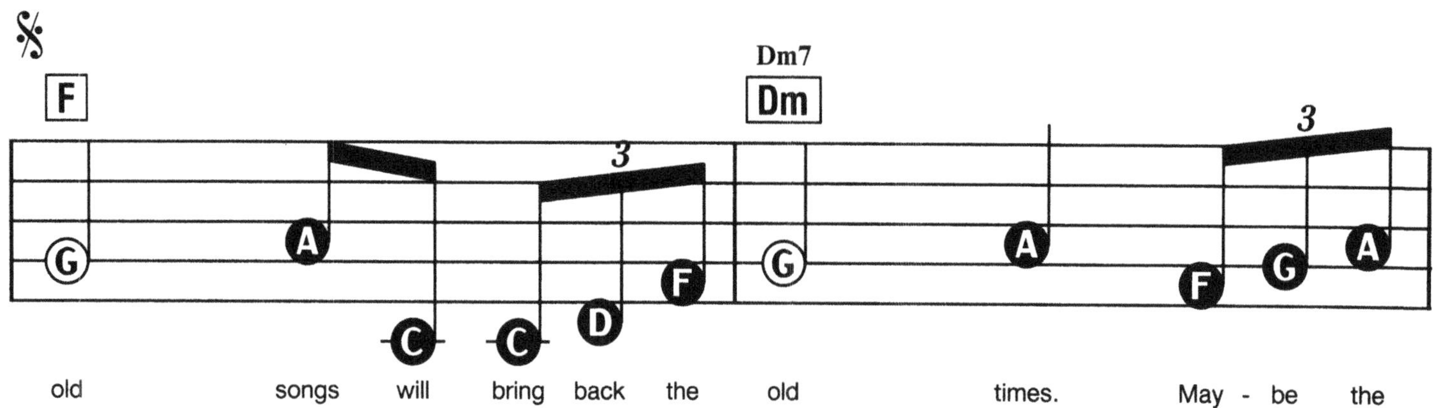
Dm7
F
Dm
old songs will bring back the old times. May - be the

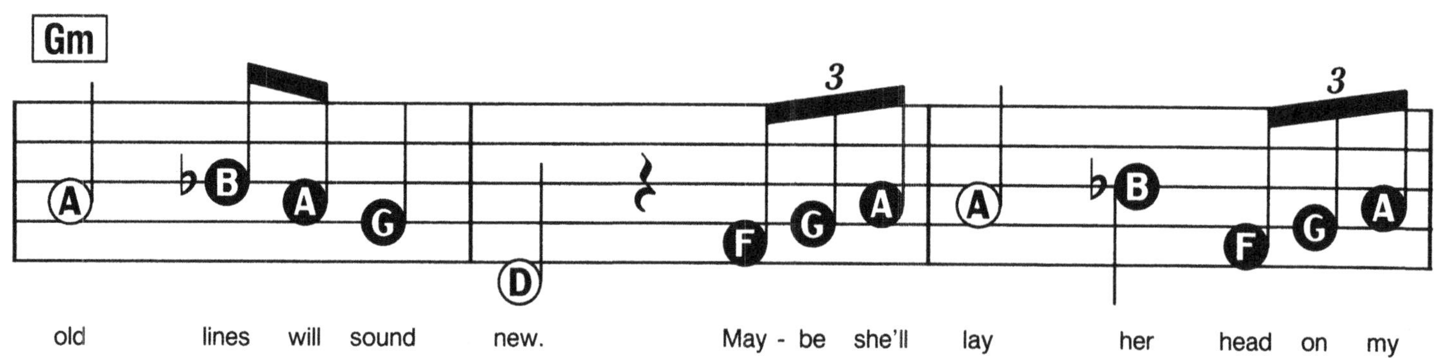
Gm
old lines will sound new. May - be she'll lay her head on my

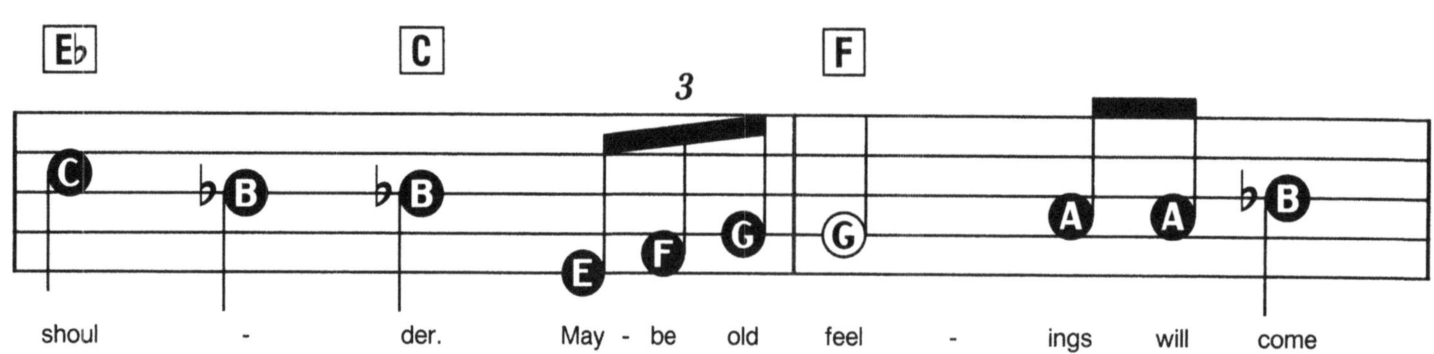
E♭
C
F
shoul - der. May - be old feel - ings will come

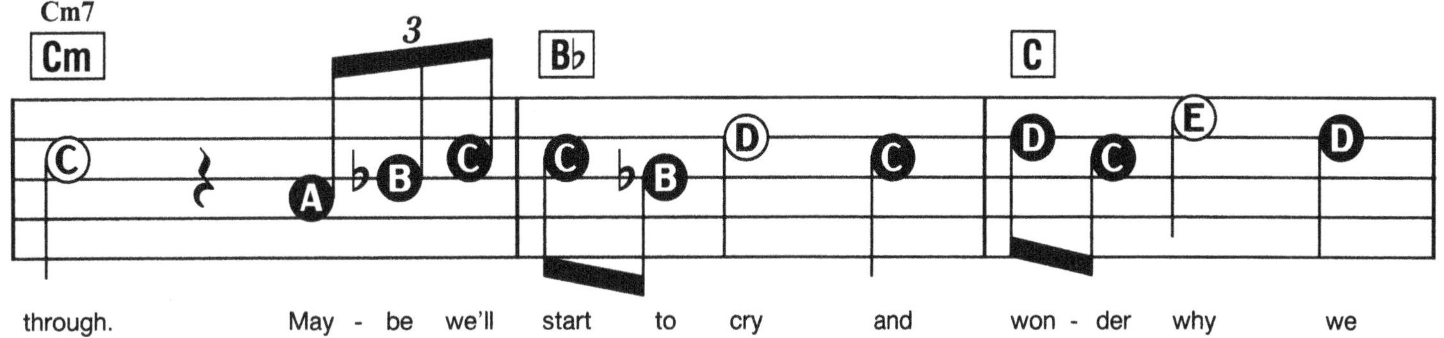
Cm7
Cm
3
Bb
C
C
A
B
C
C
B
D
C
D
C
E
D
through. May - be we'll start to cry and won - der why we

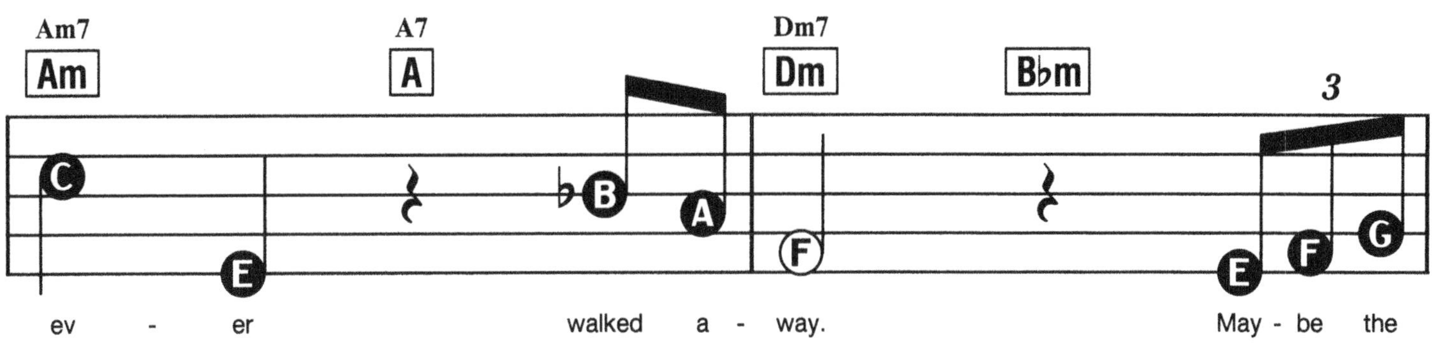
Am7
Am
A7
A
Dm7
Dm
Bbm
3
C
E
B
A
F
E
F
G
ev - er walked a - way. May - be the

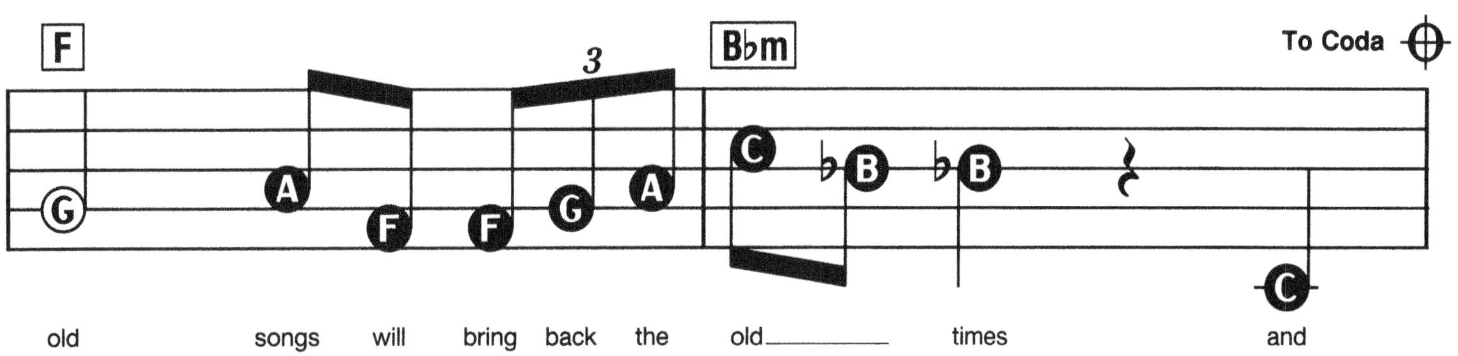
F
Bbm
To Coda
3
G
A
F
F
G
A
C
B
B
C
old songs will bring back the old times and

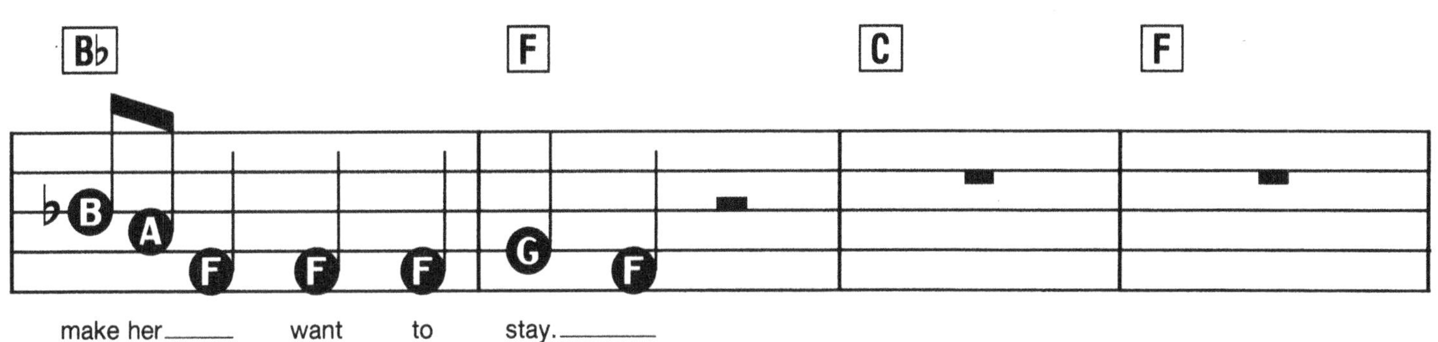
Bb
F
C
F
B
A
F
F
F
G
F
make her want to stay.

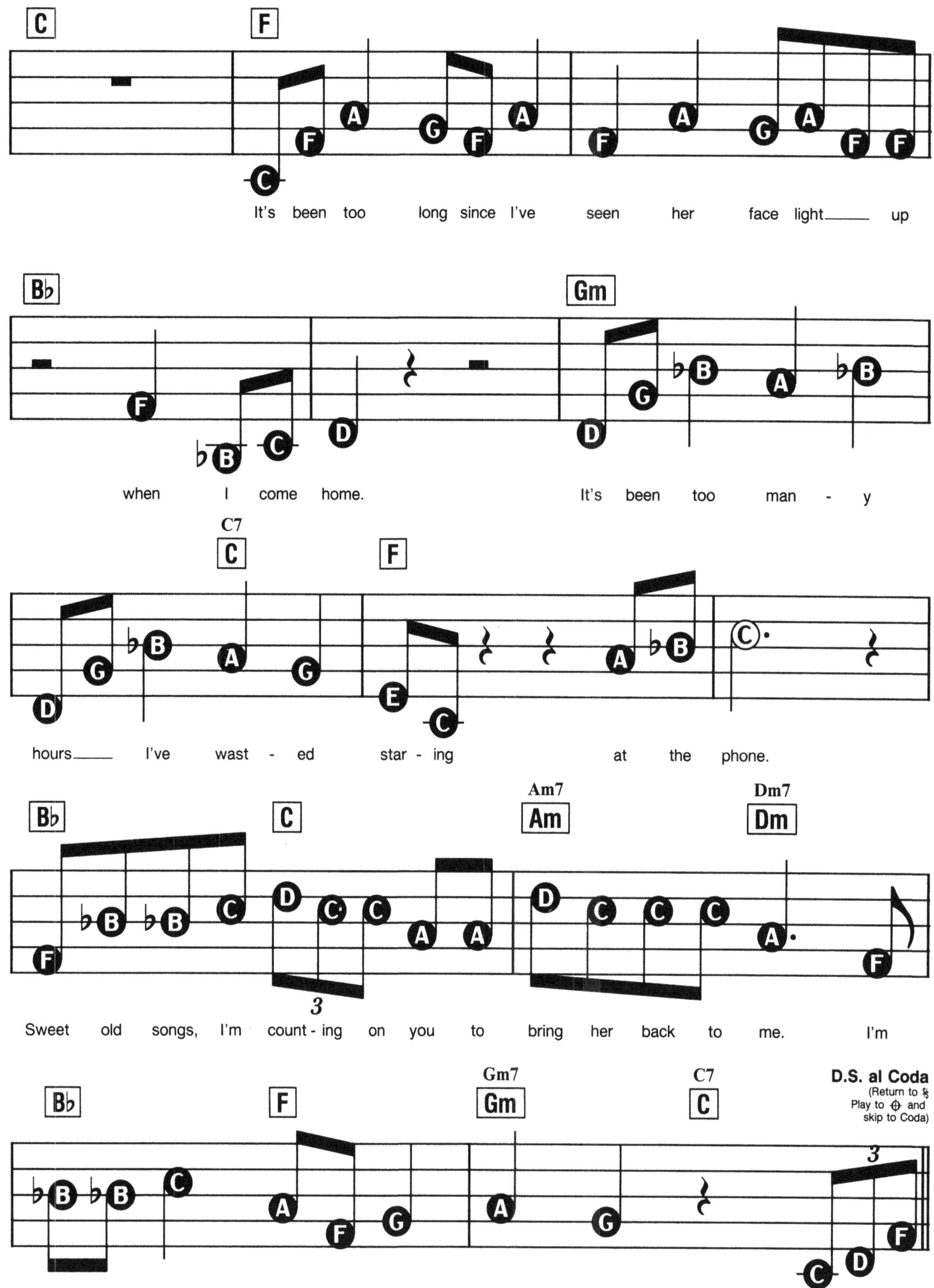
C
F
It's been too long since I've seen her face light up
B♭
Gm
when I come home. It's been too man - y
C7
C
F
hours I've wast - ed star - ing at the phone.
B♭
C
Am7
Am
Dm7
Dm
Sweet old songs, I'm count - ing on you to bring her back to me. I'm
B♭
F
Gm7
Gm
C7
C
D.S. al Coda
(Return to 𝄋
Play to ⊕ and
skip to Coda)
ti - red of lis - t'ning a - lone. May - be the

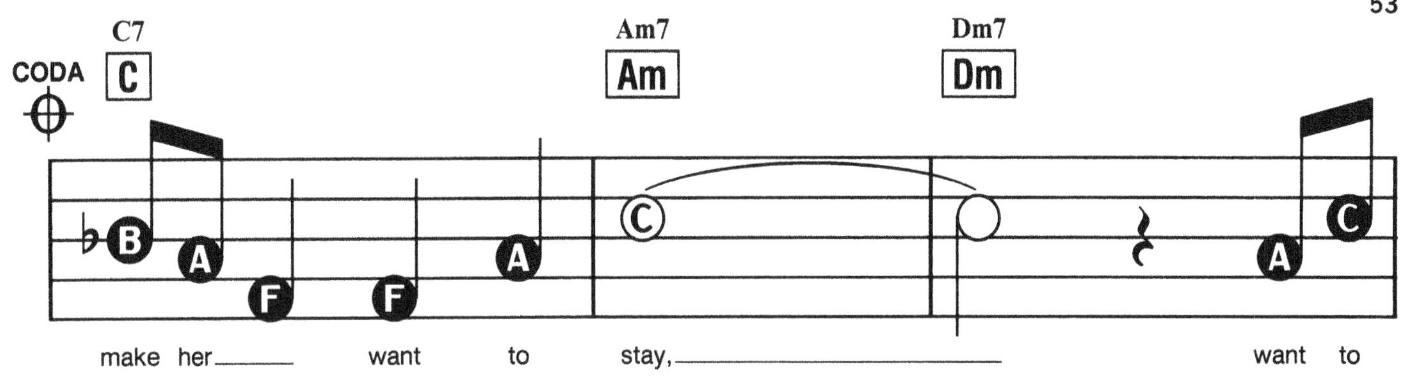
CODA
C7 C
Am7 Am
Dm7 Dm
make her want to stay, want to

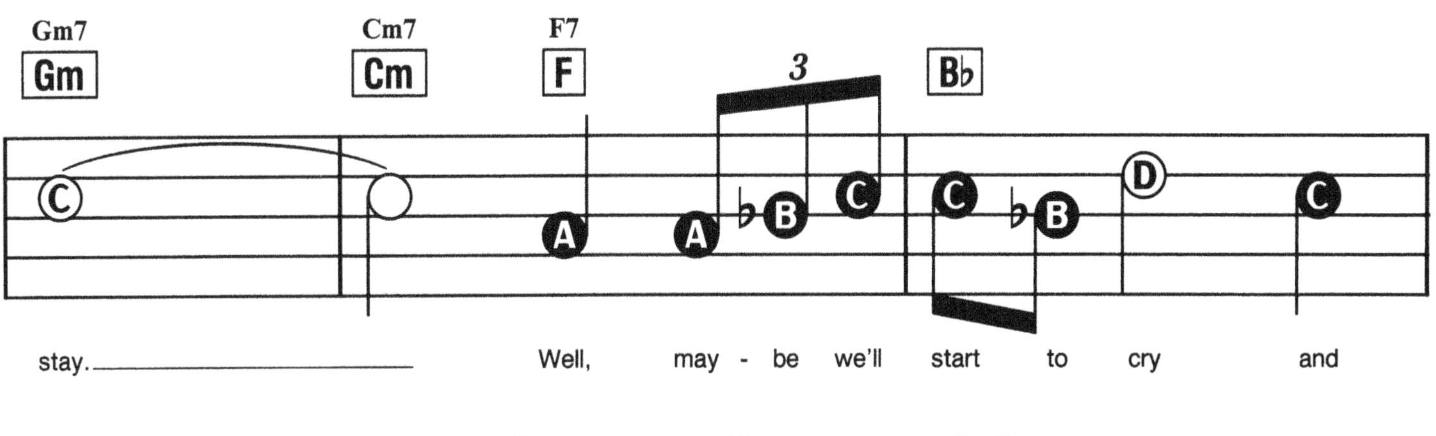
Gm7 Gm
Cm7 Cm
F7 F
B♭
stay. Well, may - be we'll start to cry and

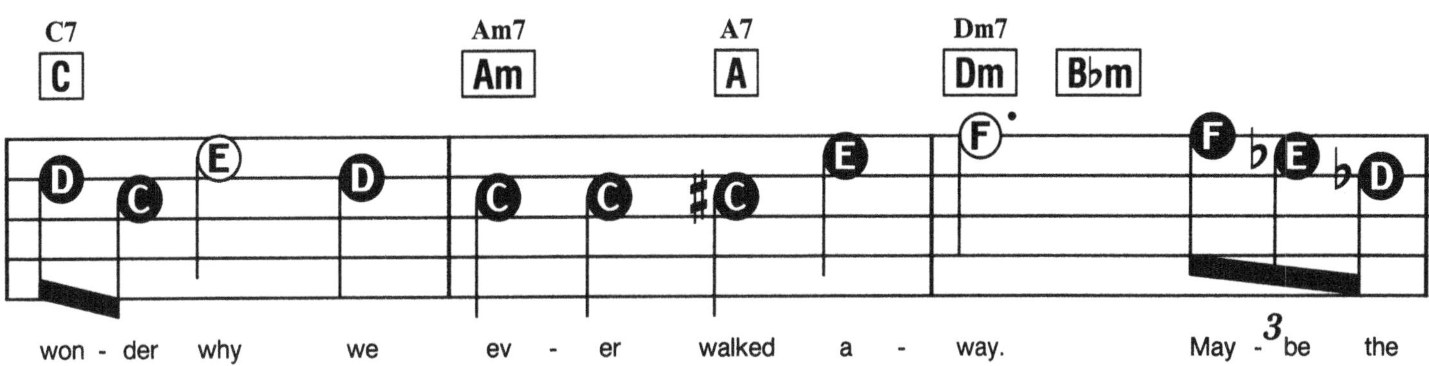
C7 C
Am7 Am
A7 A
Dm7 Dm
B♭m
won - der why we ev - er walked a - way. May - be the

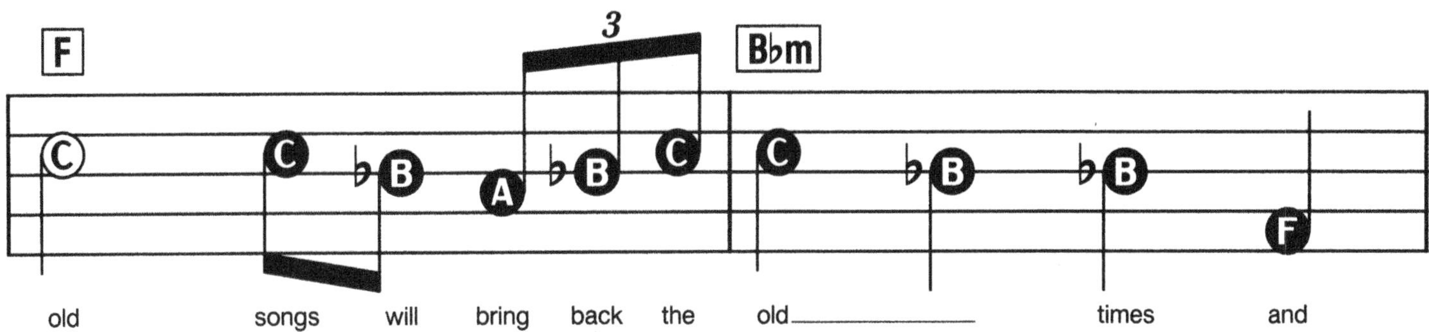
F
B♭m
old songs will bring back the old times and

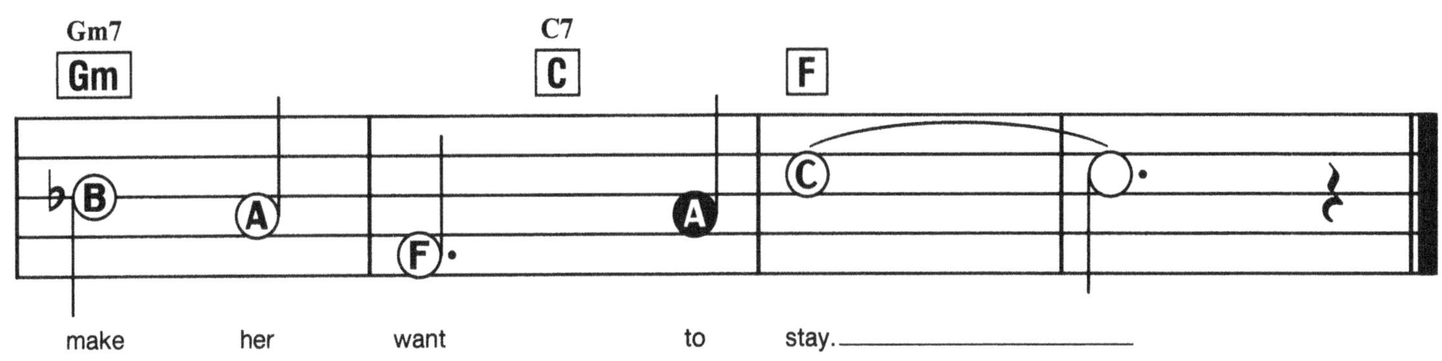
Gm7 Gm
C7 C
F
make her want to stay.

Memory

(From "CATS")

Registration 3
Rhythm: 6/8 March

Text by Trevor Nunn after T.S. Eliot
Music by Andrew Lloyd Webber

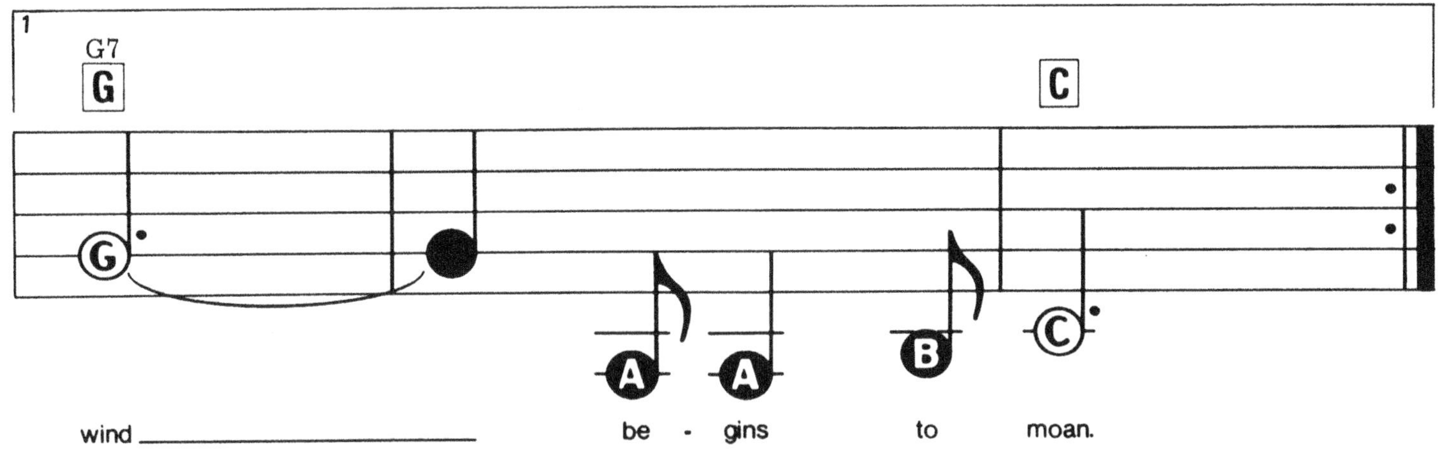
1
G7
G
C
G
A
A
B
C
wind
be - gins
to
moan.

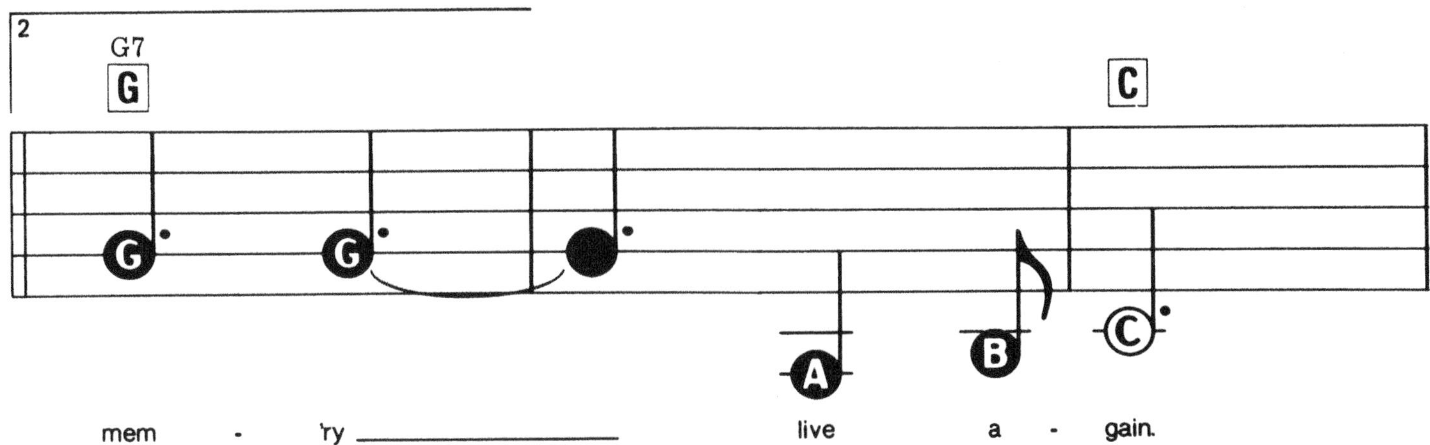
2
G7
G
C
G
G
A
B
C
mem - 'ry
live
a - gain.

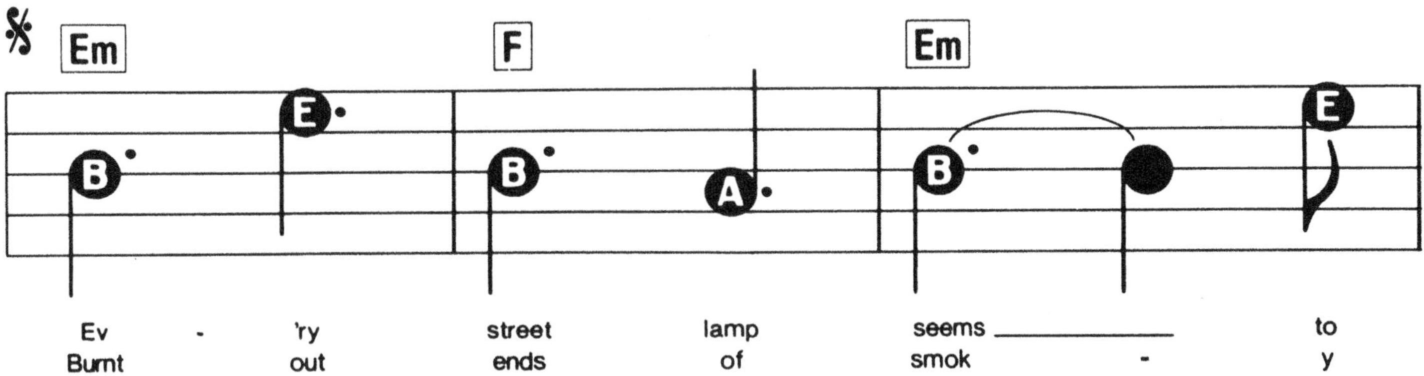
Em
F
Em
B
E
B
A
B
E
Ev - 'ry street lamp seems to
Burnt out ends of smok - y

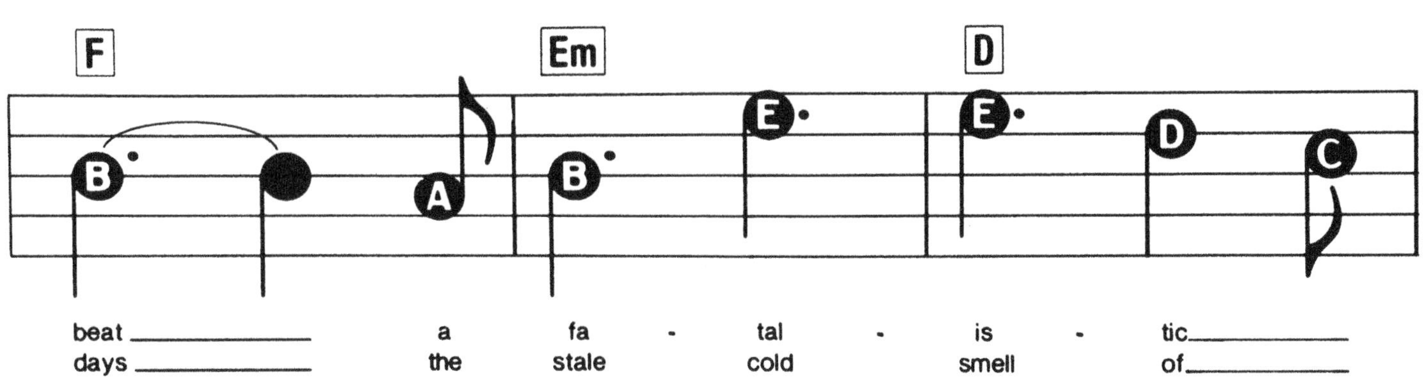
F
Em
D
B
A
B
E
E
D
C
beat a fa - tal - is - tic
days the stale cold smell of

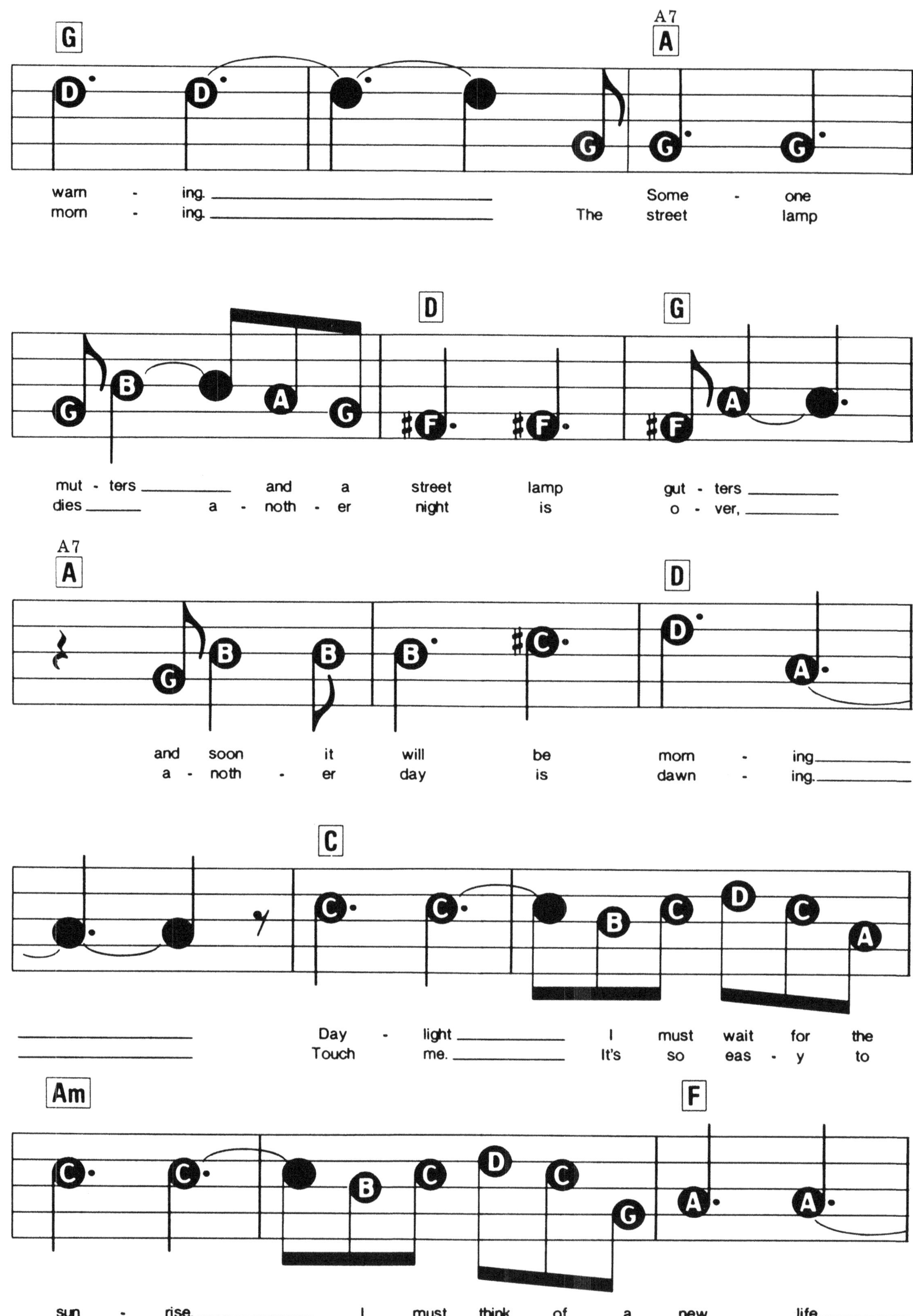
G
A7
A
D D C C G G G
warn - ing. Some - one
morn - ing. The street lamp
D
G
G B A G F F F A
mut - ters and a street lamp gut - ters
dies a - noth - er night is o - ver,
A7
A
D
G B B B C D A
and soon it will be morn - ing
a - noth - er day is dawn - ing.
C
C C B C D C A
Day - light I must wait for the
Touch me. It's so eas - y to
Am
F
C C B C D C G A A
sun - rise, I must think of a new life
leave me All a - lone with the mem - 'ry

Em
And I must - n't give in.
of my days in the sun.
When the
If you
Dm7
Dm
Am
dawn comes to - night will be a mem - o - ry too
touch me you'll un - der - stand what hap - pi - ness is.
G7
G
To Coda
And a new day
Look a new day
C
D.S. al Coda
(Return to
Play to and skip to Coda)
will be - gin
CODA
C
has be - gun

New York City Rhythm

Registration 1
Rhythm: Rock or Disco

Words and Music by
Barry Manilow and Marty Panzer

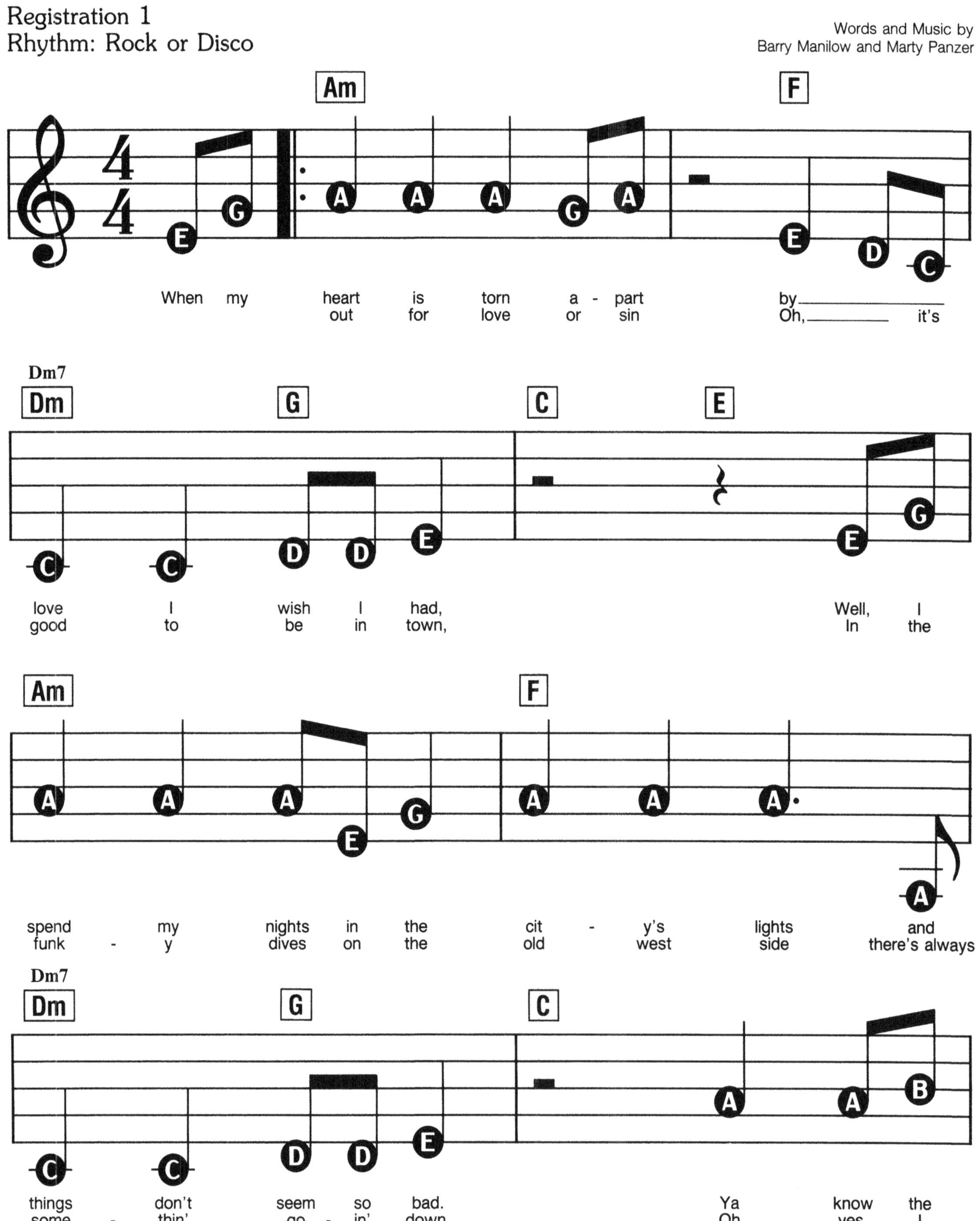

Dm
Am
Dm
move - ment seems to soothe me, and the tem - po takes con -
live my life with strang - ers, and the dan - ger's al - ways
Am
Dm7
Dm
C
F
D
trol, and I lose my blues when the New York Cit - y
there, but when I hit Broad - way and it's time to play, ya
C
Fm
Am
rhy - thm fills my soul;
know that I don't care;
it's the New York Cit - y
Em7
Em
F
rhy - thm run - nin' thru' my life, the
Am
Em7
Em
Dm7
Dm
G
pound - in' beat of the cit - y streets that keeps my dreams a - live.

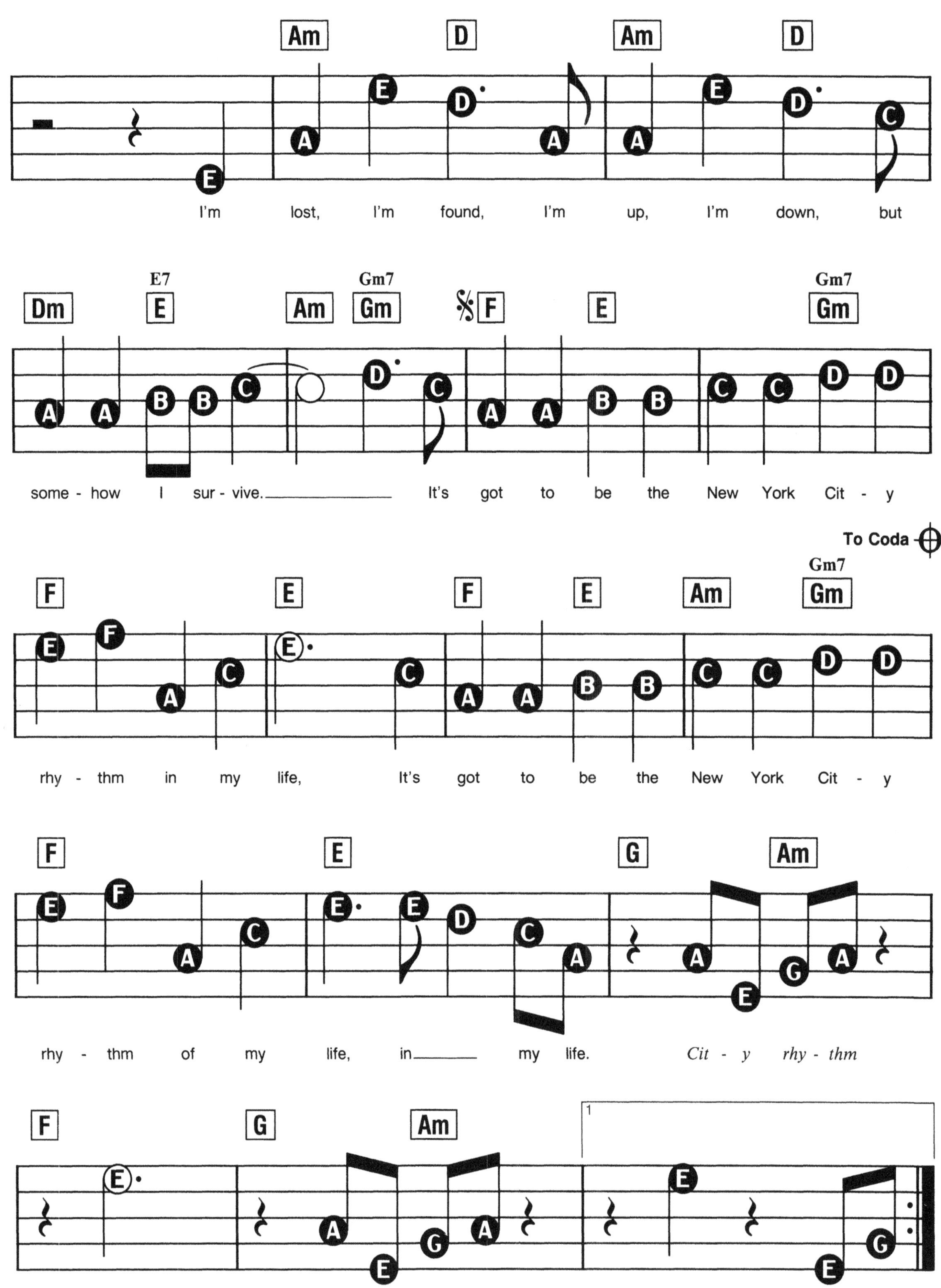
Am
D
Am
D
I'm lost, I'm found, I'm up, I'm down, but
Dm
E7
E
Am
Gm7
Gm
F
E
Gm7
Gm
some - how I sur - vive.
It's got to be the New York Cit - y
To Coda
F
E
F
E
Am
Gm7
Gm
rhy - thm in my life,
It's got to be the New York Cit - y
F
E
G
Am
rhy - thm of my life, in my life.
Cit - y rhy - thm
F
G
Am
1
Oo
Cit - y rhy - thm
Oo
When I'm

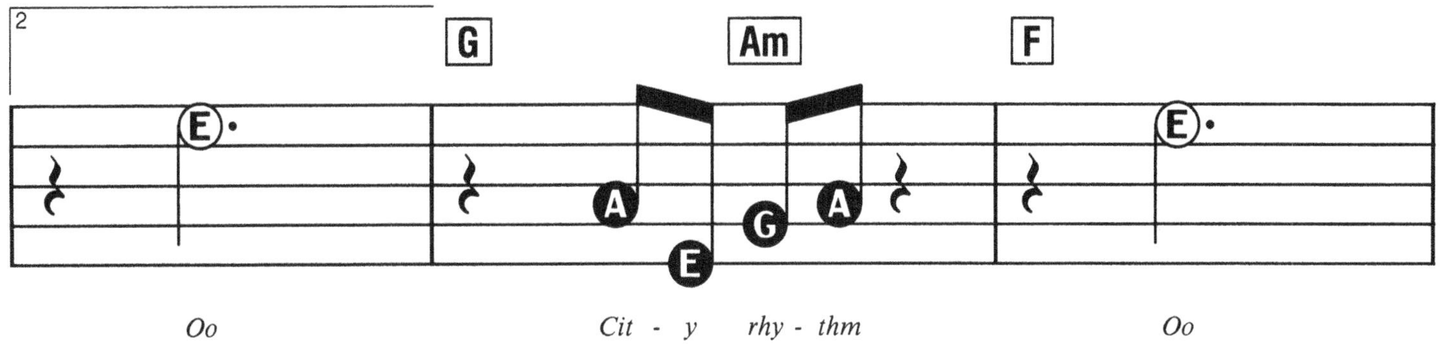
2
G
Am
F
Oo
Cit - y rhy - thm
Oo

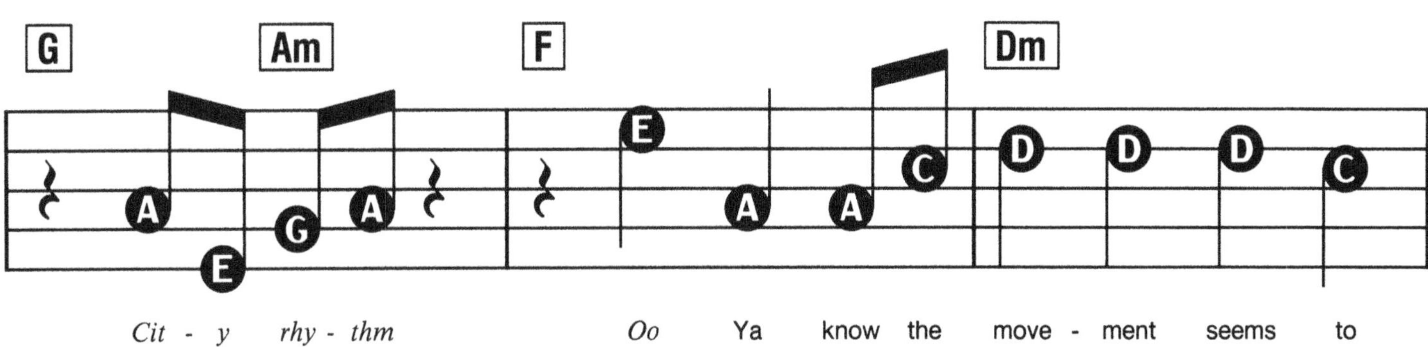
G
Am
F
Dm
Cit - y rhy - thm
Oo Ya know the move - ment seems to

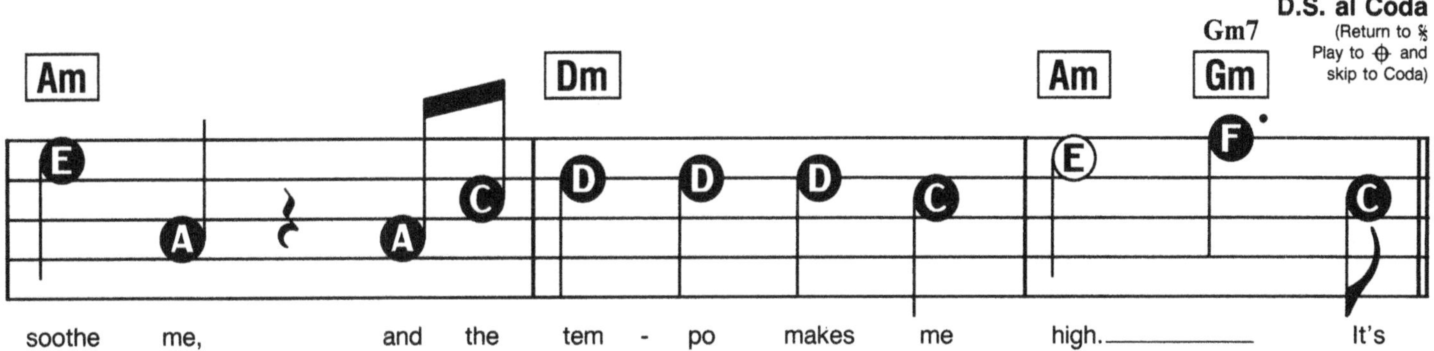
Am
Dm
Am
Gm7
Gm
D.S. al Coda
(Return to 𝄋
Play to ⊕ and
skip to Coda)
soothe me, and the tem - po makes me high. It's

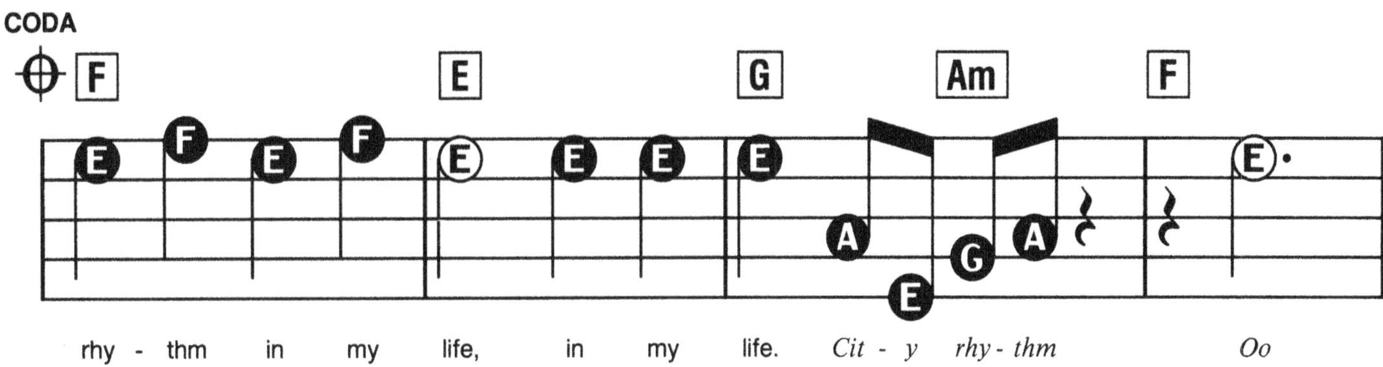
CODA
F
E
G
Am
F
rhy - thm in my life, in my life. Cit - y rhy - thm Oo

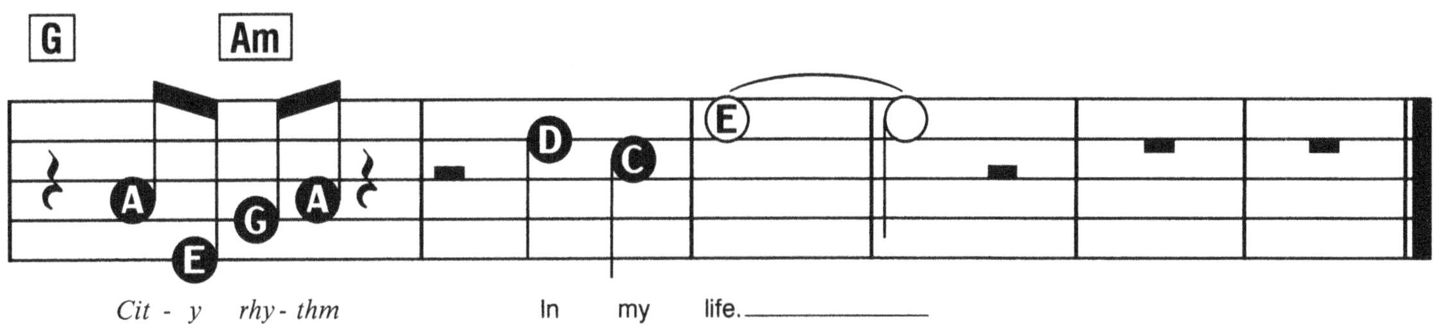
G
Am
Cit - y rhy - thm In my life.

One Voice

Registration 5
Rhythm: Rock or Ballad

Words and Music by
Barry Manilow

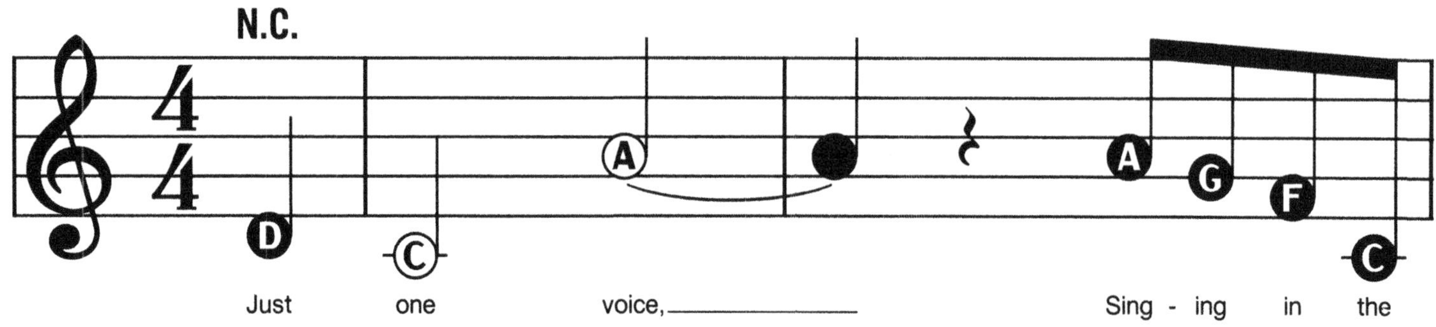

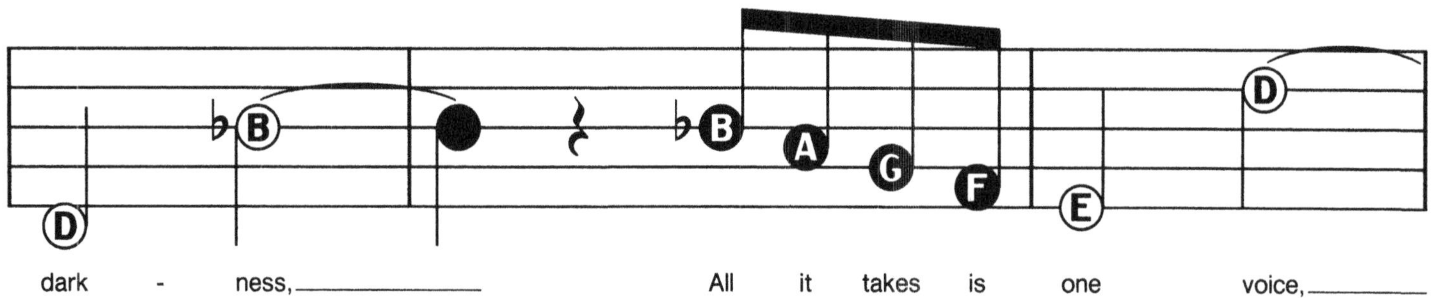

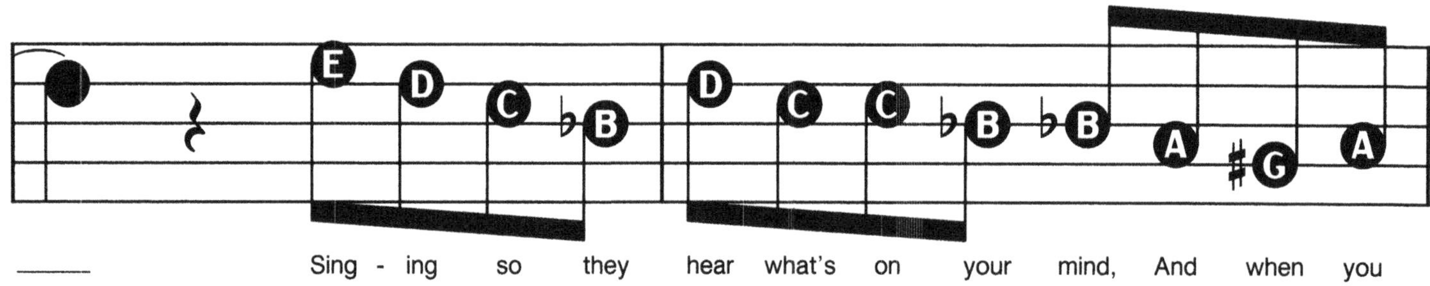

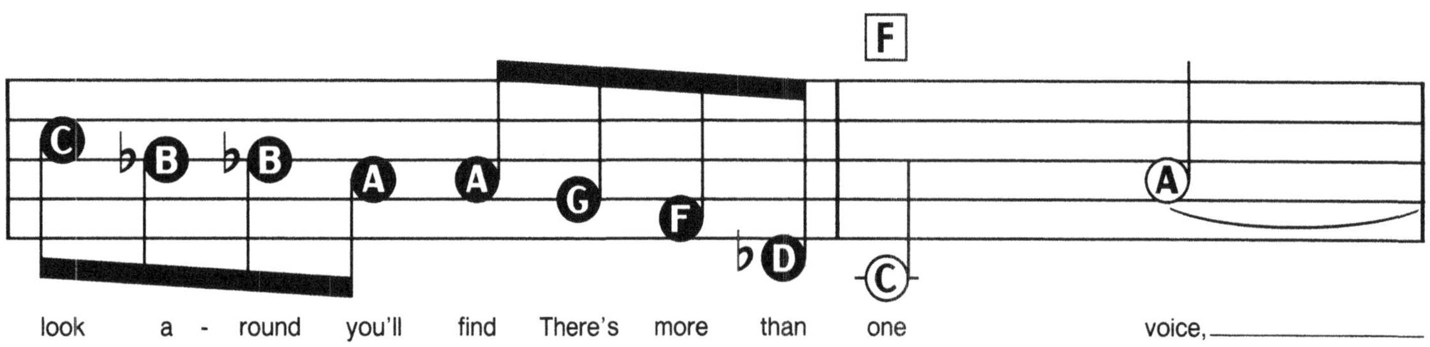

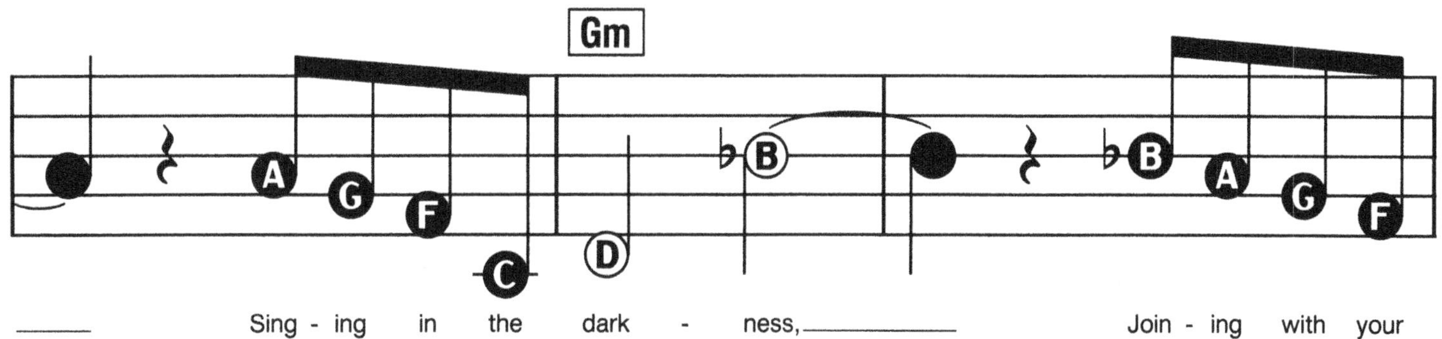
Gm
A G F C D B B B A G F
Sing - ing in the dark - ness,
Join - ing with your

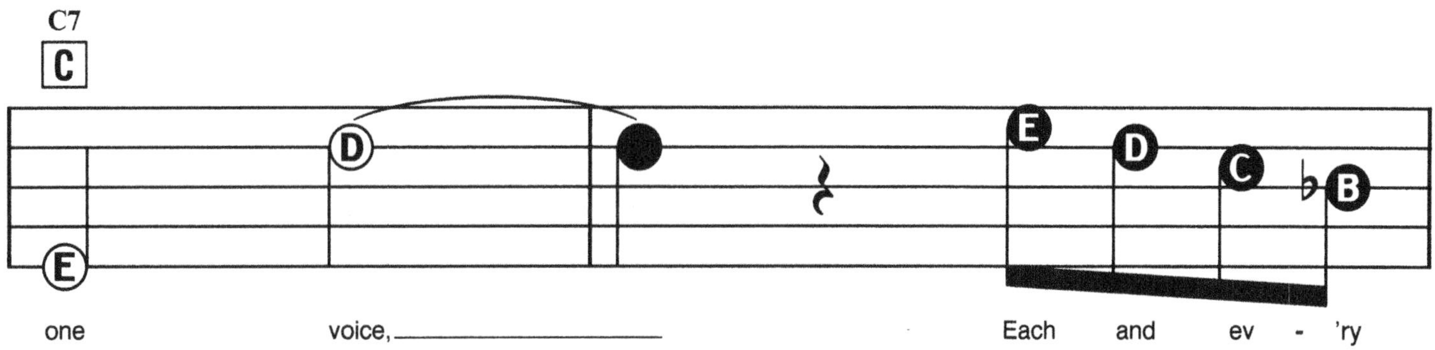
C7
C
E D E D C B
one voice,
Each and ev - 'ry

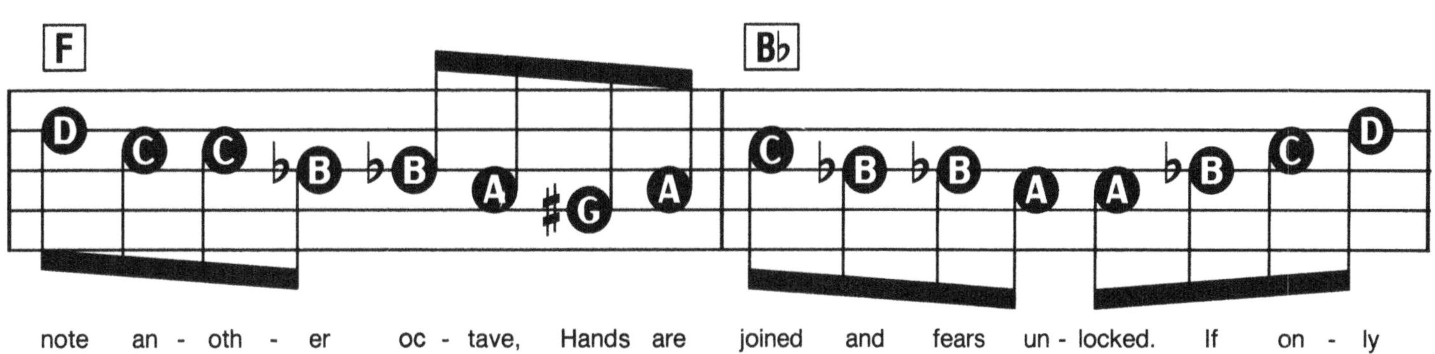
F
Bb
D C C B B A G A C B B A A B C D
note an - oth - er oc - tave, Hands are joined and fears un - locked. If on - ly

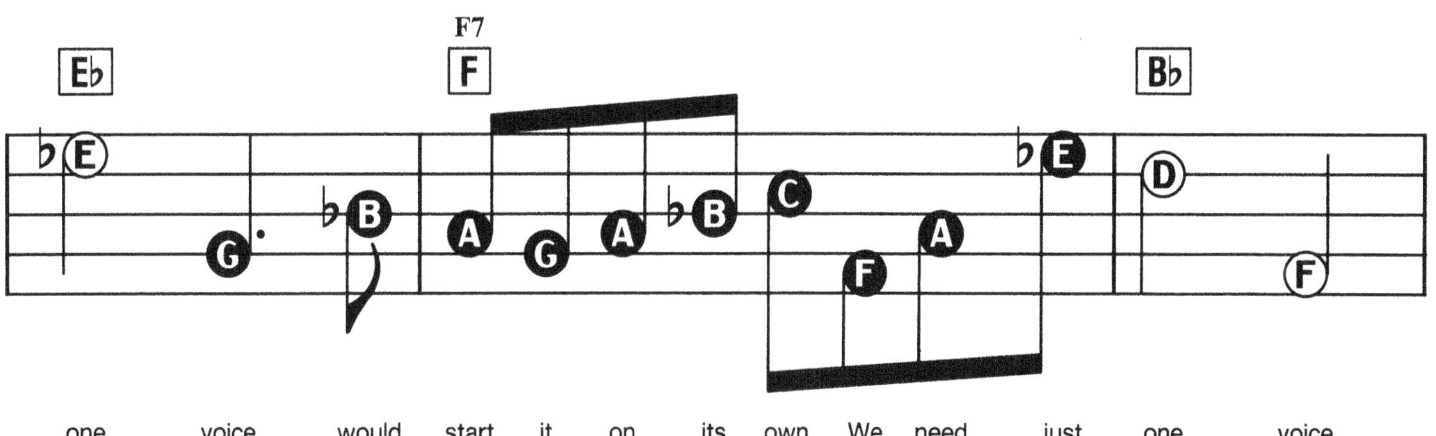
Eb
F7
F
Bb
E G B A G A B C F A E D F
one voice would start it on its own, We need just one voice

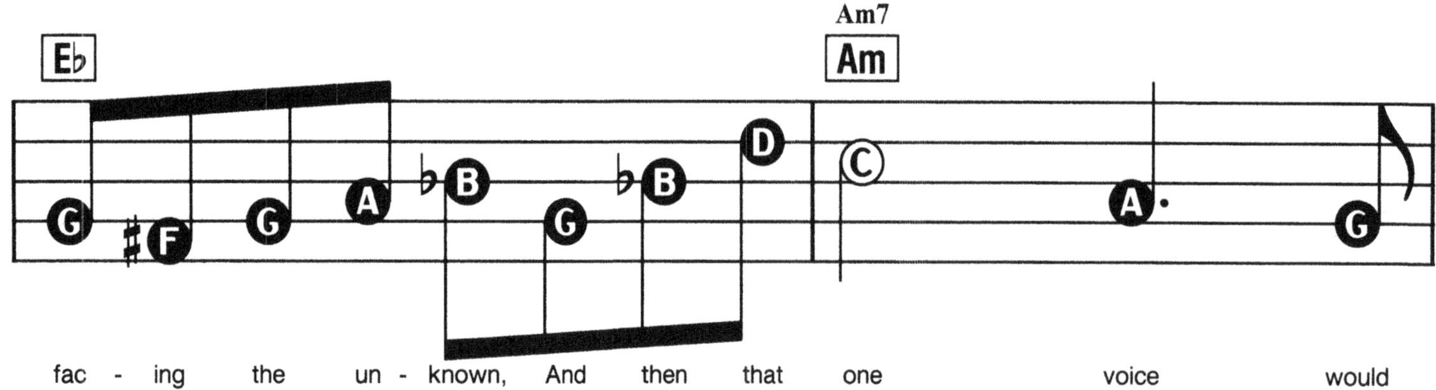
E♭
Am7
Am
G ♯F G A ♭B G ♭B D C A G
fac - ing the un - known, And then that one voice would

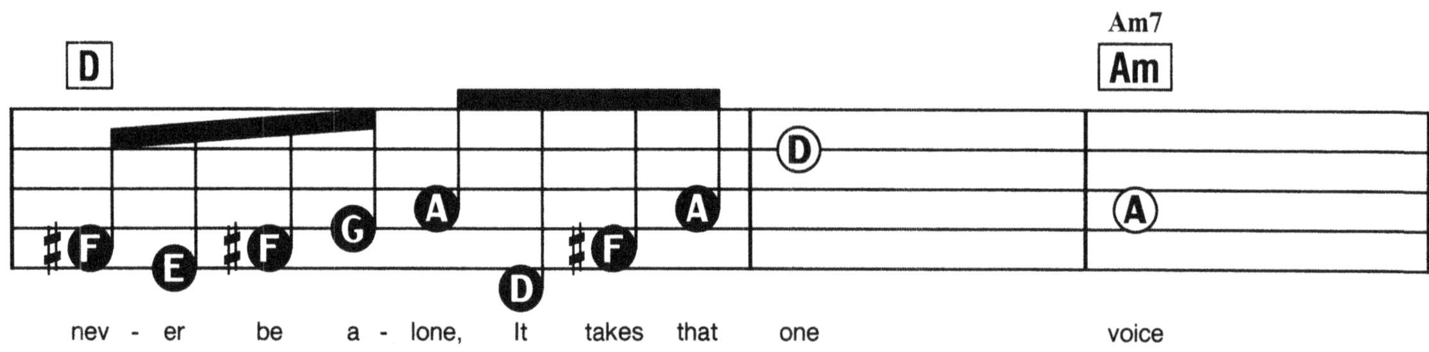
D
Am7
Am
♯F E ♯F G A D ♯F A D A
nev - er be a - lone, It takes that one voice

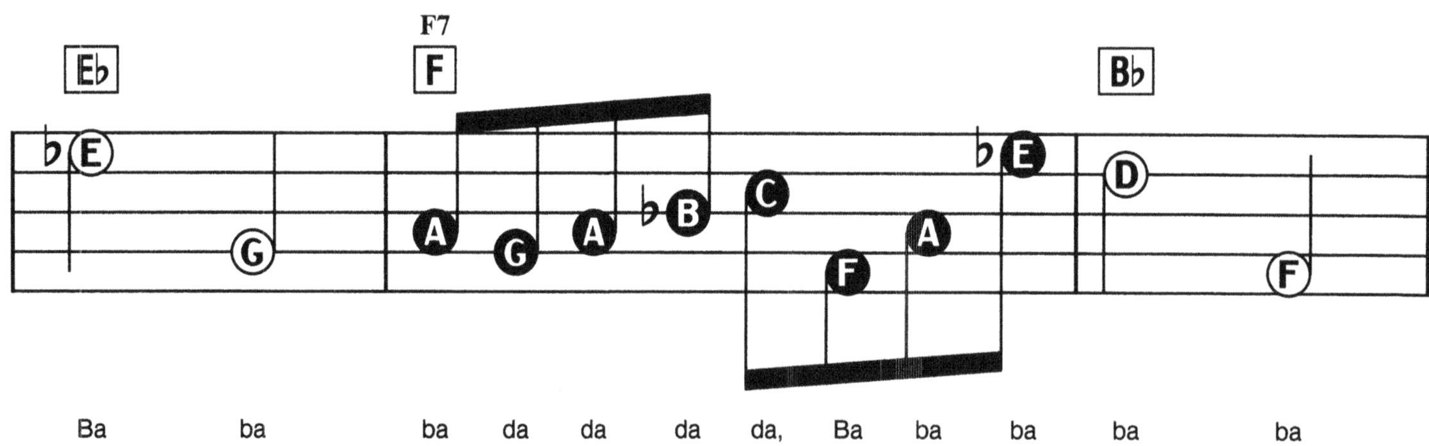
E♭
F7
F
B♭
♭E G A G A ♭B C F A ♭E D F
Ba ba ba da da da da, Ba ba ba ba ba

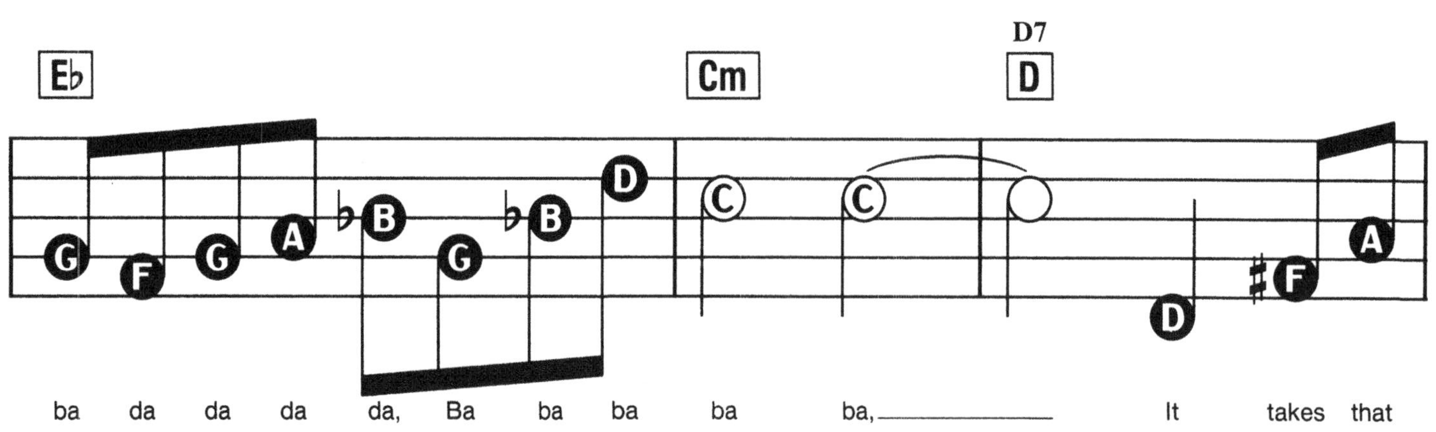
E♭
Cm
D7
D
G F G A ♭B G ♭B D C C D ♯F A
ba da da da da, Ba ba ba ba ba, It takes that

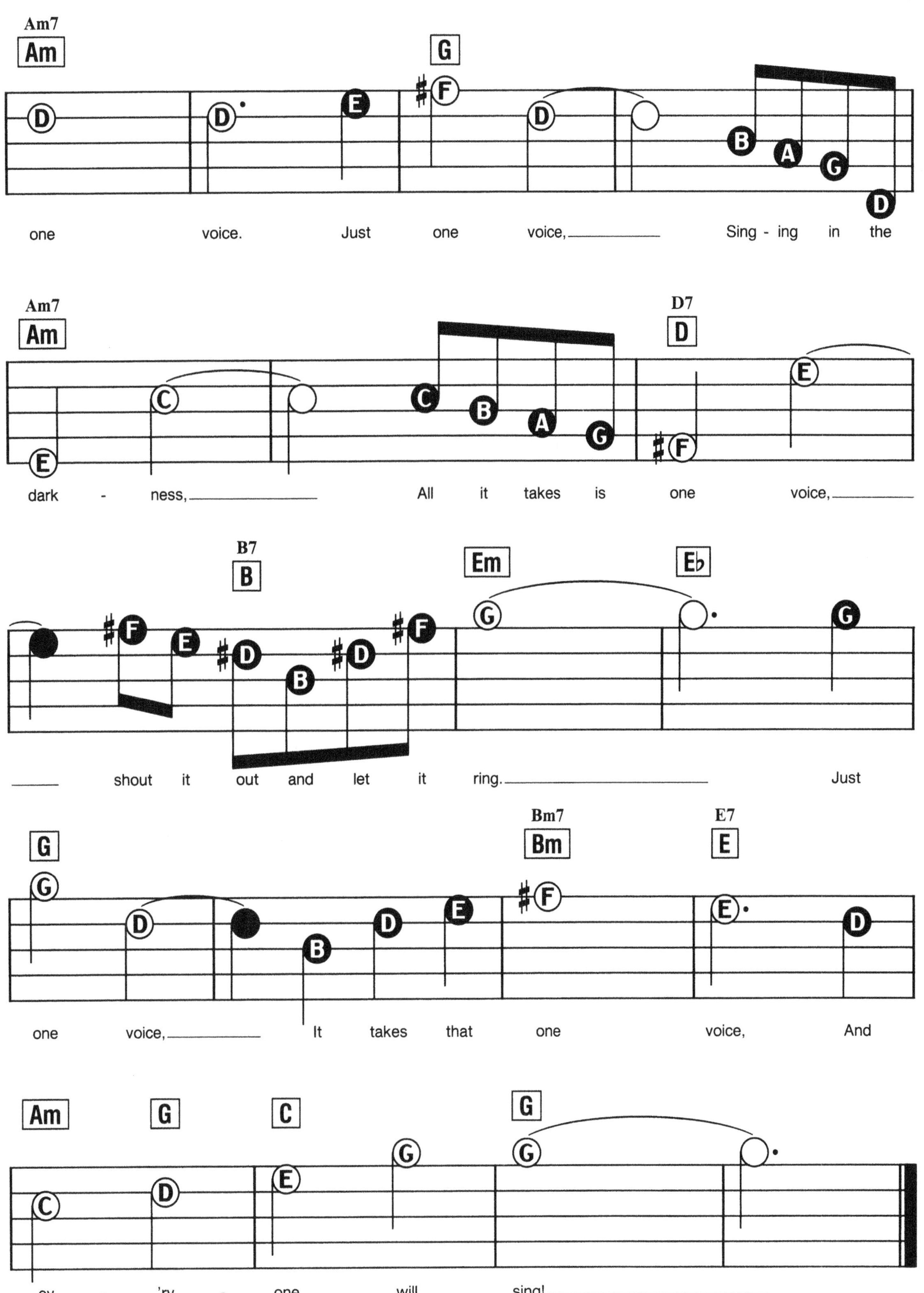
Am7 Am G
one voice. Just one voice, Sing - ing in the
Am7 Am D7 D
dark - ness, All it takes is one voice,
B7 B Em E♭
shout it out and let it ring. Just
G Bm7 Bm E7 E
one voice, It takes that one voice, And
Am G C G
ev - 'ry - one will sing!

Paradise Cafe

Registration 2
Rhythm: Ballad or Rock

Words by Bruce Sussman and Jack Feldman
Music by Barry Manilow

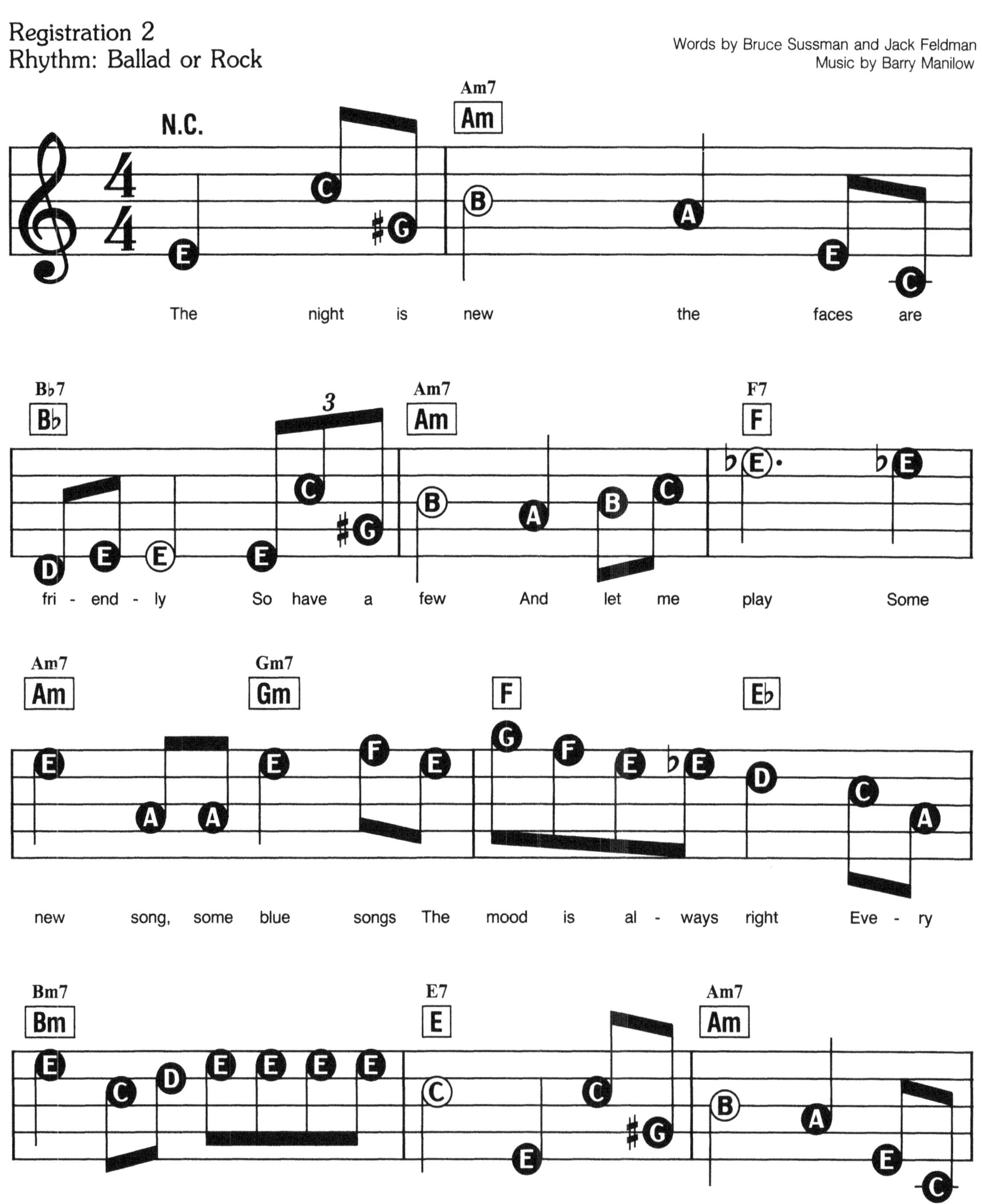

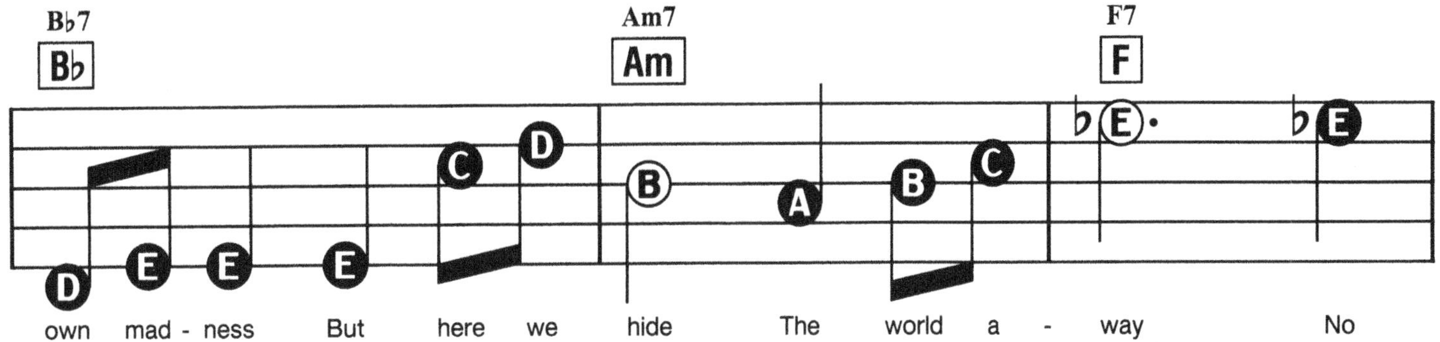
B♭7
B♭
Am7
Am
F7
F
D E E E C D
B A B C
E E
own mad - ness But here we hide The world a - way No

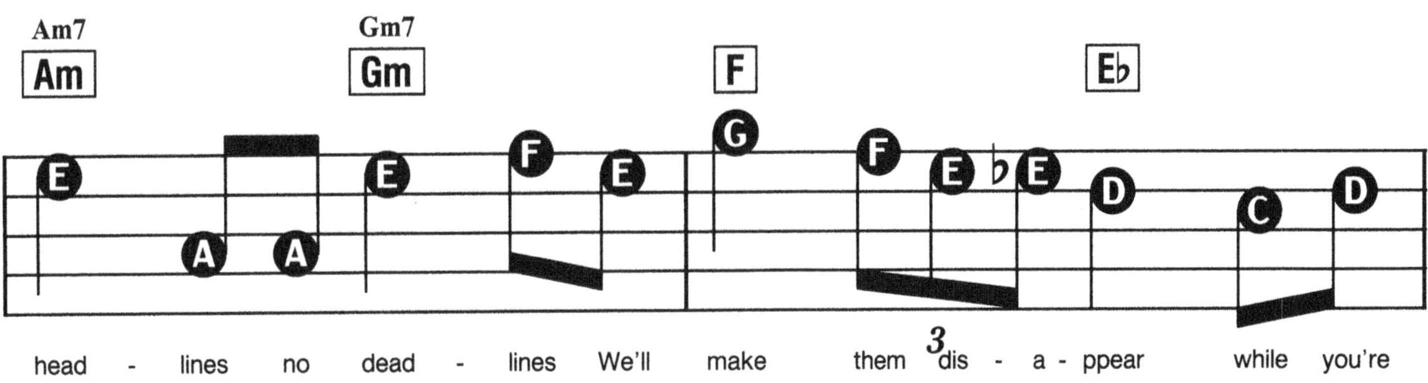
Am7
Am
Gm7
Gm
F
E♭
E A A E F E
G F E E D C D
3
head - lines no dead - lines We'll make them dis - a - ppear while you're

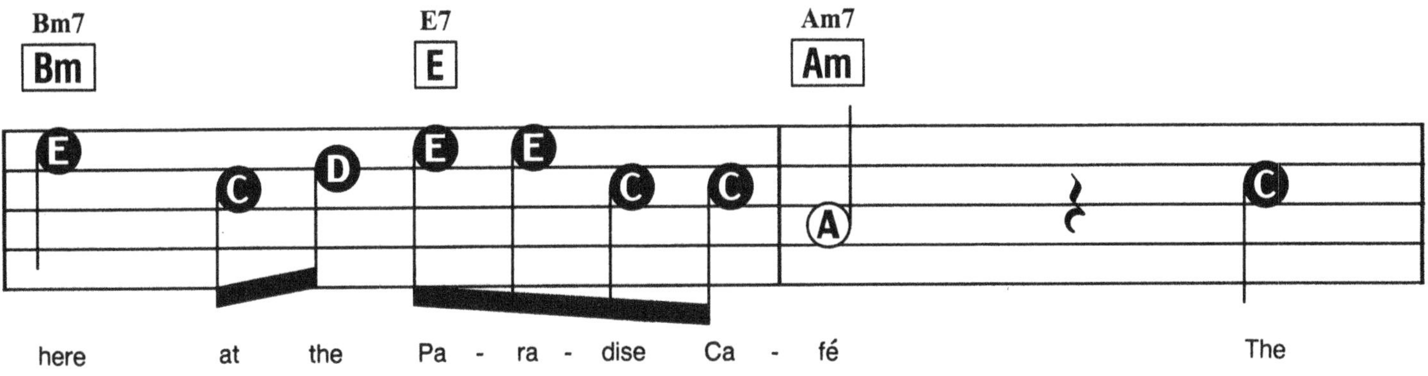
Bm7
Bm
E7
E
Am7
Am
E C D E E C C
A C
here at the Pa - ra - dise Ca - fé The

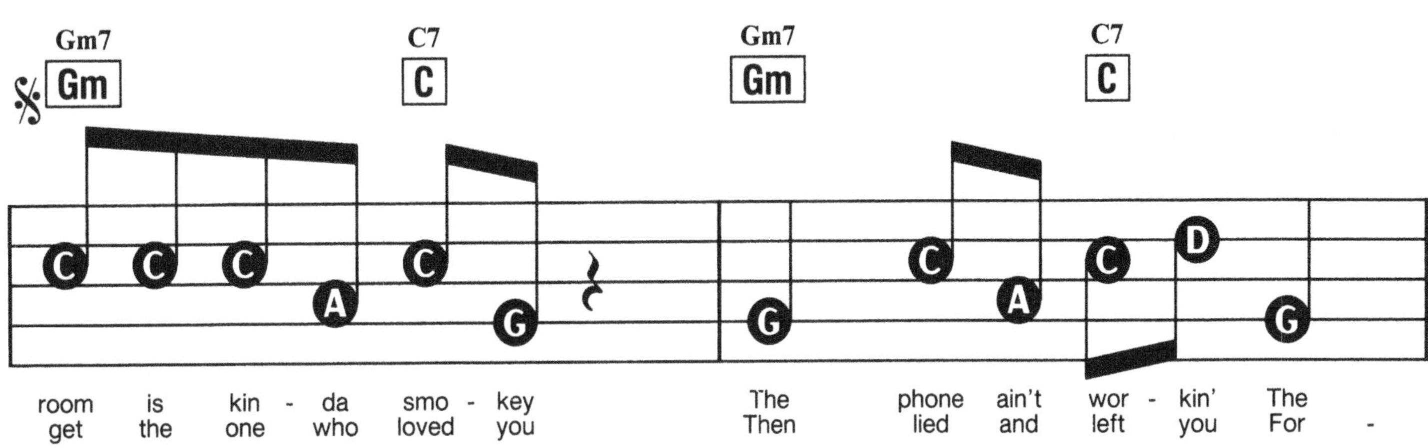
Gm7
Gm
C7
C
Gm7
Gm
C7
C
C C C A C G
G C A C D G
room is kin - da smo - key The phone ain't wor - kin' The
get the one who loved you Then lied and left you For -

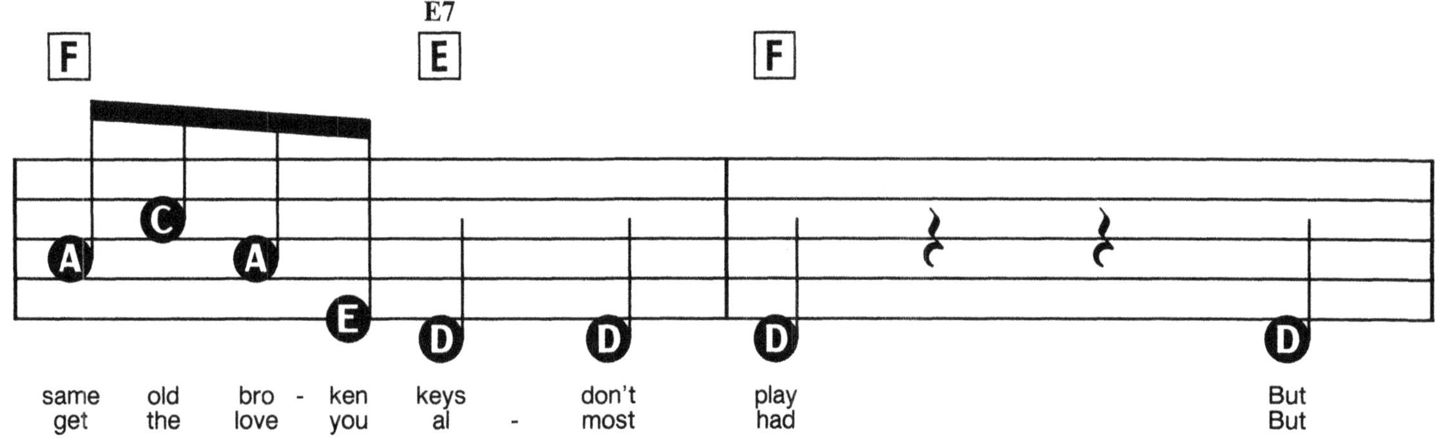
E7
F
E
F
A C A E D D D D
same old bro - ken keys don't play But
get the love you al - most had But

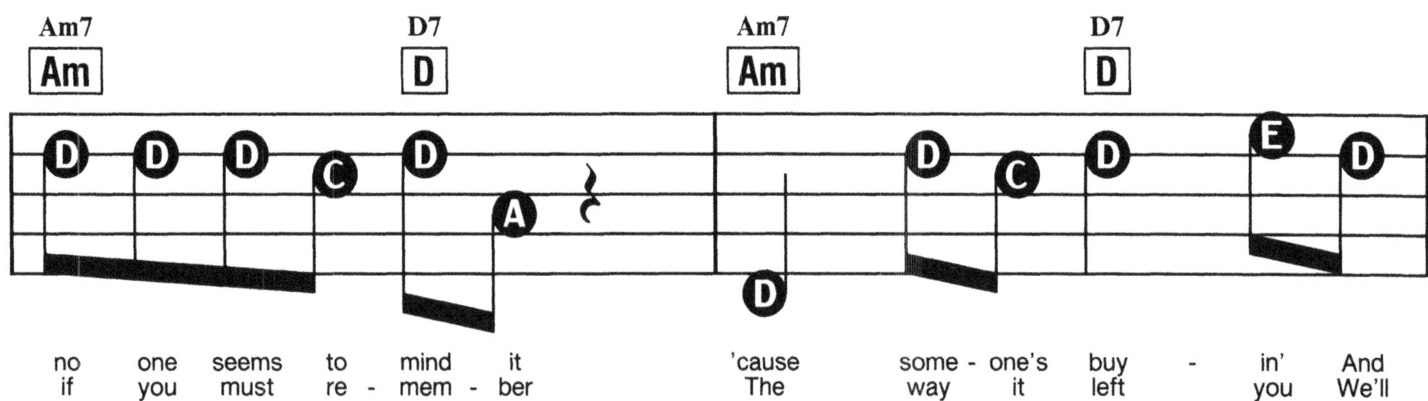
Am7
Am
D7
D
Am7
Am
D7
D
D D D C D A D D C D E D
no one seems to mind it 'cause some - one's buy - in' And
if you must re - mem - ber The way it left you We'll

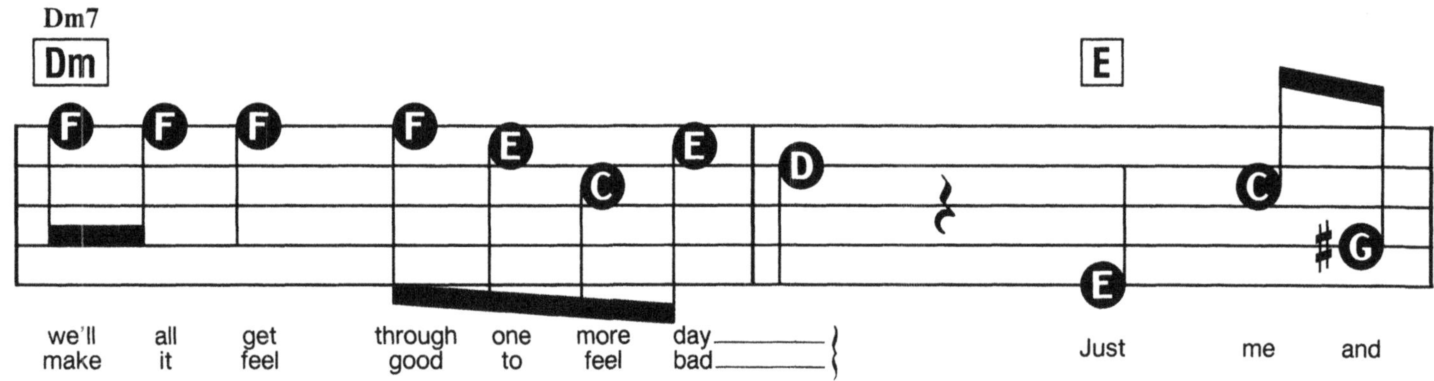
Dm7
Dm
E
F F F F E C E D E C G
we'll all get through one more day
make it feel good to feel bad
Just me and

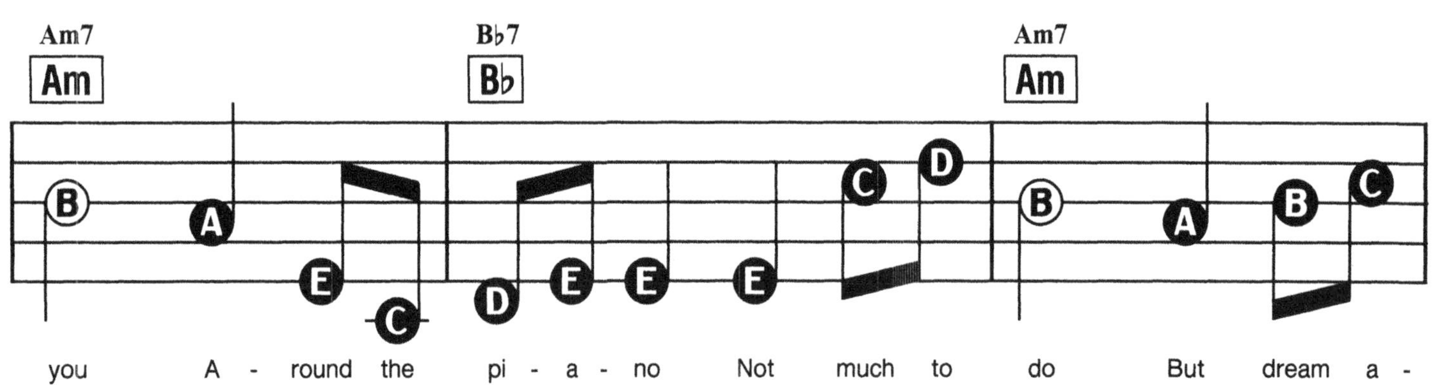
Am7
Am
B♭7
B♭
Am7
Am
B A E C D E E E C D B A B C
you A - round the pi - a - no Not much to do But dream a -

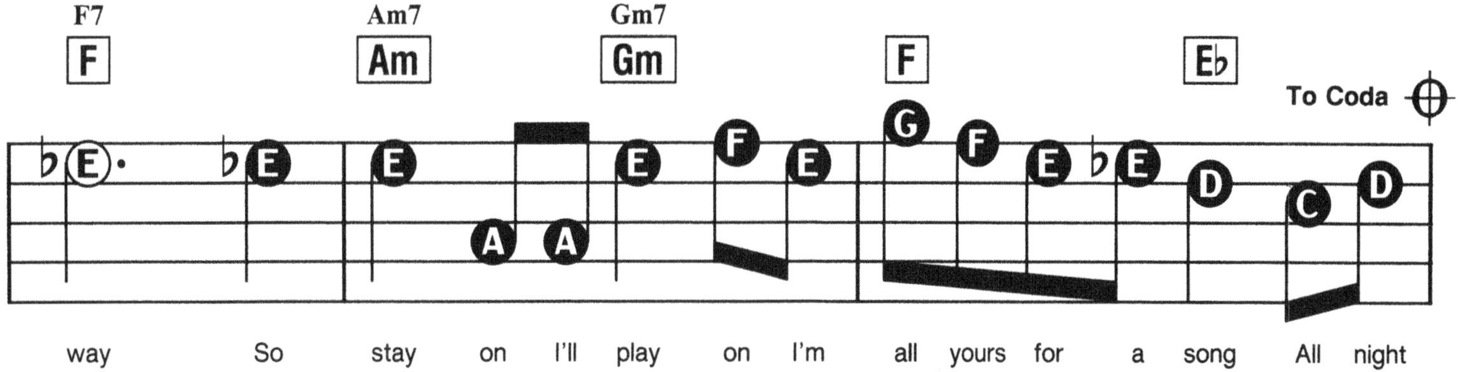
F7 Am7 Gm7
F Am Gm F E♭
To Coda
way So stay on I'll play on I'm all yours for a song All night

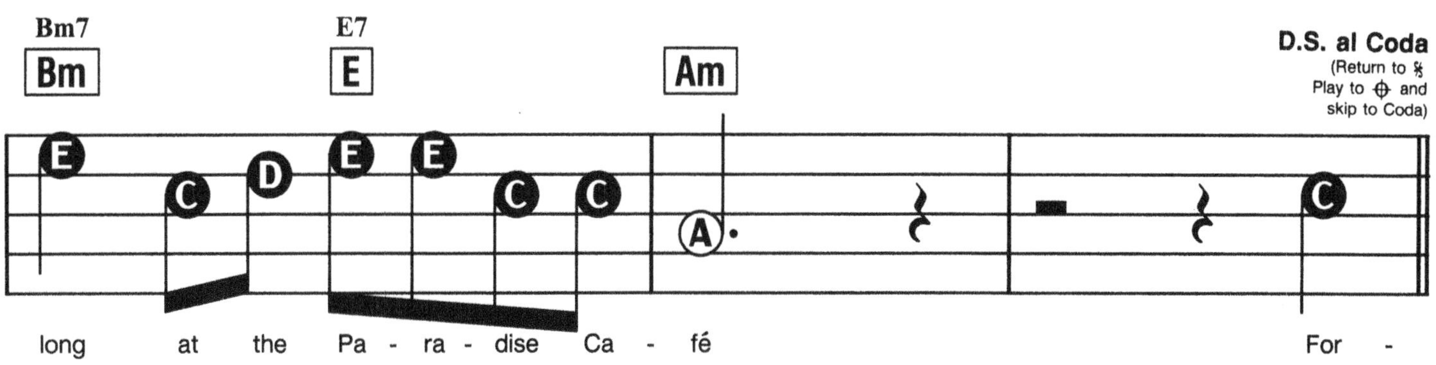
Bm7 E7
Bm E Am
D.S. al Coda
(Return to 𝄋
Play to 𝄌 and
skip to Coda)
long at the Pa - ra - dise Ca - fé For -

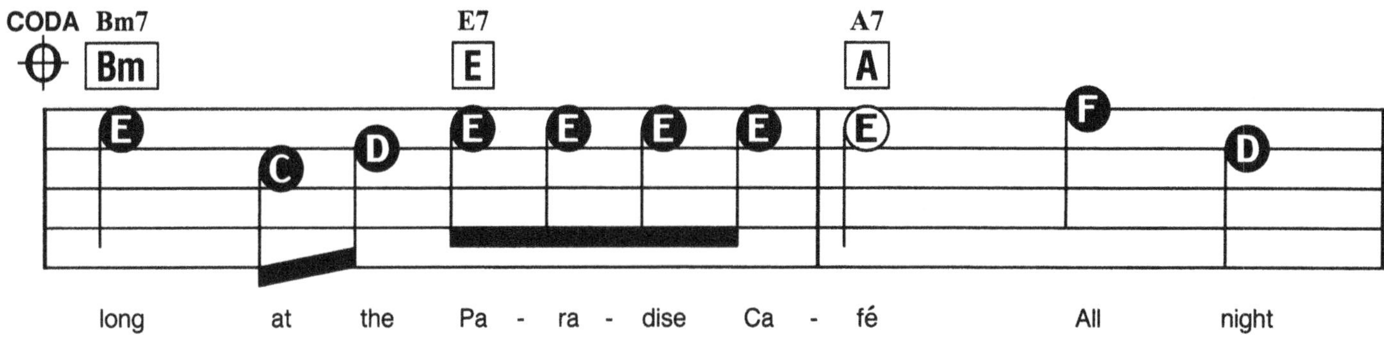
CODA Bm7 E7 A7
Bm E A
long at the Pa - ra - dise Ca - fé All night

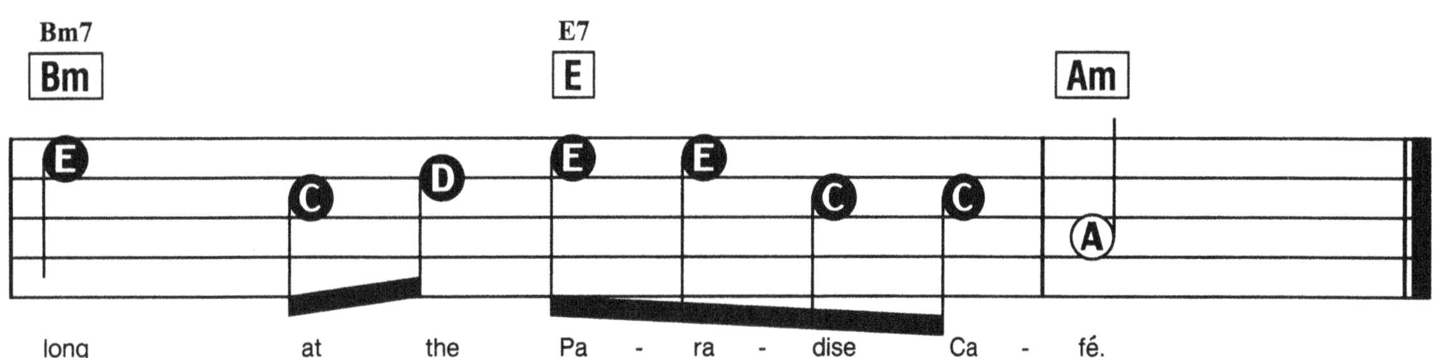
Bm7 E7
Bm E Am
long at the Pa - ra - dise Ca - fé.

Ships

Registration 7
Rhythm: Ballad or Rock

Words and Music by
Ian Hunter

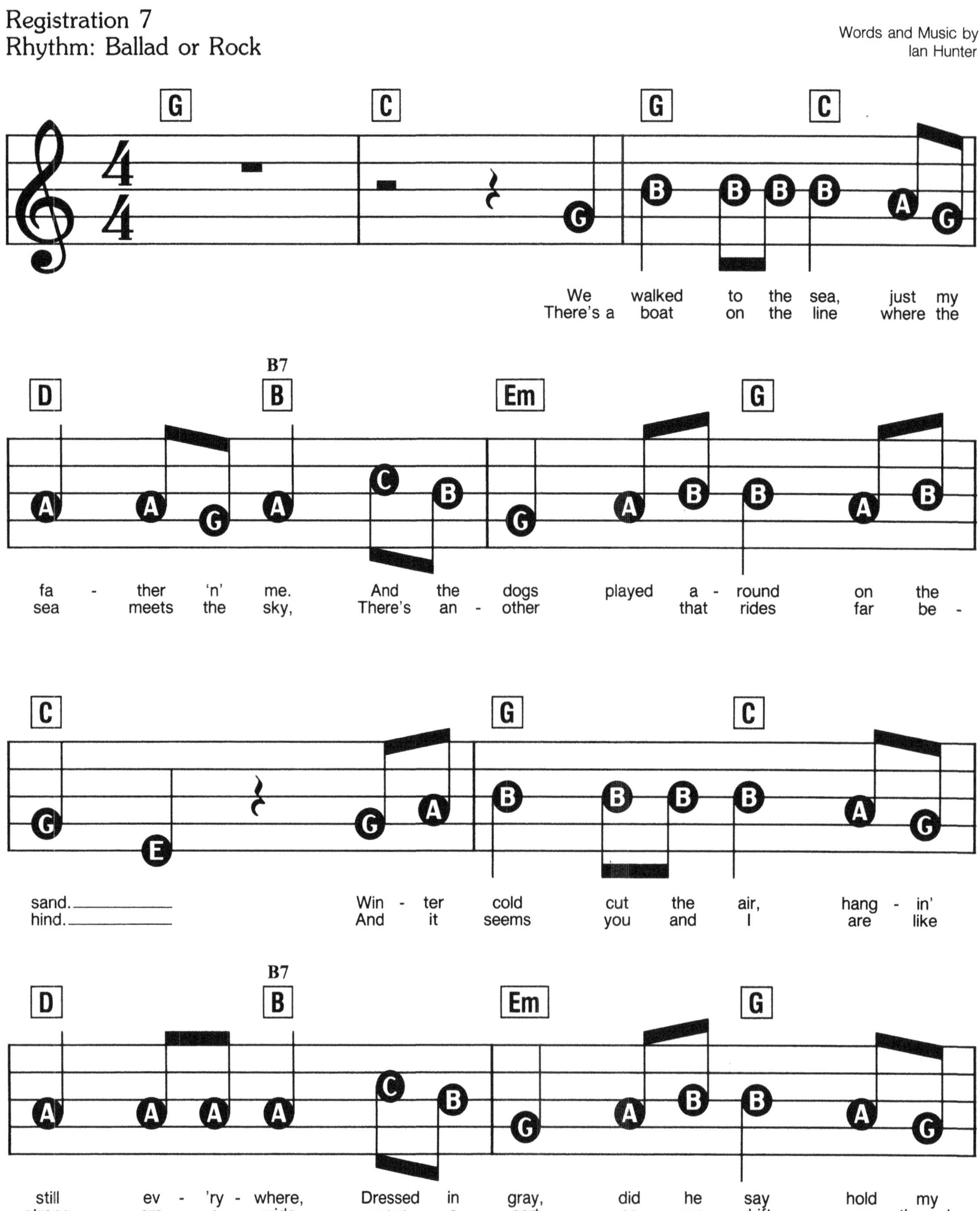

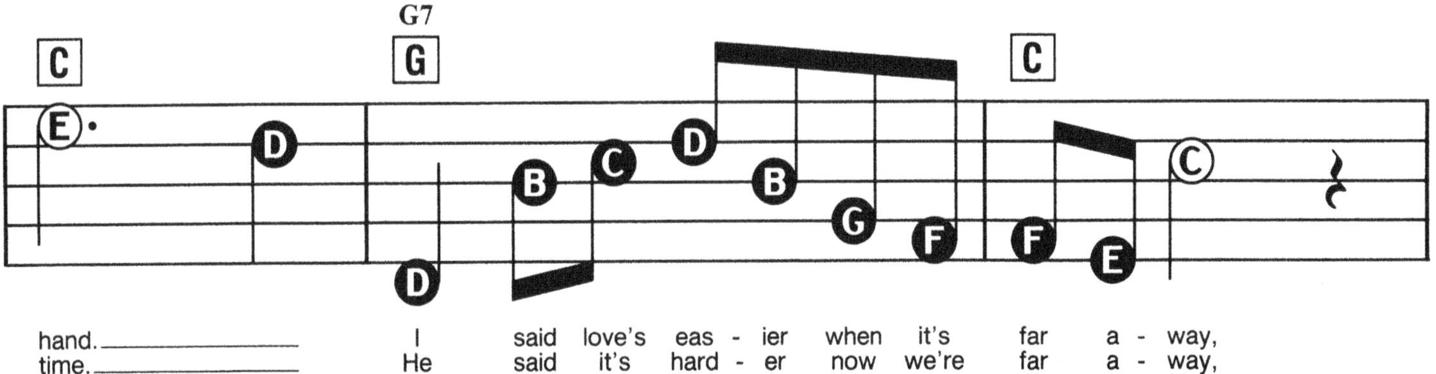
C
G7
G
C
E D D B C D B G F F E C
hand.
time.
I said love's eas - ier when it's far a - way,
He said it's hard - er now we're far a - way,

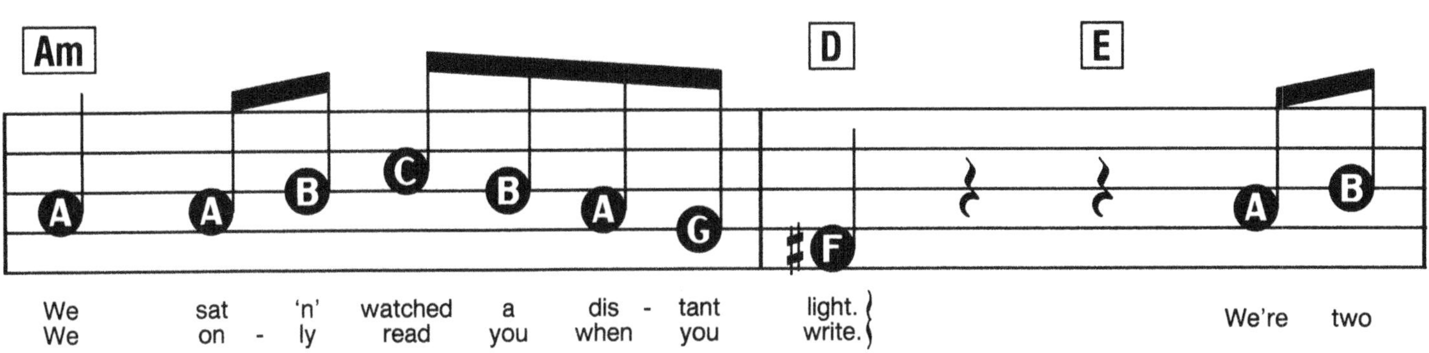
Am
D
E
A A B C B A G F A B
We sat 'n' watched a dis - tant light.
We on - ly read you when you write.
We're two

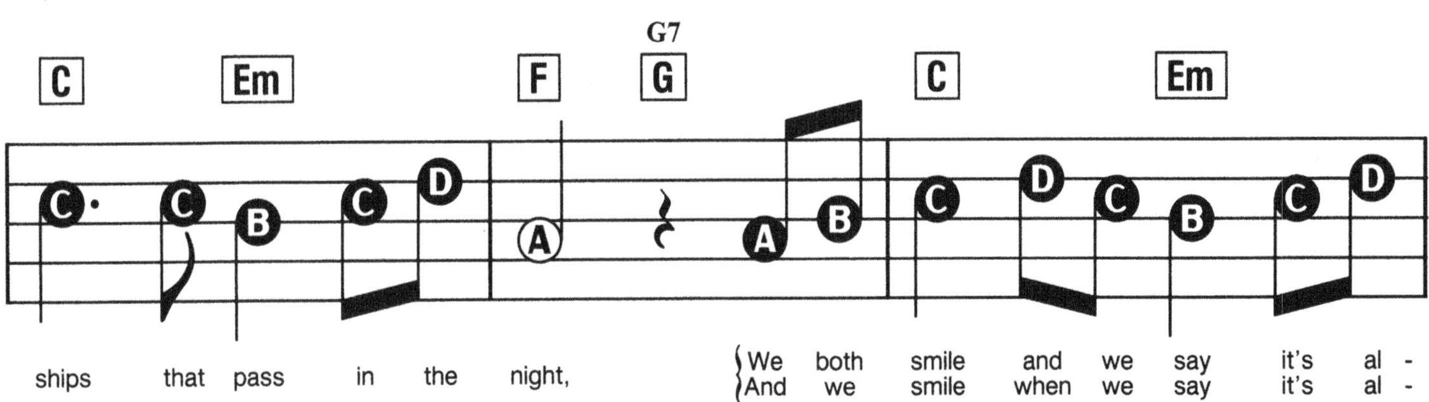
C
Em
F
G7
G
C
Em
C C B C D A A B C D C B C D
ships that pass in the night,
We both smile and we say it's al -
And we smile when we say it's al -

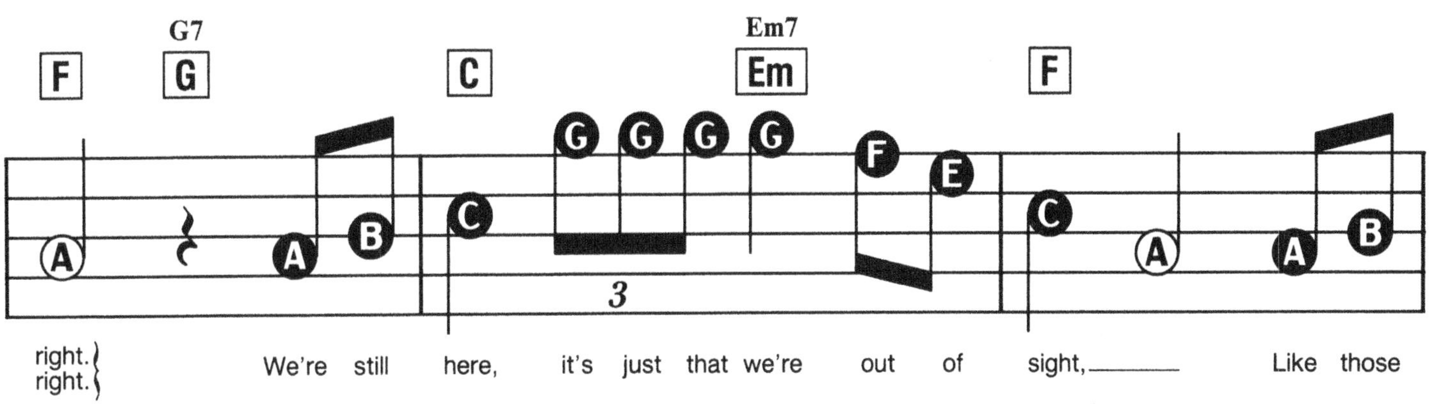
F
G7
G
C
Em7
Em
F
A A B C G G G G F E C A A B
3
right.
right.
We're still here, it's just that we're out of sight,
Like those

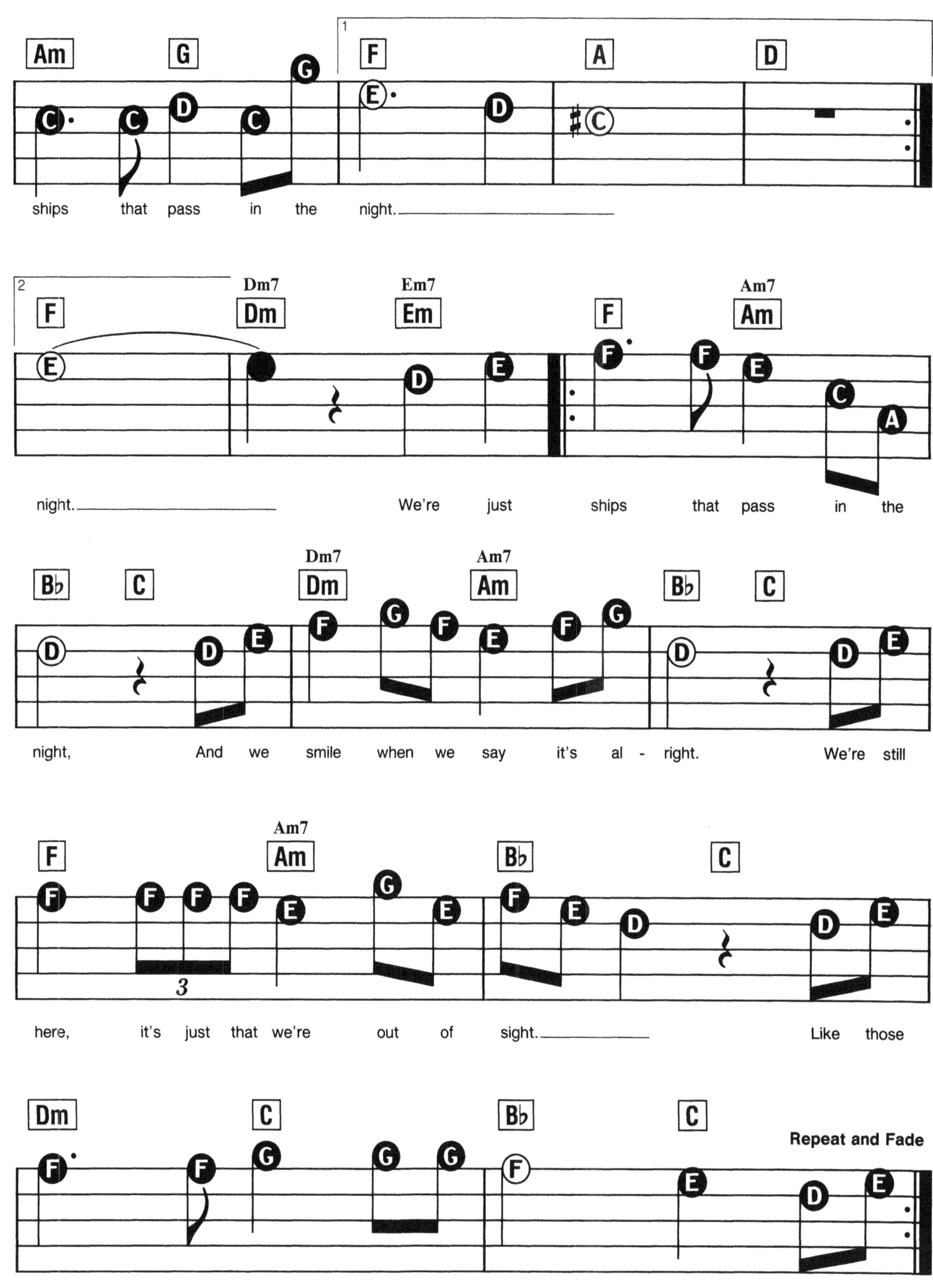
Am
G
1
F
A
D
ships that pass in the night.
2
F
Dm7
Dm
Em7
Em
F
Am7
Am
night. We're just ships that pass in the
B♭
C
Dm7
Dm
Am7
Am
B♭
C
night, And we smile when we say it's al - right. We're still
F
Am7
Am
B♭
C
3
here, it's just that we're out of sight. Like those
Dm
C
B♭
C
Repeat and Fade
ships that pass in the night. We're just

This One's For You

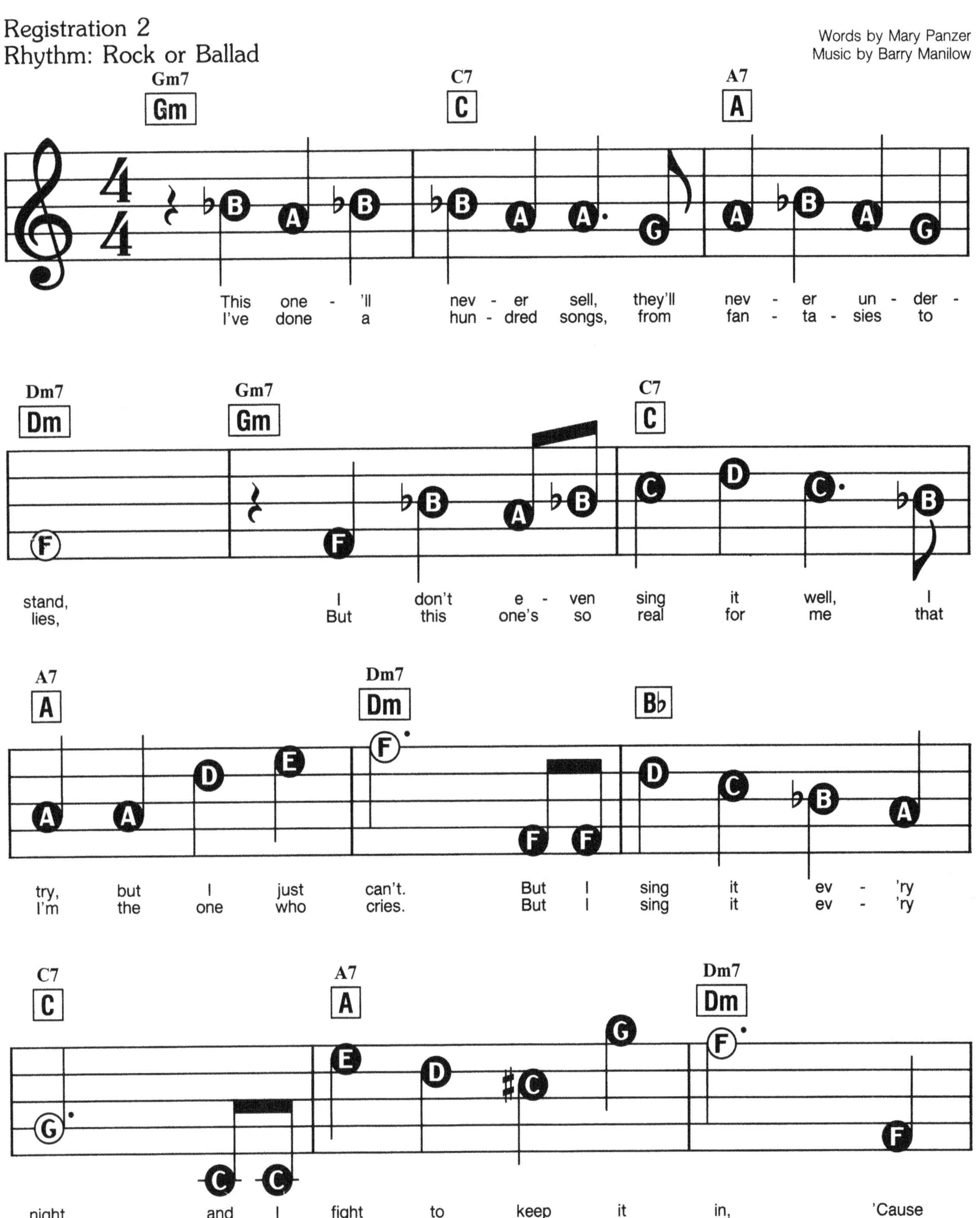

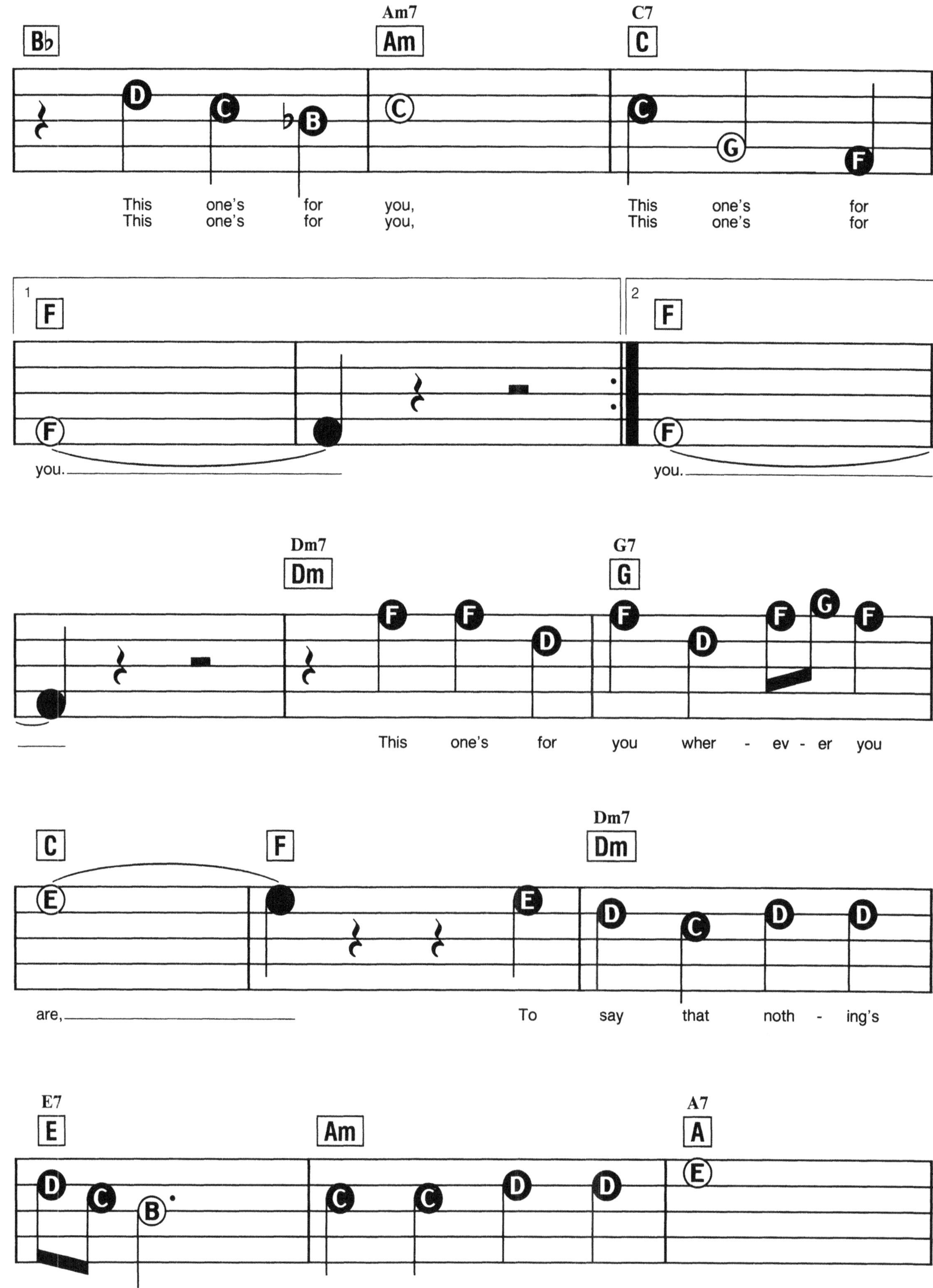
Am7
C7
B♭
Am
C
This one's for you,
This one's for you,
This one's for
This one's for
1
2
F
you.
you.
Dm7
G7
Dm
G
This one's for you wher - ev - er you
C
F
Dm7
Dm
are,
To say that noth - ing's
E7
A7
E
Am
A
been the same since we've been a - part.

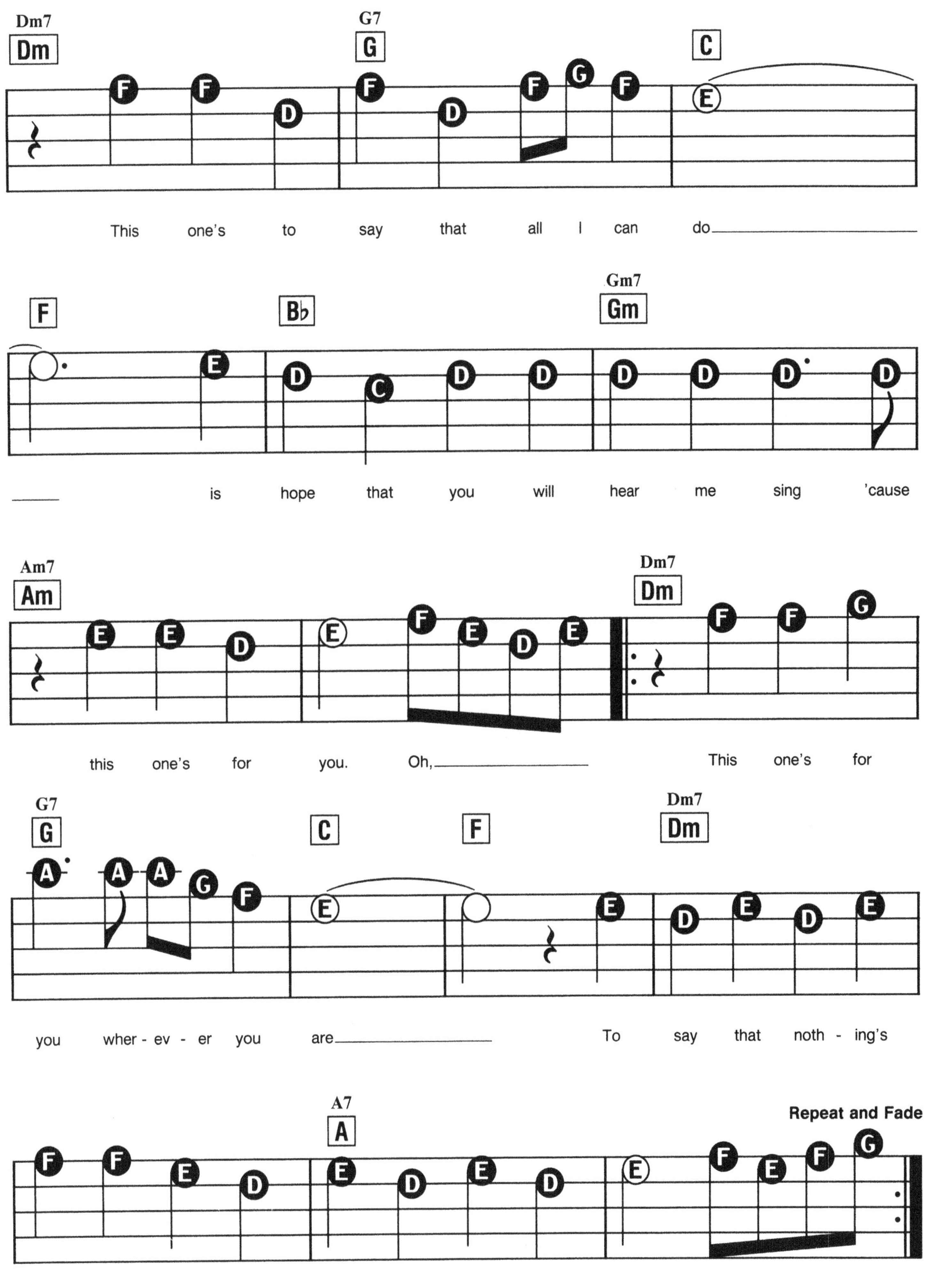
Dm7
Dm
G7
G
C
F F D F D F G F E
This one's to say that all I can do
F
Bb
Gm7
Gm
E D C D D D D D D
is hope that you will hear me sing 'cause
Am7
Am
Dm7
Dm
E E D E F E D E F F G
this one's for you. Oh,
This one's for
G7
G
C
F
Dm7
Dm
A A A G F E E D E D E
you wher - ev - er you are
To say that noth - ing's
A7
A
Repeat and Fade
F F E D E D E D E F E F G
been the same since we've been a - part. Oh,

Some Kind Of Friend

Registration 4
Rhythm: Rock or Disco

Words by Adrienne Anderson
Music by Barry Manilow

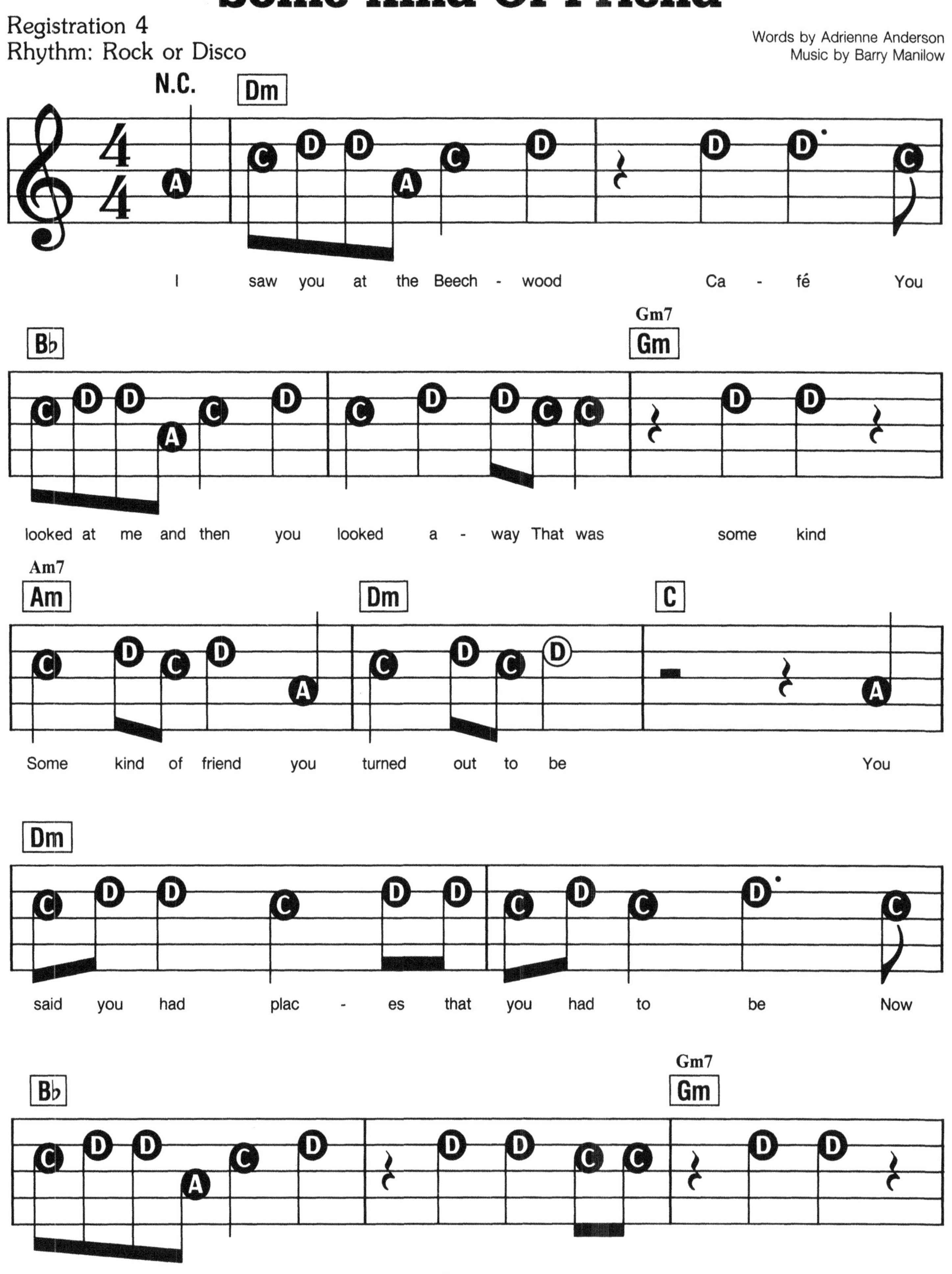

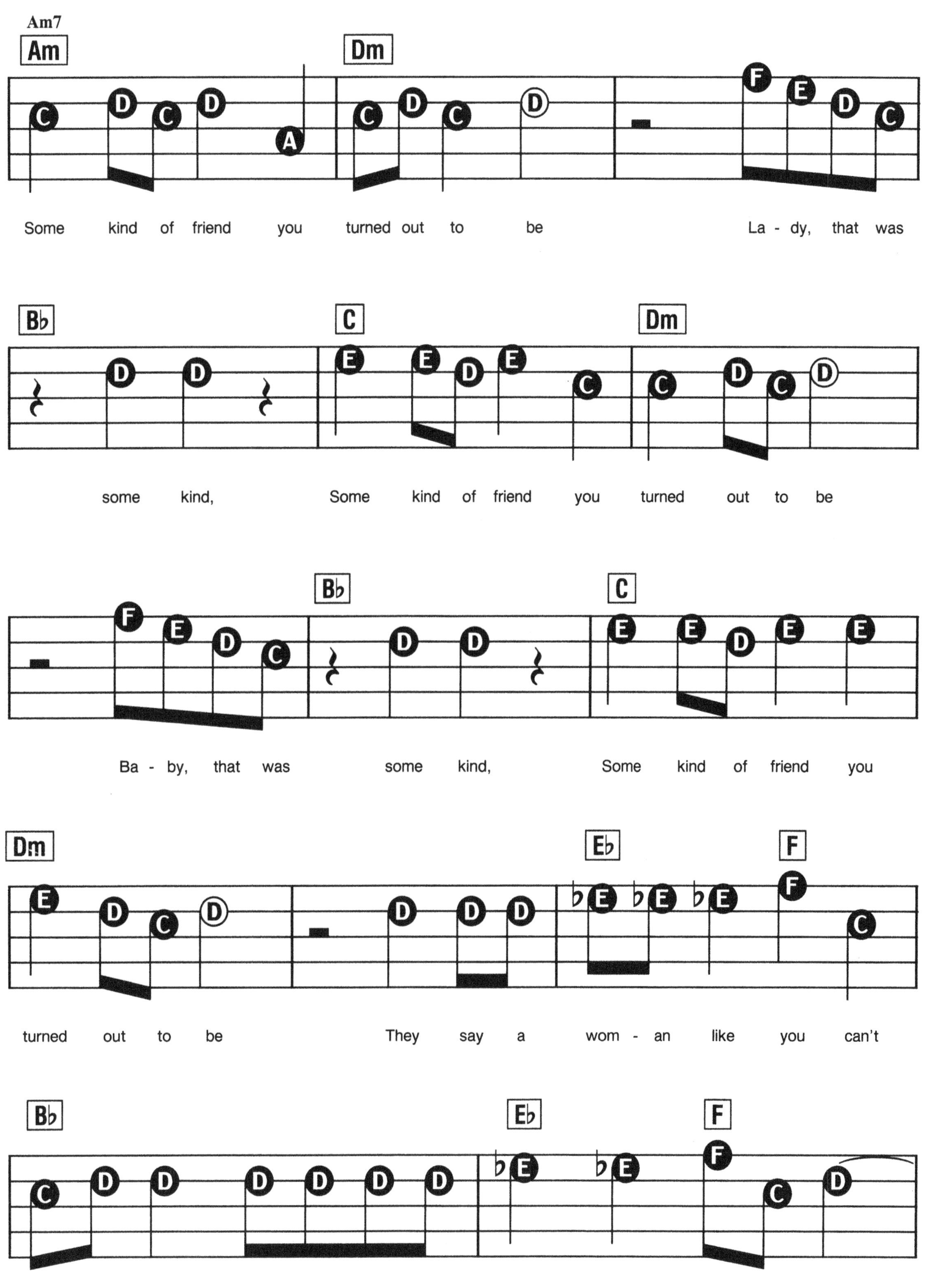
Am7
Am
Dm
Some kind of friend you turned out to be La - dy, that was
B♭
C
Dm
some kind, Some kind of friend you turned out to be
B♭
C
Ba - by, that was some kind, Some kind of friend you
Dm
E♭
F
turned out to be They say a wom - an like you can't
B♭
E♭
F
get e - nough Got your Mas - e - ra - ti built for two

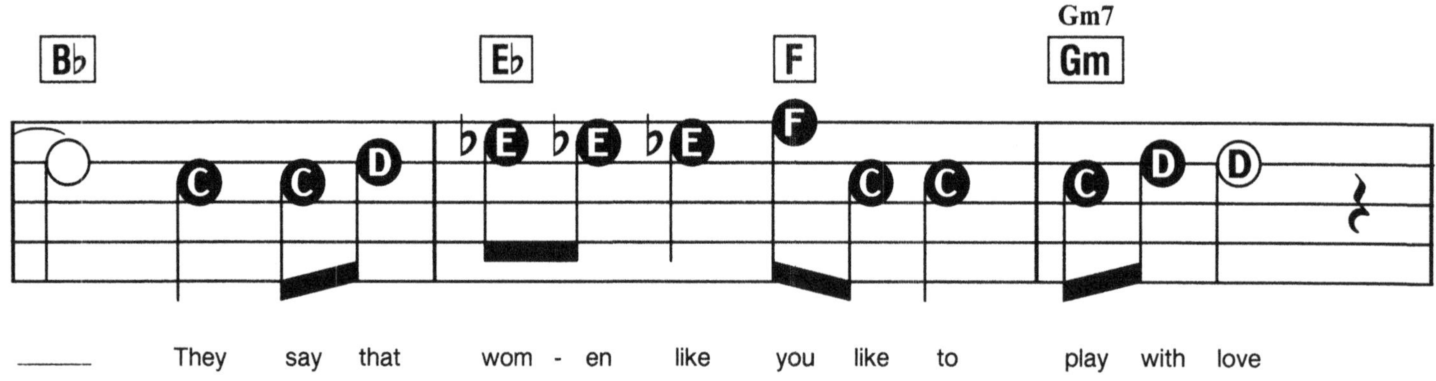
Gm7
B♭
E♭
F
Gm
They say that wom - en like you like to play with love

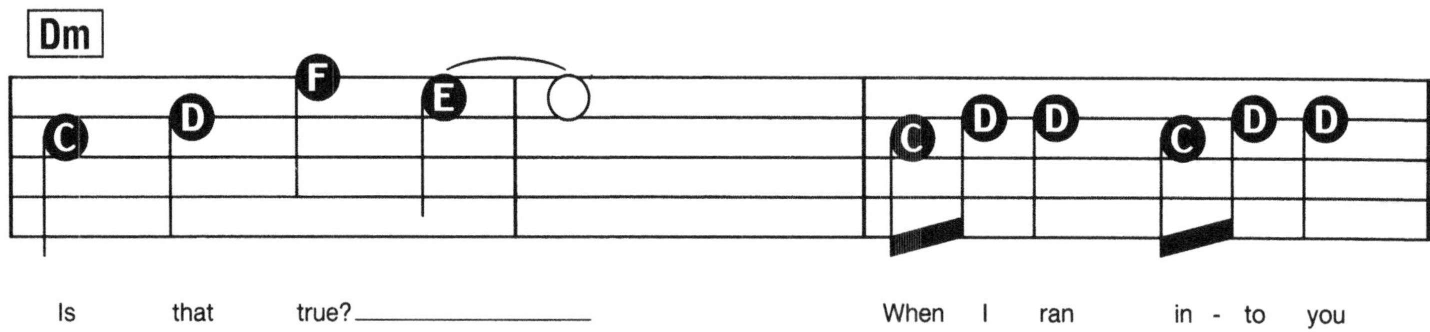
Dm
Is that true?
When I ran in - to you

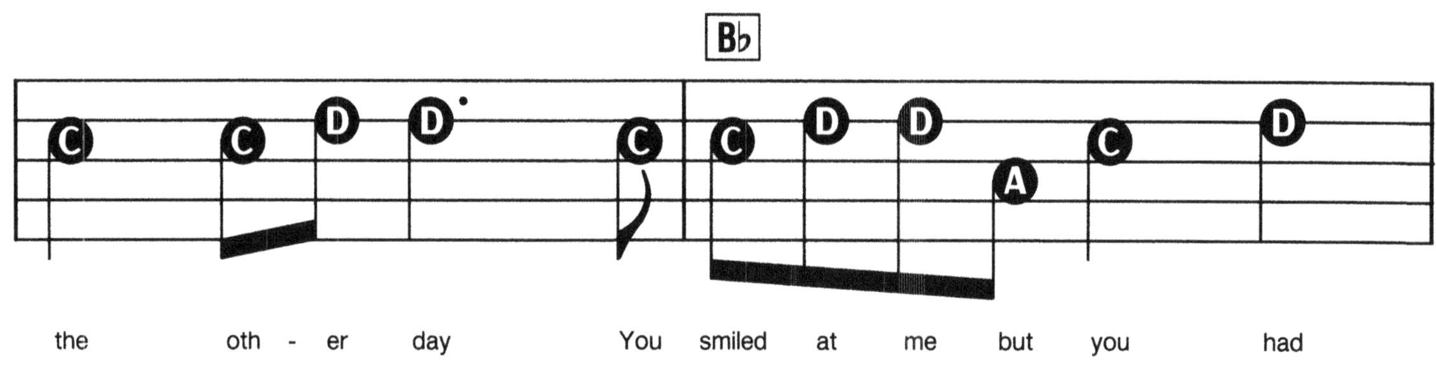
B♭
the oth - er day You smiled at me but you had

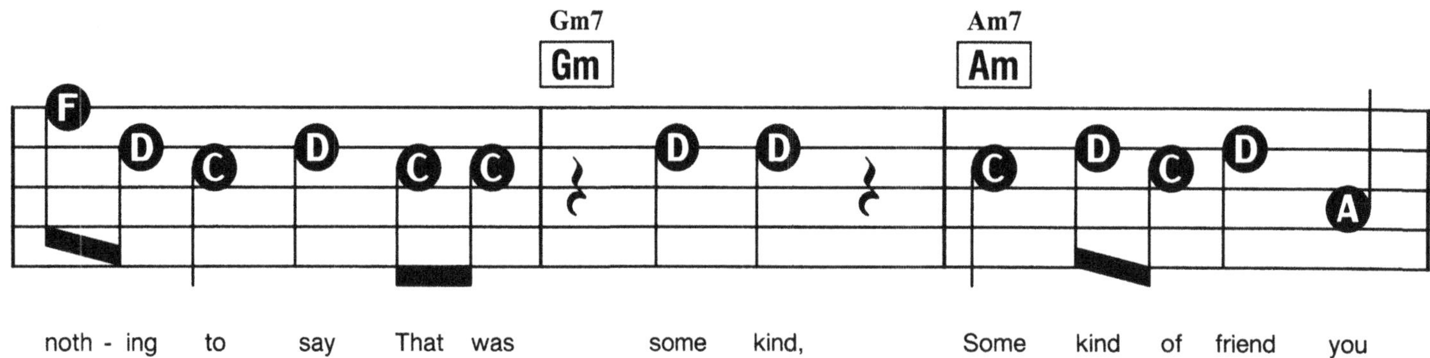
Gm7
Gm
Am7
Am
noth - ing to say That was some kind, Some kind of friend you

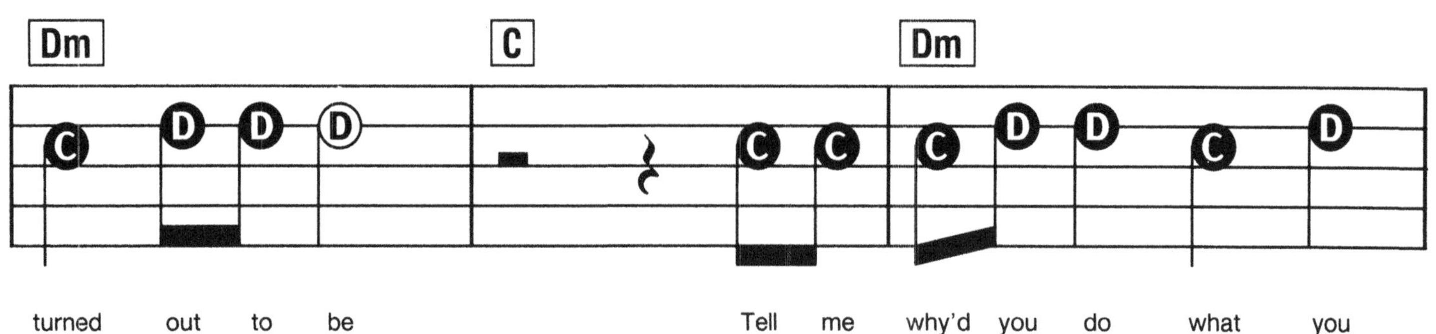
Dm
C
Dm
turned out to be Tell me why'd you do what you

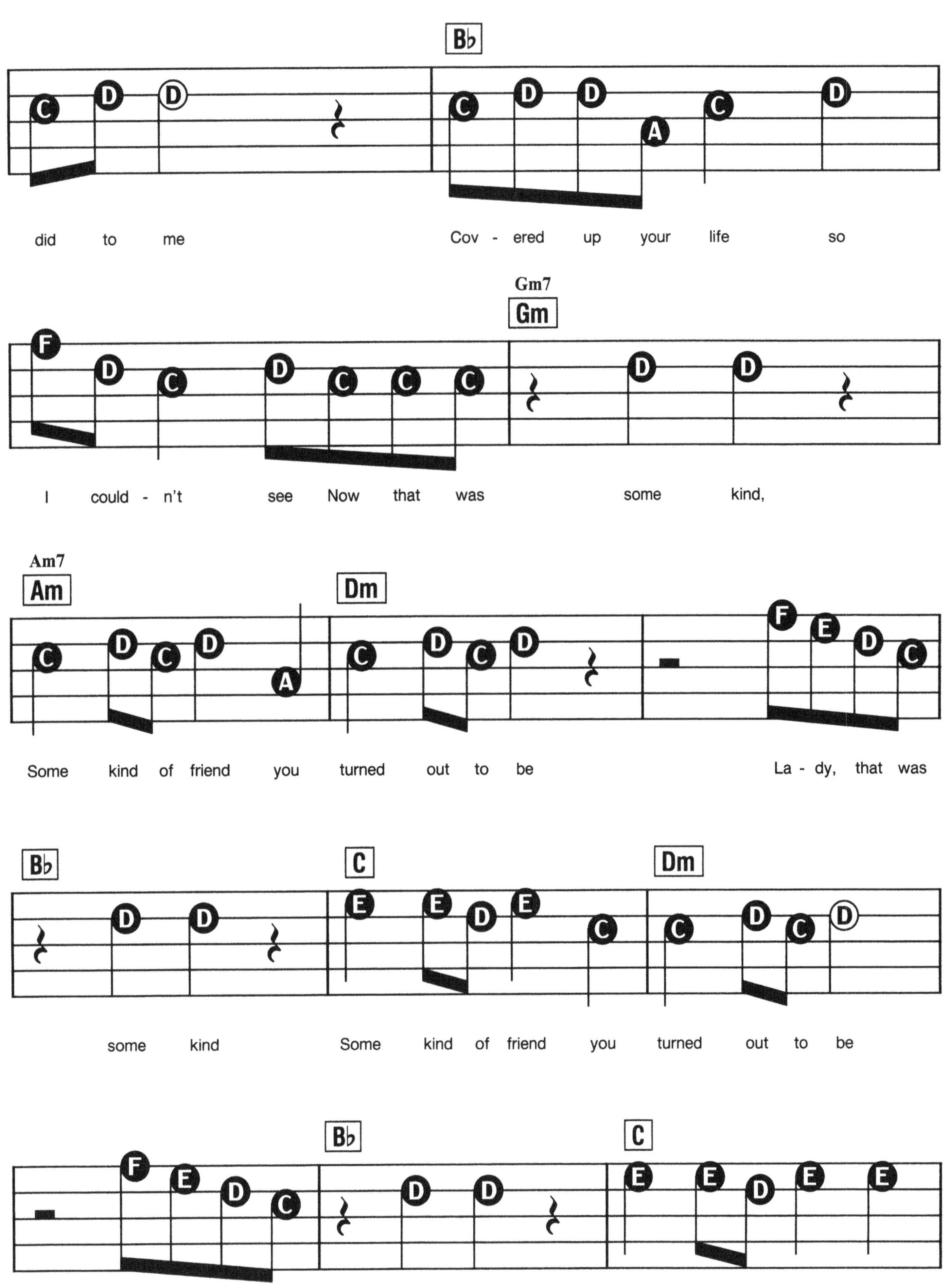
B♭
did to me
Cov - ered up your life so
Gm7
Gm
I could - n't see Now that was some kind,
Am7
Am
Dm
Some kind of friend you turned out to be La - dy, that was
B♭
C
Dm
some kind Some kind of friend you turned out to be
B♭
C
Ba - by, that was some kind Some kind of friend you

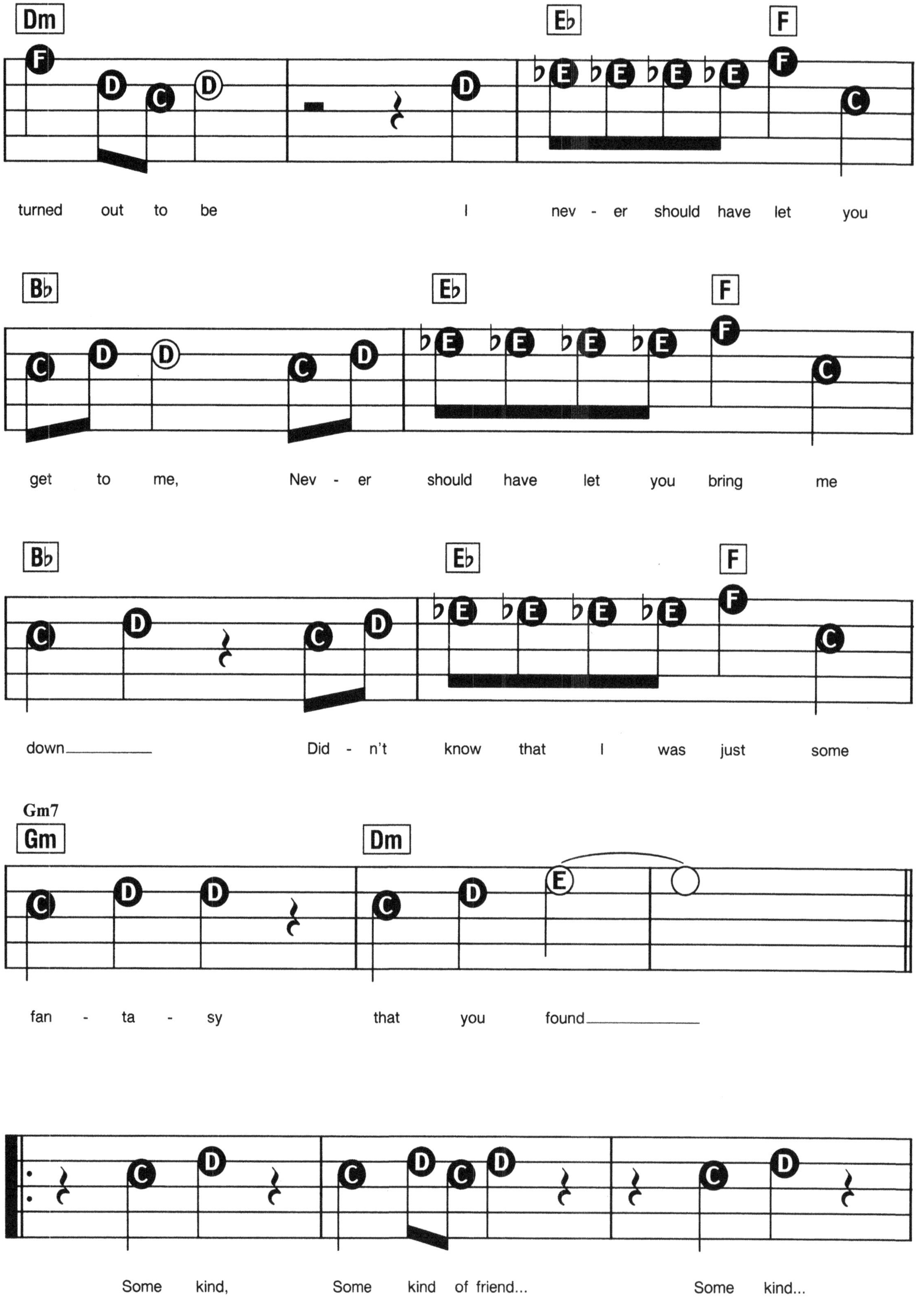

Dm Eb F

turned out to be I nev - er should have let you

Bb Eb F

get to me, Nev - er should have let you bring me

Bb Eb F

down Did - n't know that I was just some

Gm7
Gm Dm

fan - ta - sy that you found

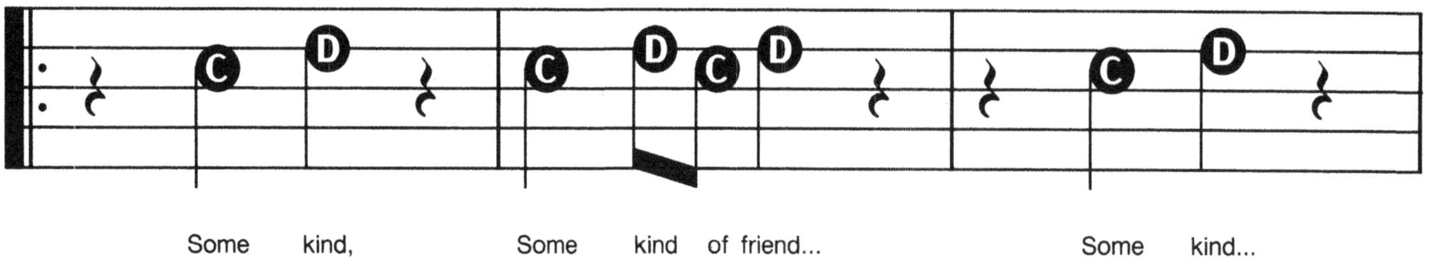

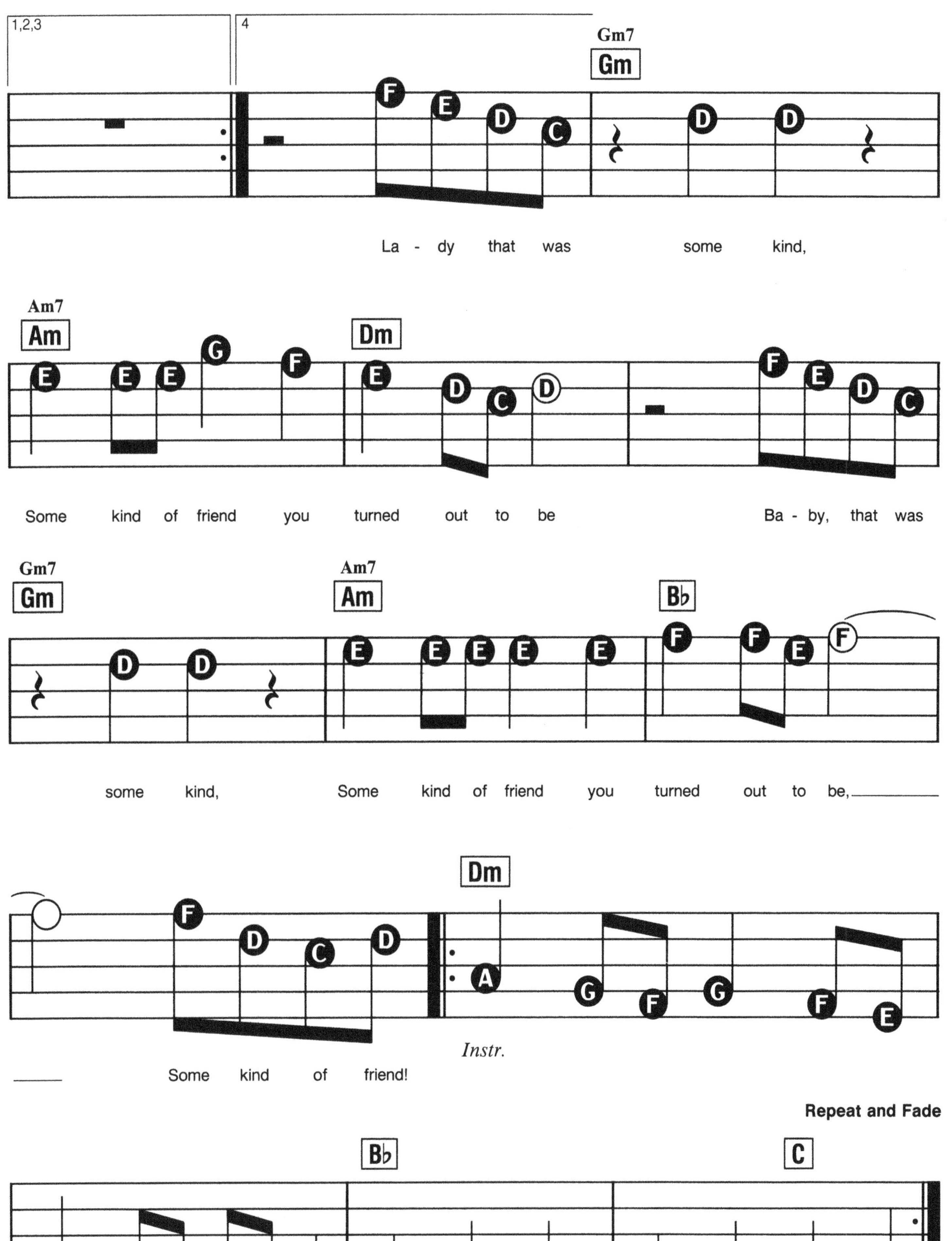
1,2,3
4
Gm7
Gm
F
E
D
C
D
D
La - dy that was some kind,
Am7
Am
E
E
E
G
F
Dm
E
D
C
D
F
E
D
C
Some kind of friend you turned out to be Ba - by, that was
Gm7
Gm
D
D
Am7
Am
E
E
E
E
E
B♭
F
F
E
F
some kind, Some kind of friend you turned out to be,
Dm
F
D
C
D
A
G
F
G
F
E
Instr.
Some kind of friend!
Repeat and Fade
B♭
C
F
E
D
E
D
C
C
D
D
C
D
D
E

Somewhere In The Night

Registration 1
Rhythm: Ballad or Rock

Words by Will Jennings
Music by Richard Kerr

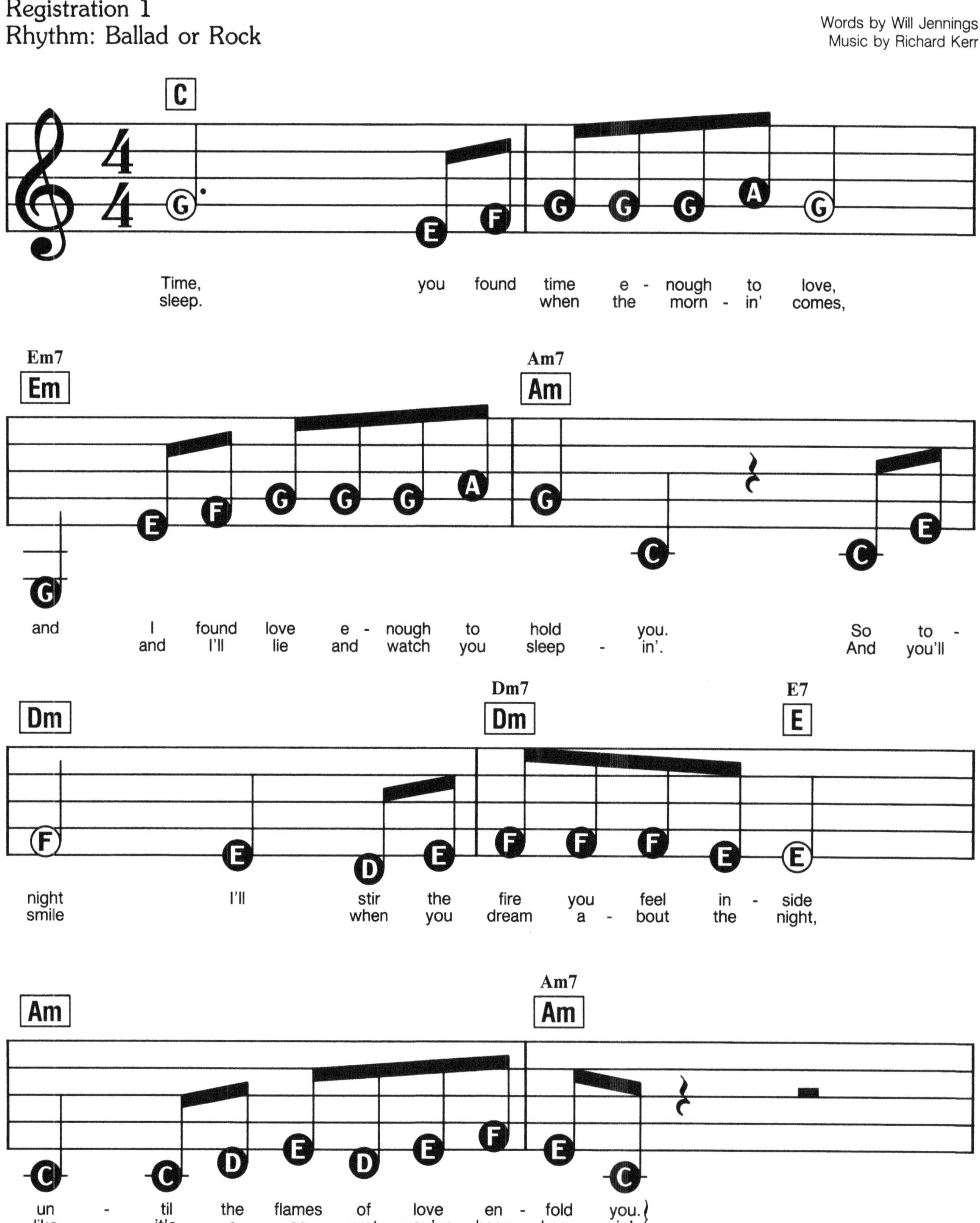

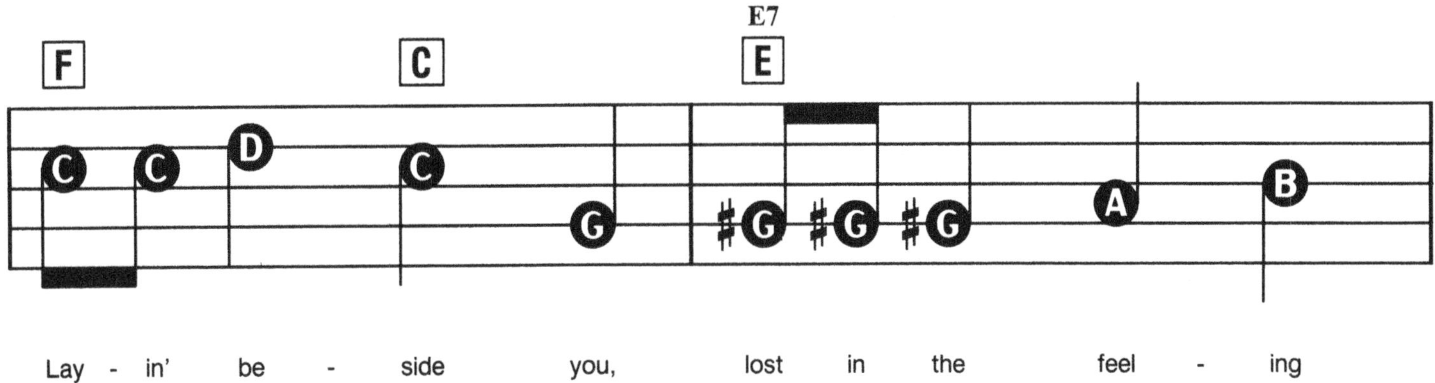
E7
F
C
E
C C D C G ♯G ♯G ♯G A B
Lay - in' be - side you, lost in the feel - ing

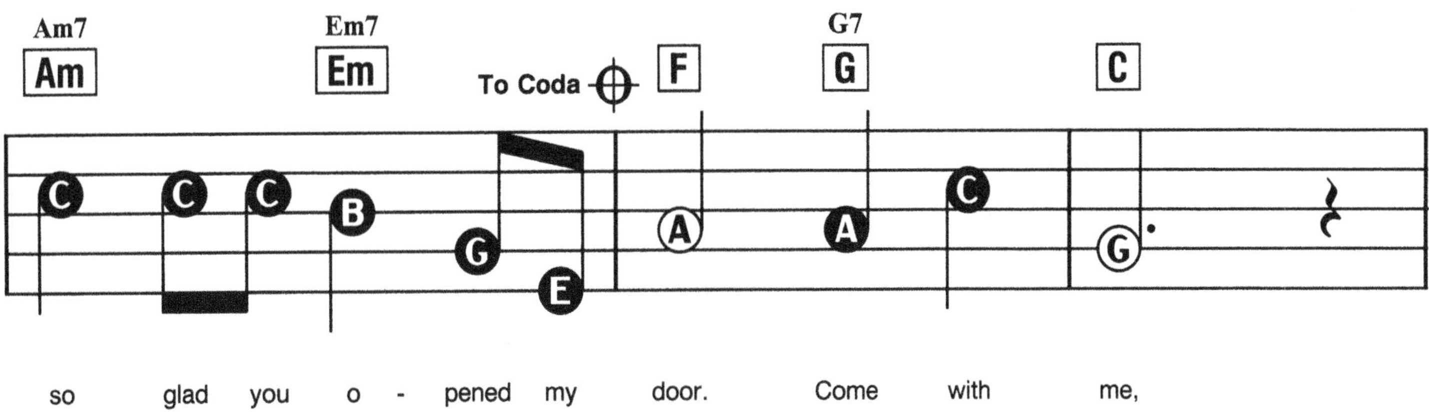
Am7
Em7
G7
Am
Em
To Coda
F
G
C
C C C B G E A A C G
so glad you o - pened my door. Come with me,

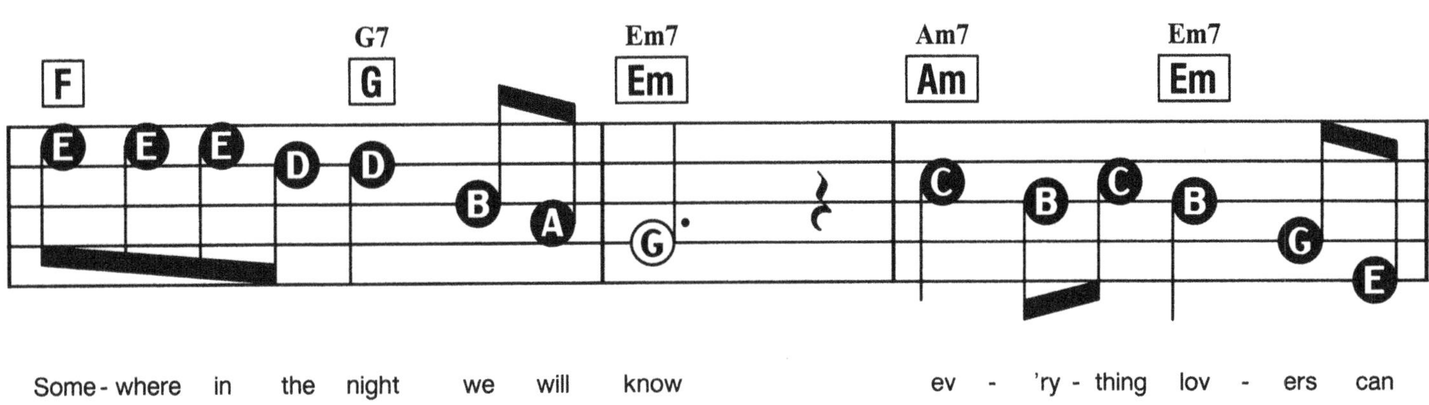
G7
Em7
Am7
Em7
F
G
Em
Am
Em
E E E D D B A G C B C B G E
Some - where in the night we will know ev - 'ry - thing lov - ers can

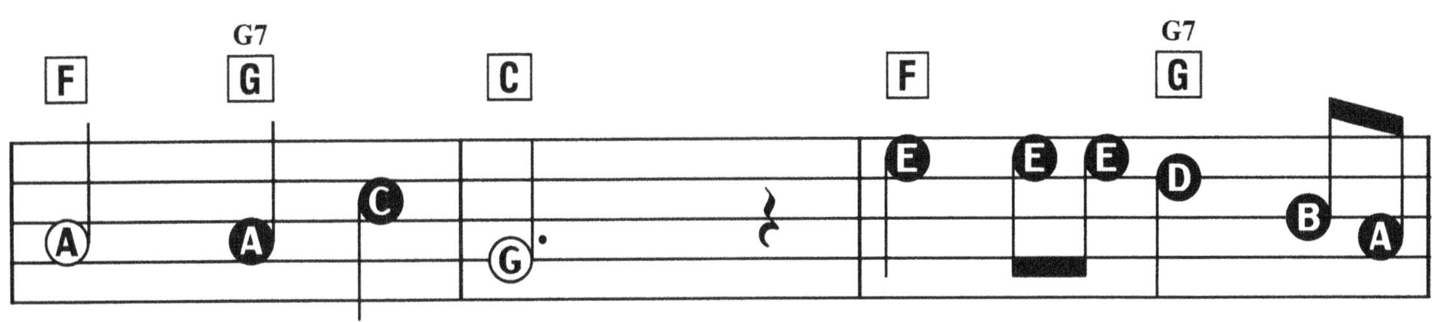
G7
G7
F
G
C
F
G
A A C G E E E D B A
know. You're my song, Mu - sic too mag - ic to

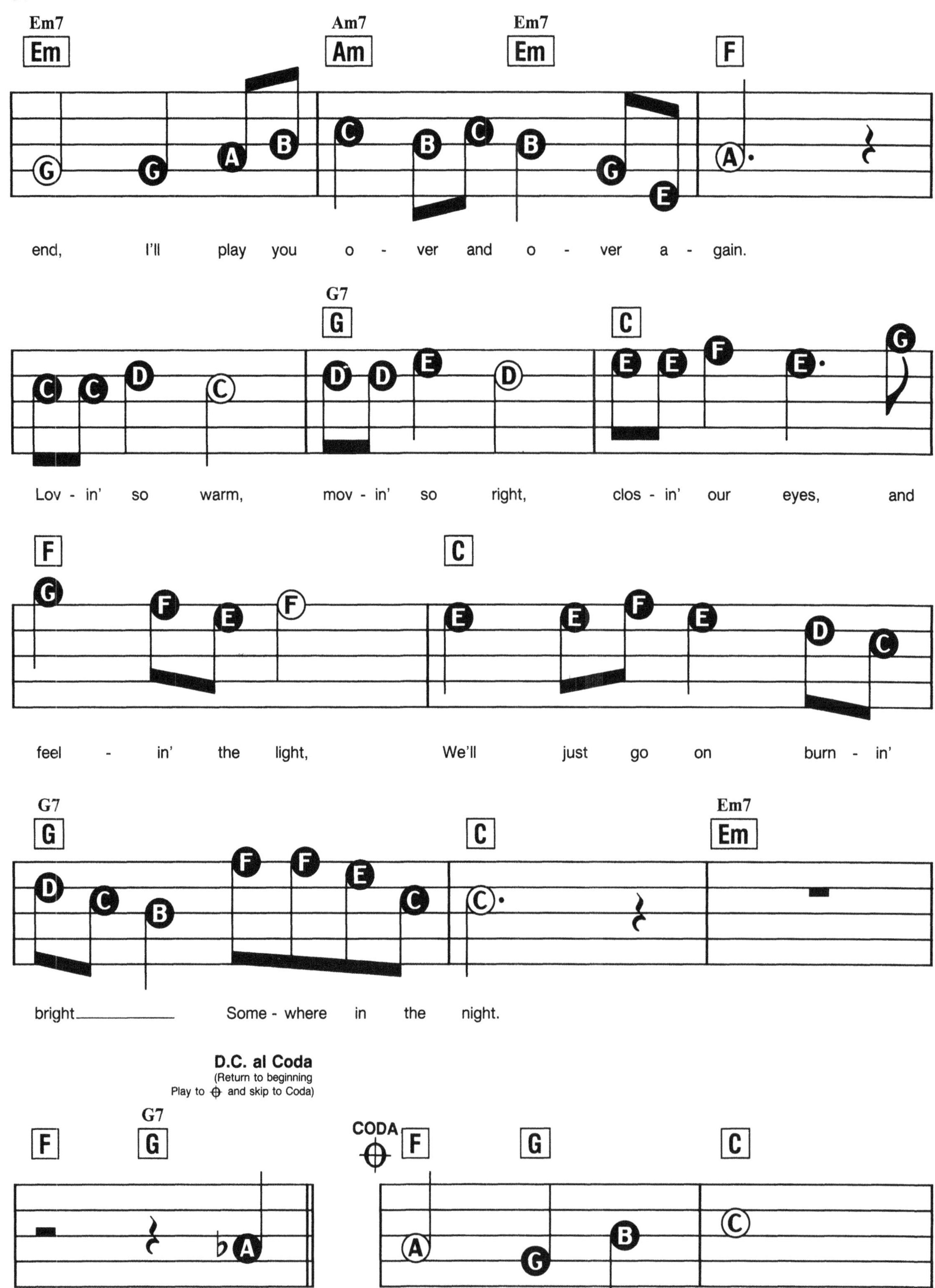
Em7
Em
Am7
Am
Em7
Em
F
G
G
A
B
C
B
C
B
G
E
A
end, I'll play you o - ver and o - ver a - gain.
G7
G
C
C
C
D
C
D
D
E
D
E
E
F
E
G
Lov - in' so warm, mov - in' so right, clos - in' our eyes, and
F
C
G
F
E
F
E
E
F
E
D
C
feel - in' the light, We'll just go on burn - in'
G7
G
C
Em7
Em
D
C
B
F
F
E
C
C
bright Some - where in the night.
D.C. al Coda
(Return to beginning
Play to ⊕ and skip to Coda)
F
G7
G
CODA
F
G
C
A
A
G
B
C
You'll door You're my song

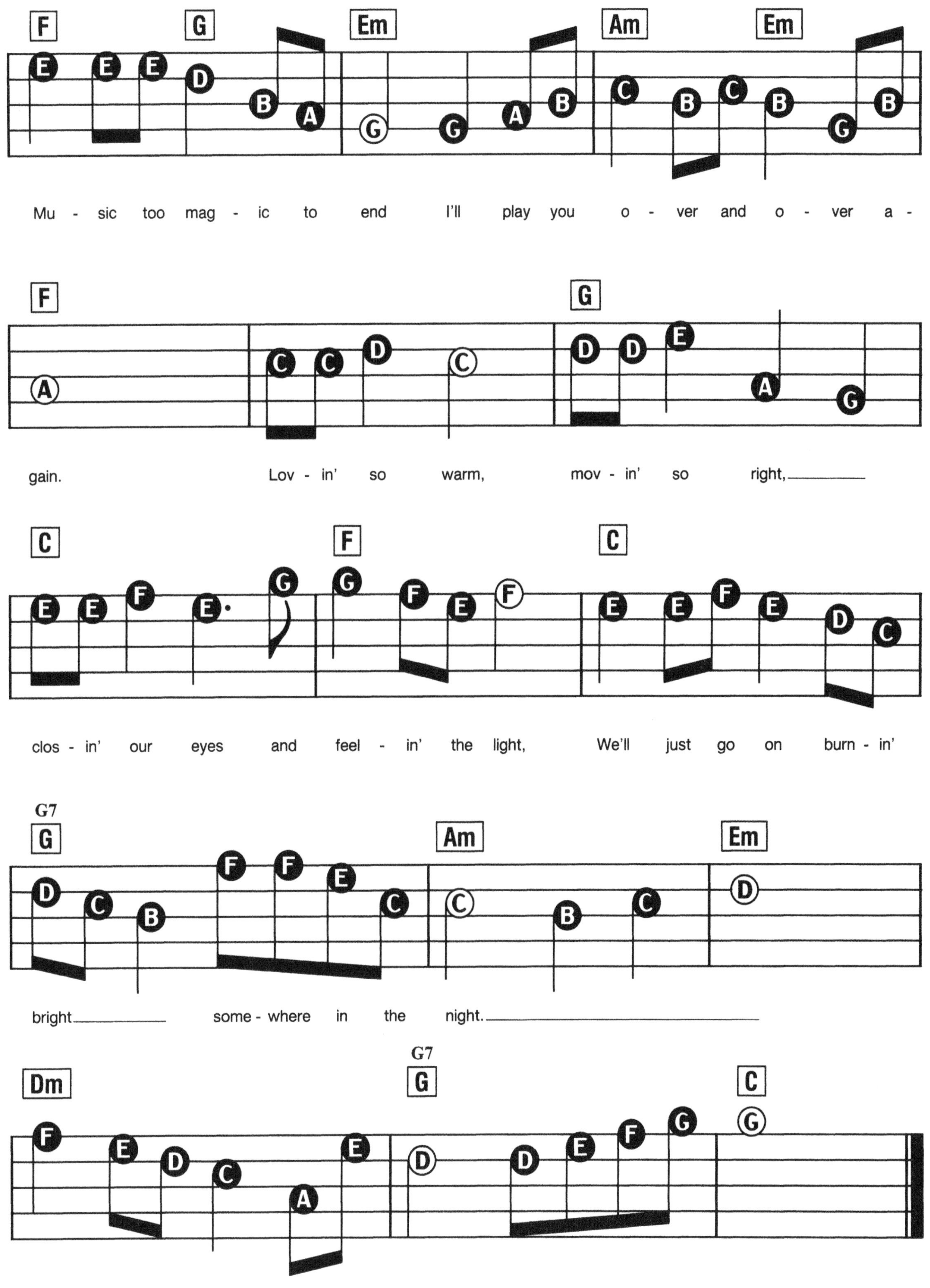
F G Em Am Em
Mu - sic too mag - ic to end I'll play you o - ver and o - ver a -
F G
gain. Lov - in' so warm, mov - in' so right,
C F C
clos - in' our eyes and feel - in' the light, We'll just go on burn - in'
G7
G Am Em
bright some - where in the night.
Dm G7 G C
We'll just go on burn - in' bright some - where in the night.

Tryin' To Get The Feeling Again

Registration 3
Rhythm: Ballad

Words and Music by
David Pomeranz

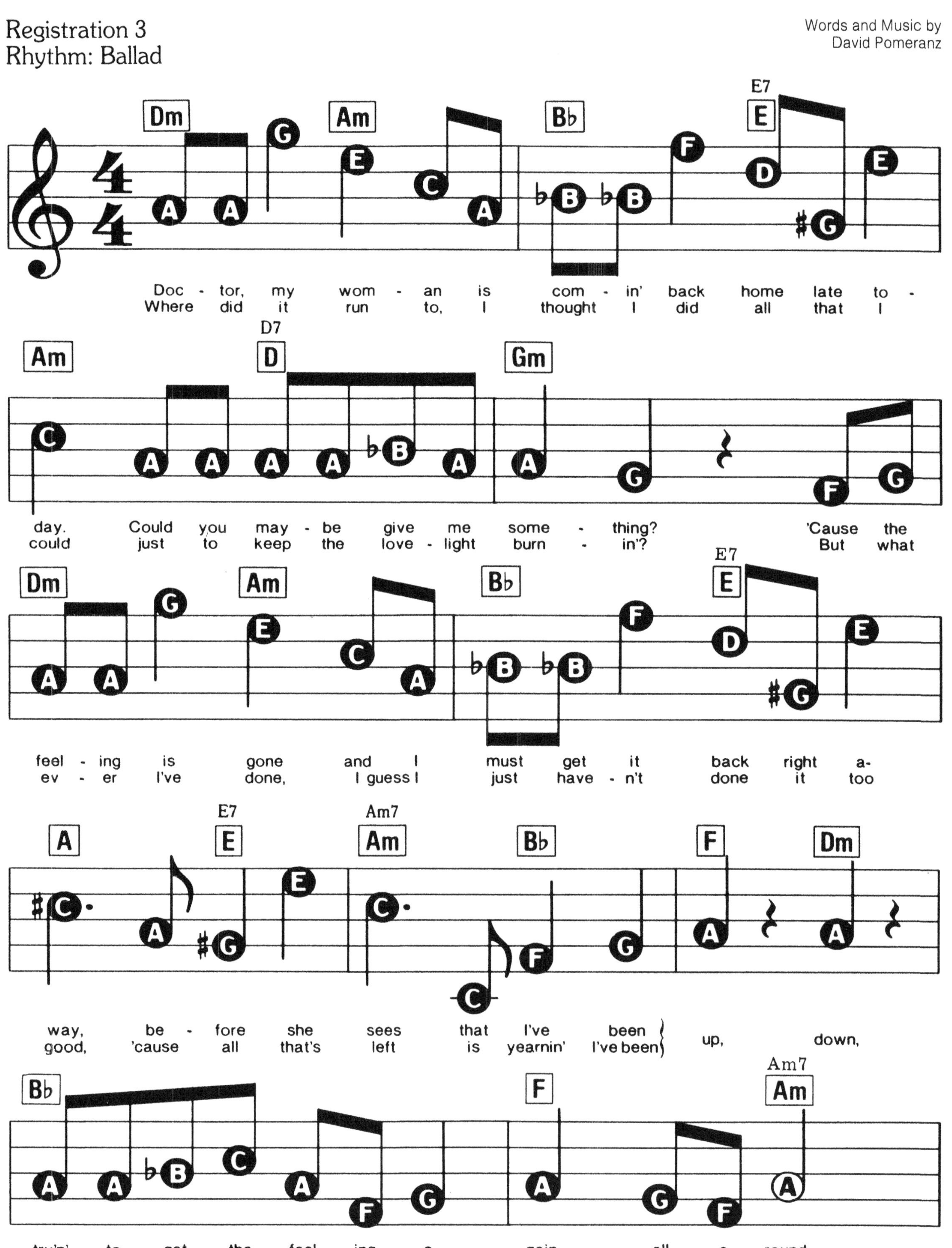

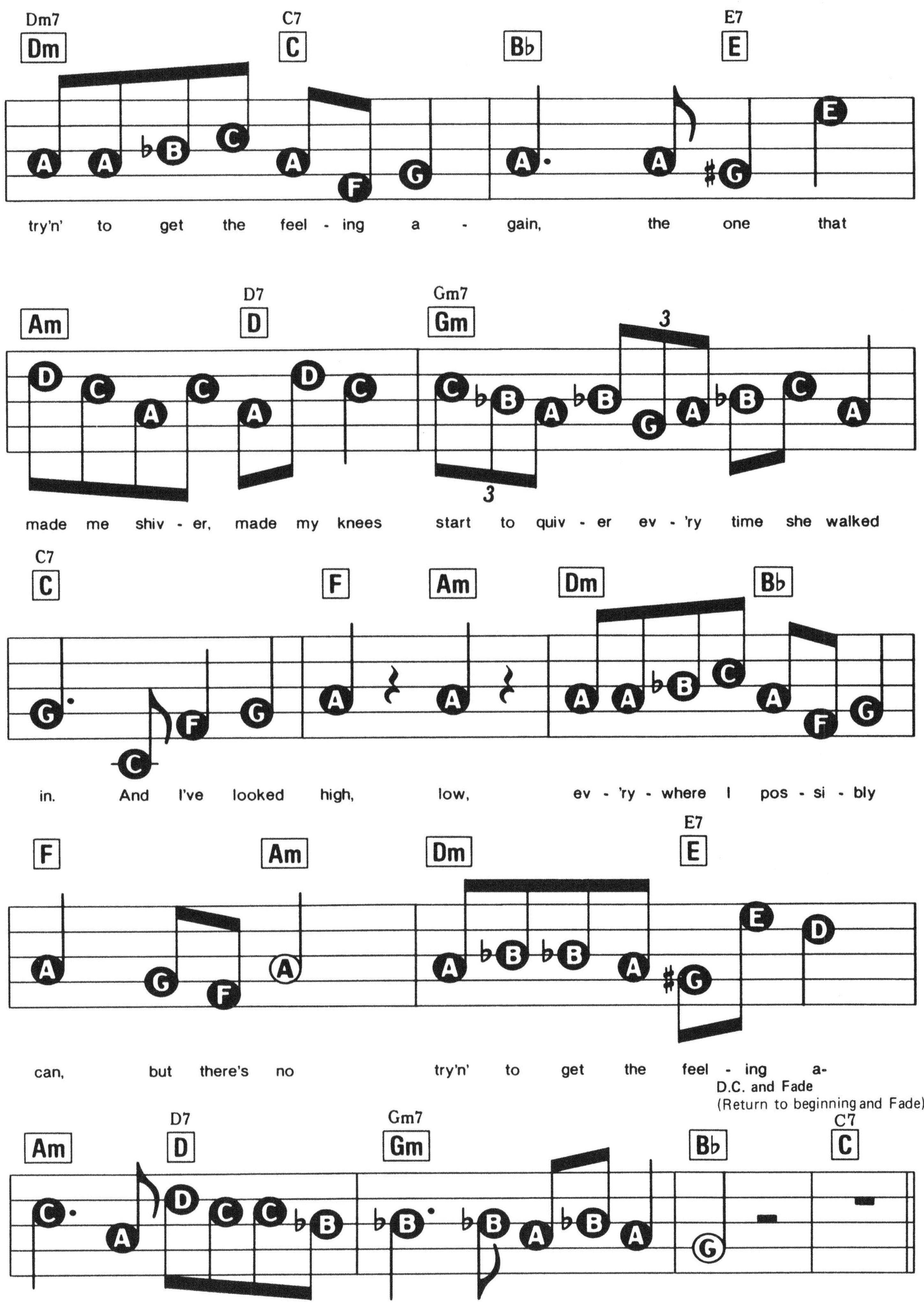
Dm7
Dm
C7
C
B♭
E7
E
try'n' to get the feel - ing a - gain, the one that
Am
D7
D
Gm7
Gm
3
made me shiv - er, made my knees start to quiv - er ev - 'ry time she walked
C7
C
F
Am
Dm
B♭
in. And I've looked high, low, ev - 'ry - where I pos - si - bly
F
Am
Dm
E7
E
can, but there's no try'n' to get the feel - ing a-
D.C. and Fade
(Return to beginning and Fade)
Am
D7
D
Gm7
Gm
B♭
C7
C
gain. It seemed to dis - ap - pear as fast as it came.

Weekend In New England

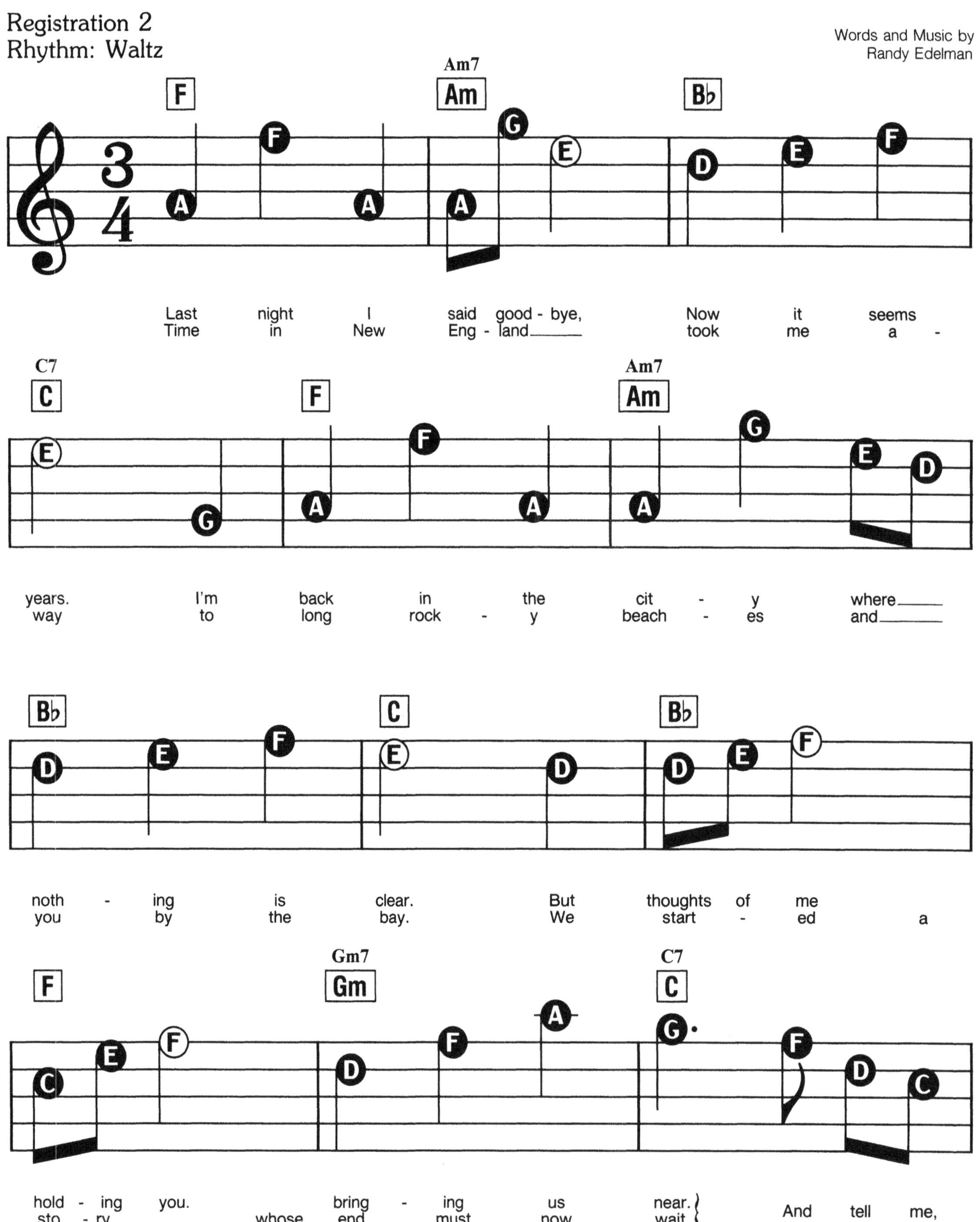

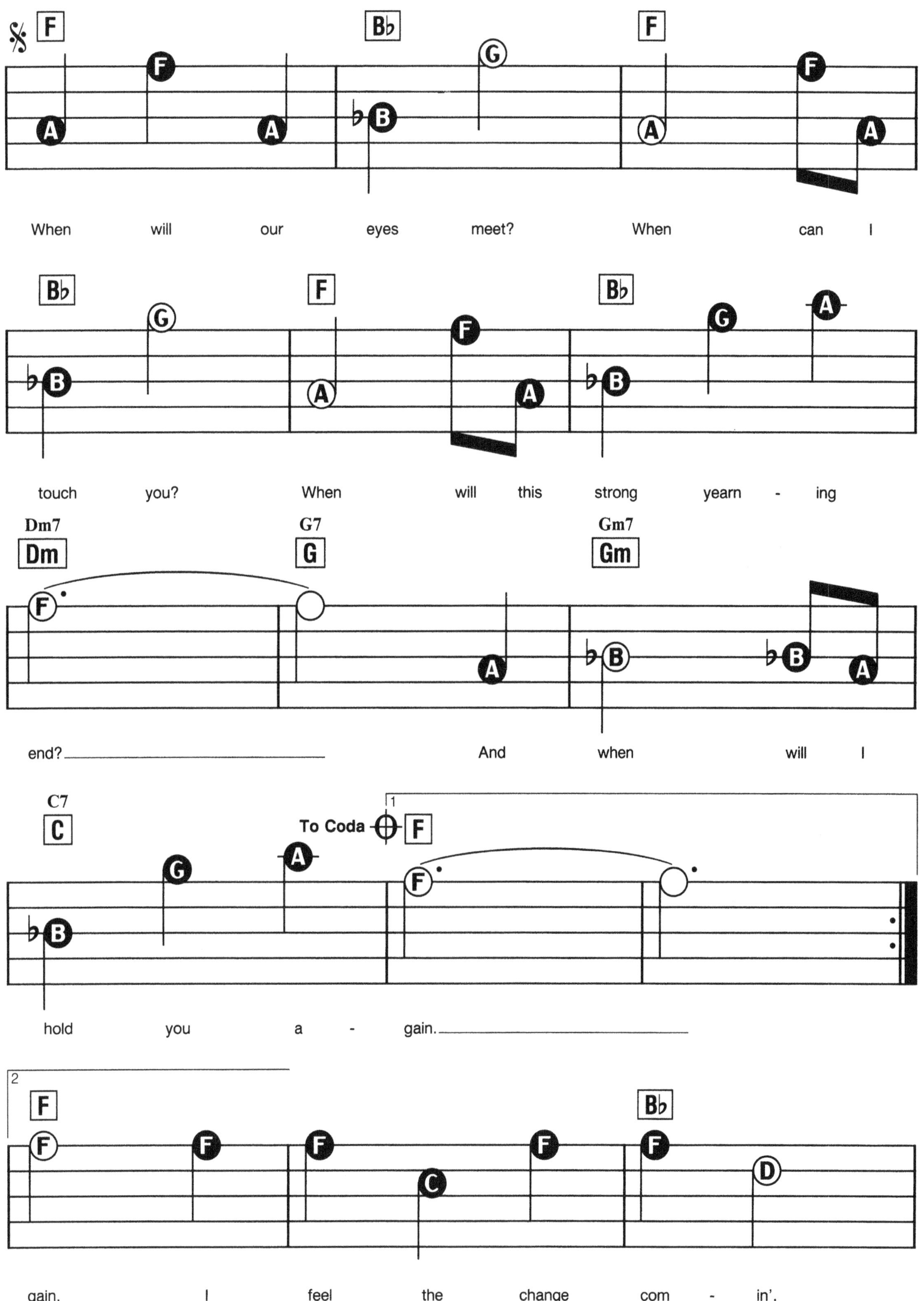
F
Bb
F
When will our eyes meet? When can I
Bb
F
Bb
touch you? When will this strong yearn - ing
Dm7
Dm
G7
G
Gm7
Gm
end? And when will I
C7
C
To Coda
1
F
hold you a - gain.
2
F
Bb
gain. I feel the change com - in',

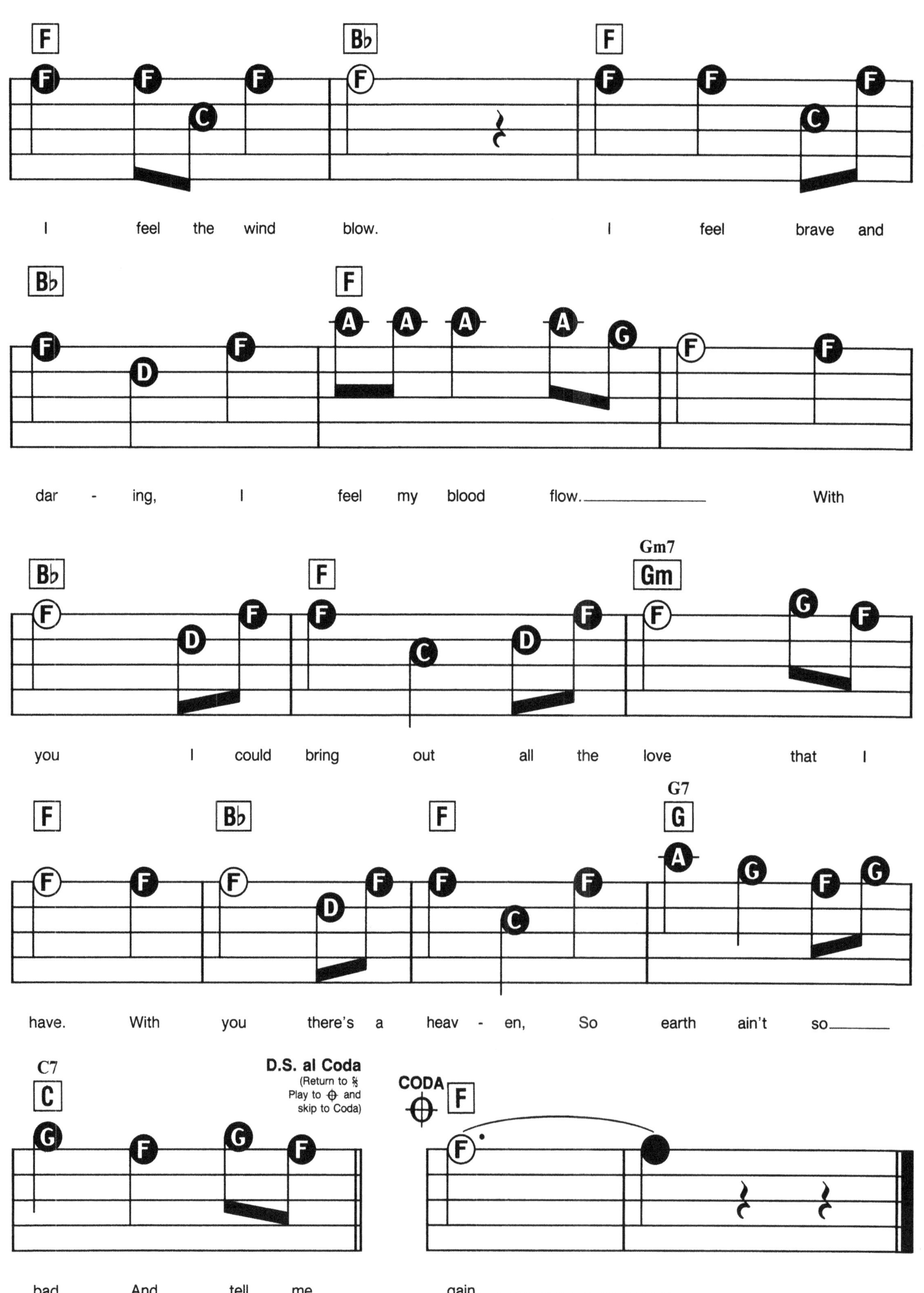
F
Bb
F
I feel the wind blow.
I feel brave and
Bb
F
dar - ing, I feel my blood flow.
With
Bb
F
Gm7
Gm
you I could bring out all the love that I
F
Bb
F
G7
G
have. With you there's a heav - en, So earth ain't so
C7
C
D.S. al Coda
(Return to 𝄋
Play to ⊕ and
skip to Coda)
CODA
F
bad. And tell me
gain.

When October Goes

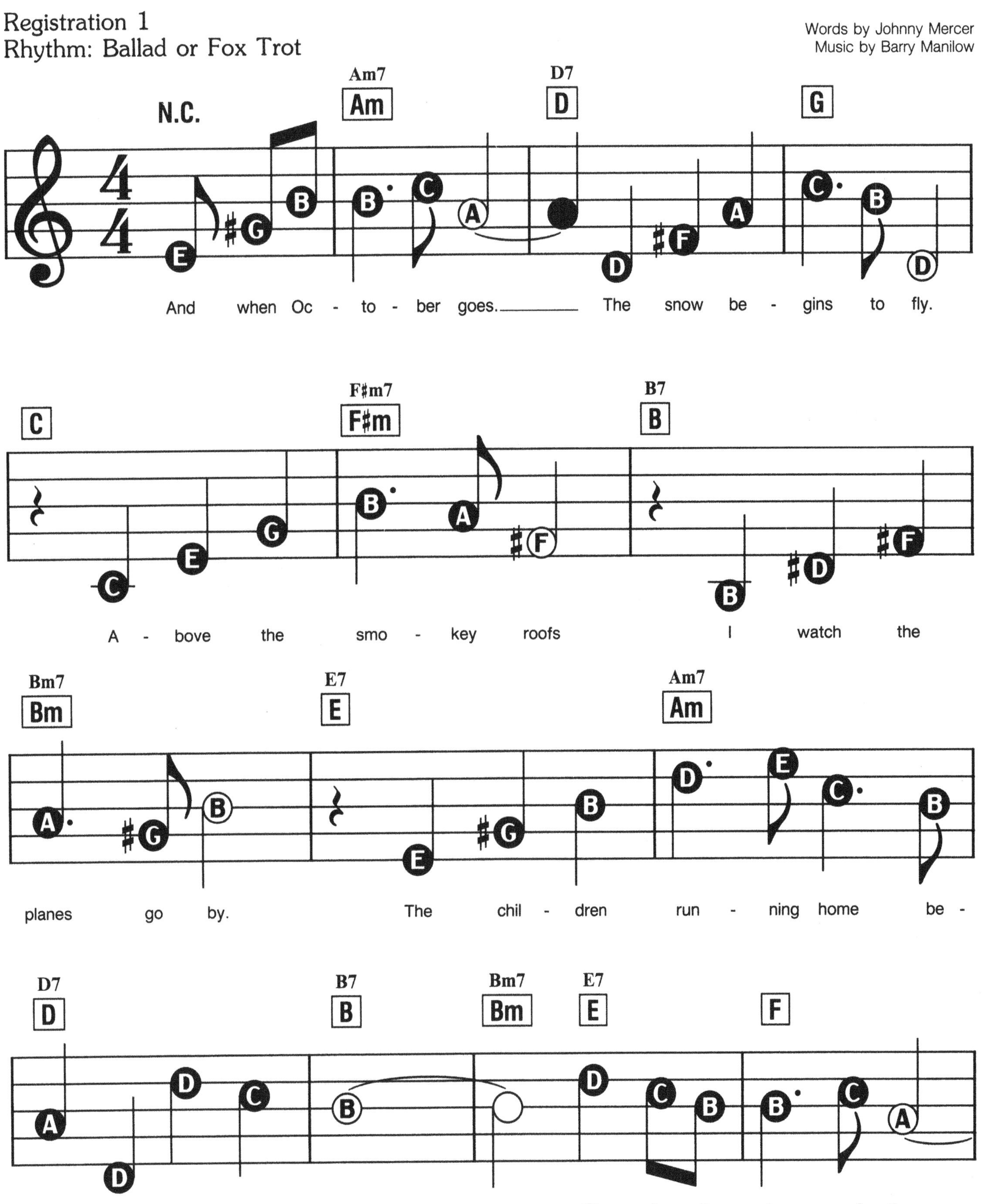

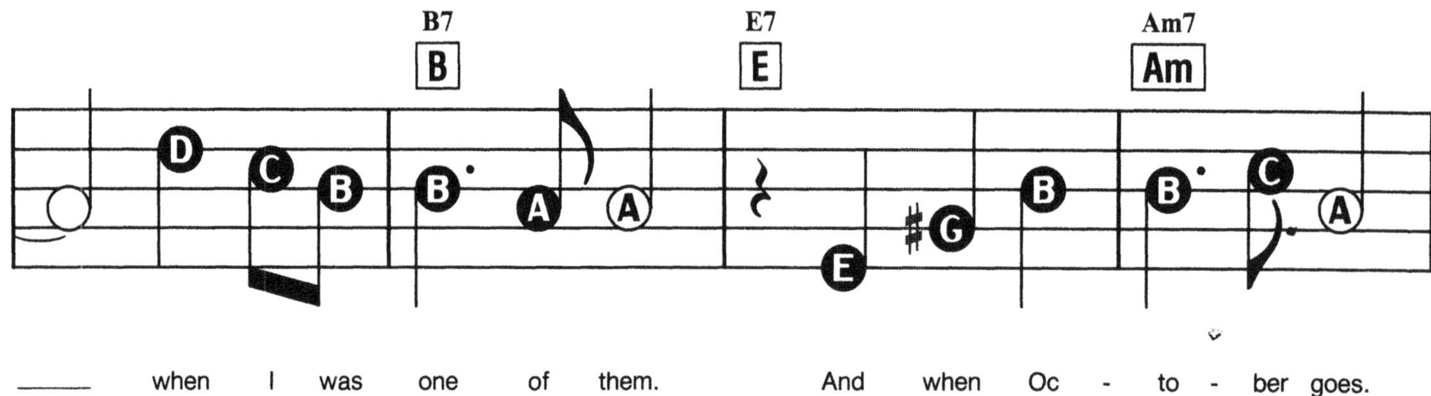
B7
B
E7
E
Am7
Am
D
C
B
B
A
A
E
G
B
B
C
A
when I was one of them. And when Oc - to - ber goes.

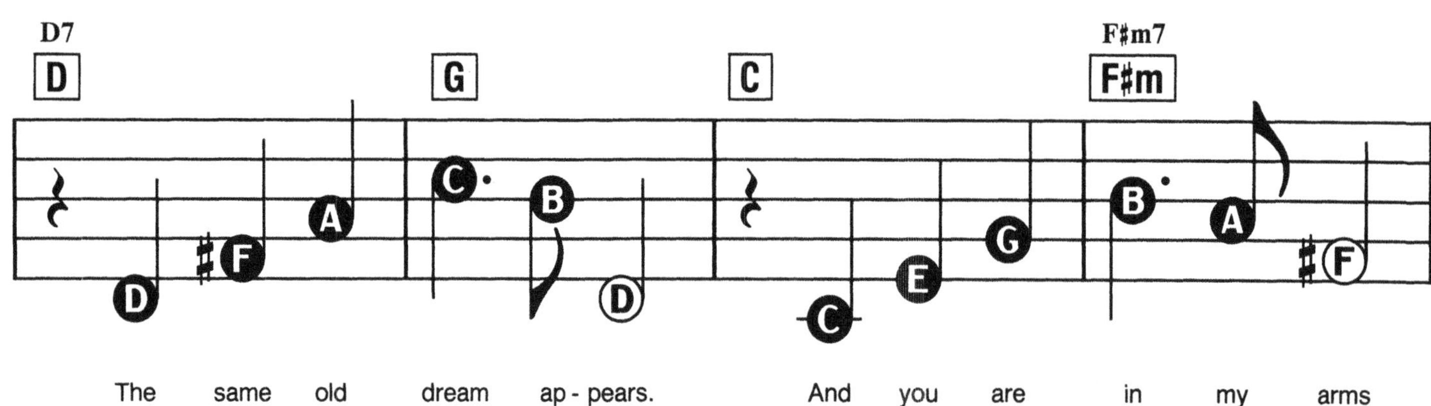
D7
D
G
C
F♯m7
F♯m
D
F
A
C
B
D
C
E
G
B
A
F
The same old dream ap - pears. And you are in my arms

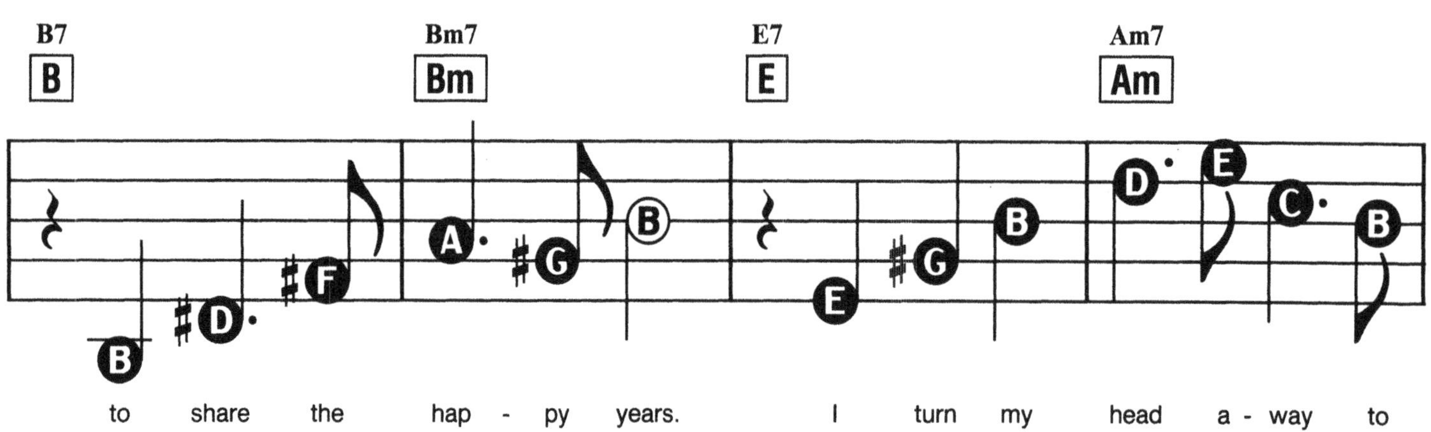
B7
B
Bm7
Bm
E7
E
Am7
Am
B
D
F
A
G
B
E
G
B
D
E
C
B
to share the hap - py years. I turn my head a - way to

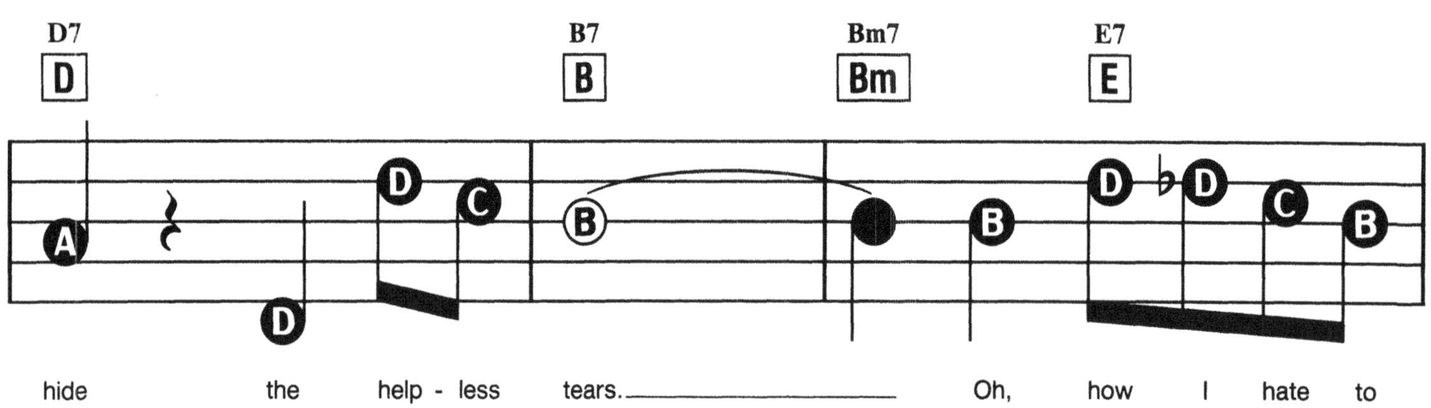
D7
D
B7
B
Bm7
Bm
E7
E
A
D
D
C
B
B
D
D
C
B
hide the help - less tears. Oh, how I hate to

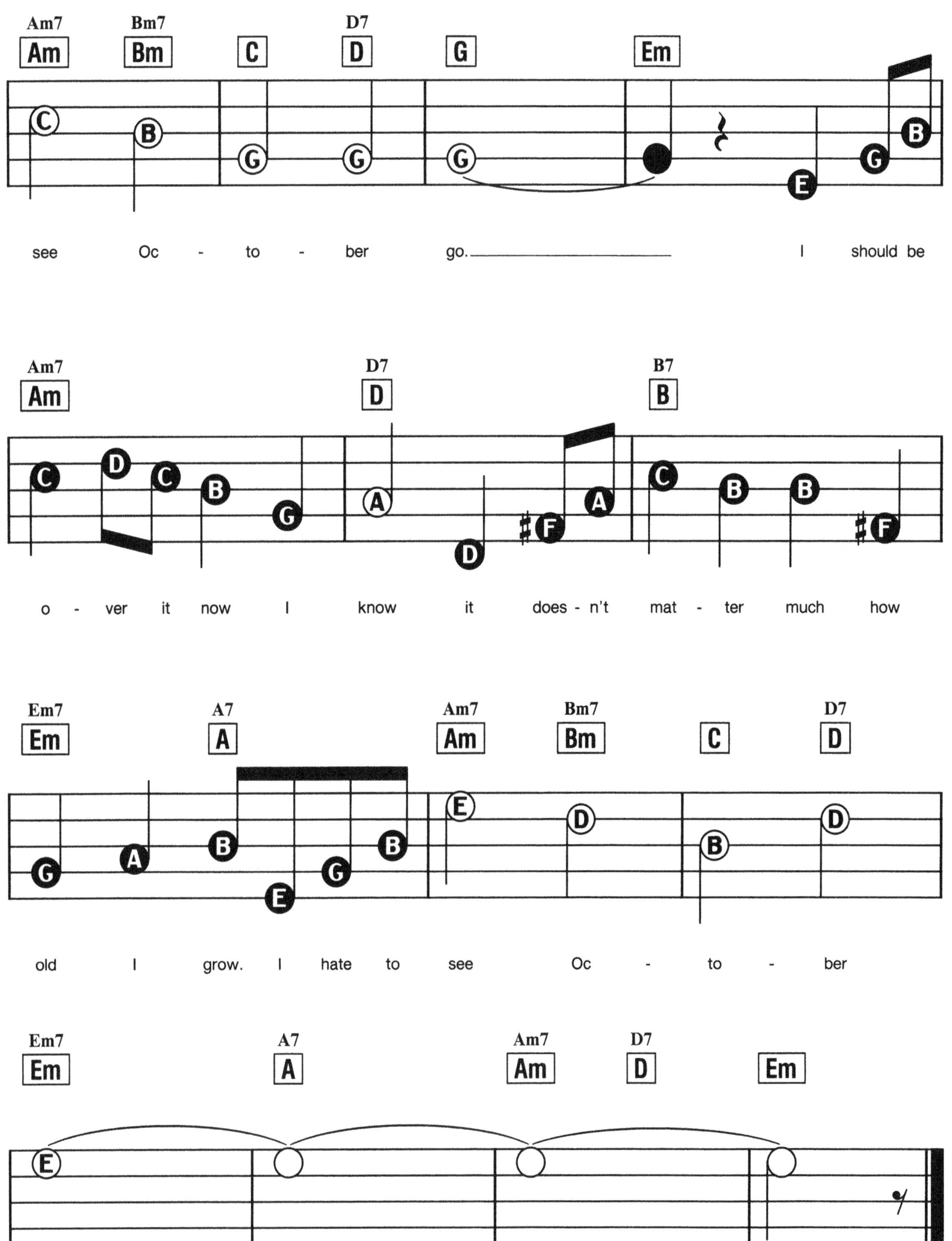
Am7 Bm7 D7
Am Bm C D G Em
C B G G G E G B
see Oc - to - ber go. I should be
Am7 D7 B7
Am D B
C D C B G A D F A C B B F
o - ver it now I know it does - n't mat - ter much how
Em7 A7 Am7 Bm7 D7
Em A Am Bm C D
G A B E G B E D B D
old I grow. I hate to see Oc - to - ber
Em7 A7 Am7 D7
Em A Am D Em
E
go.

Who Needs To Dream

Registration 2
Rhythm: Ballad or Rock

Words by Bruce Sussman and Jack Feldman
Music by Barry Manilow and Artie Butler

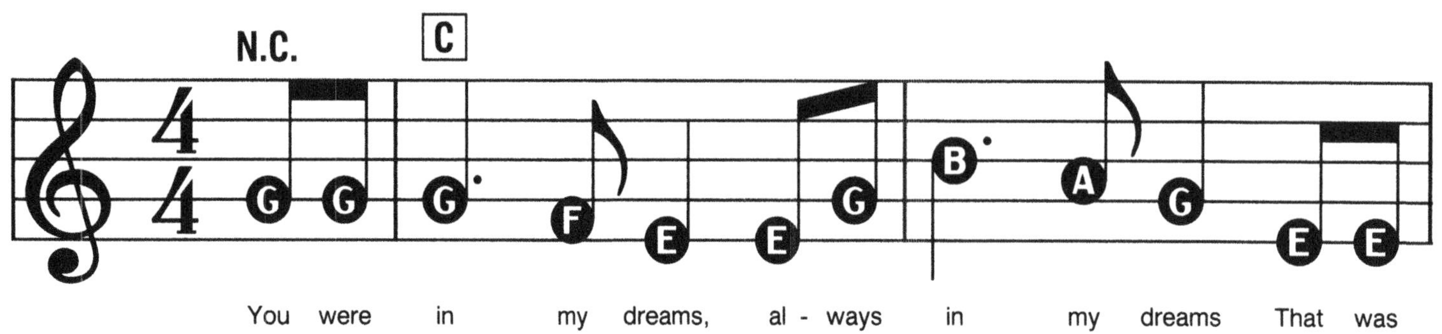

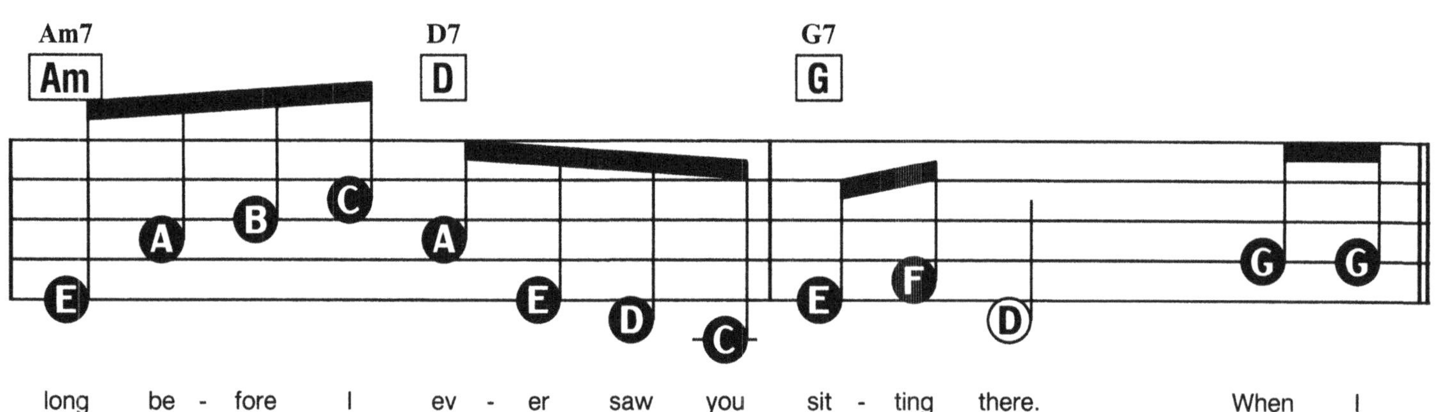

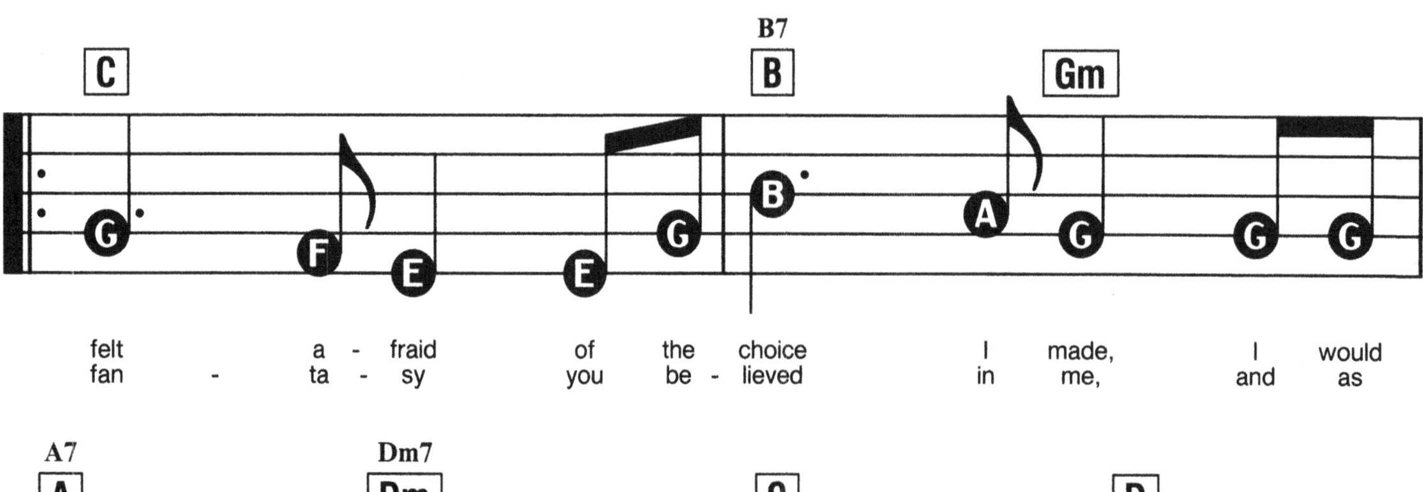

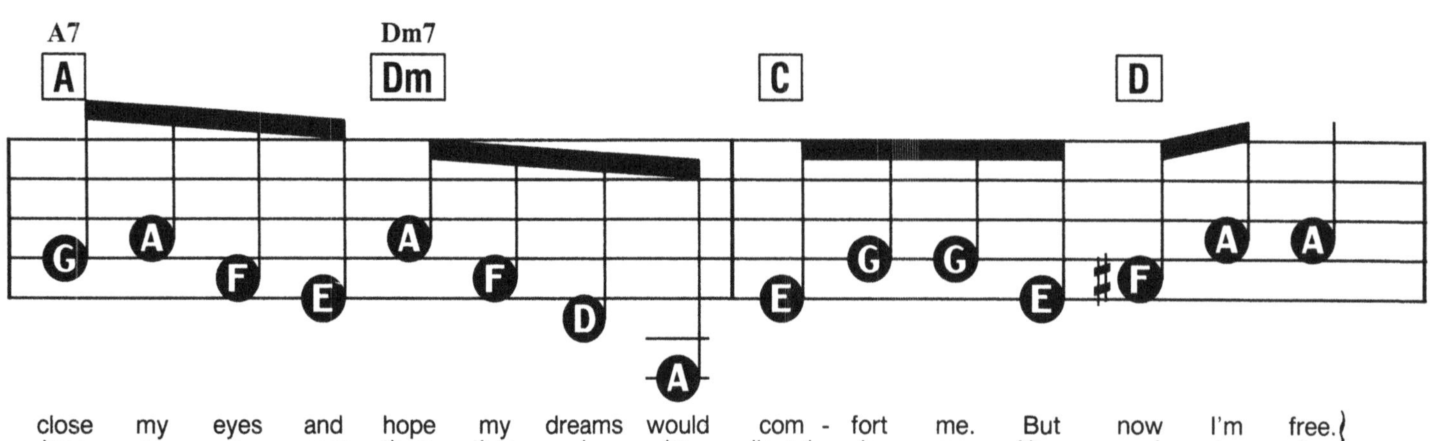

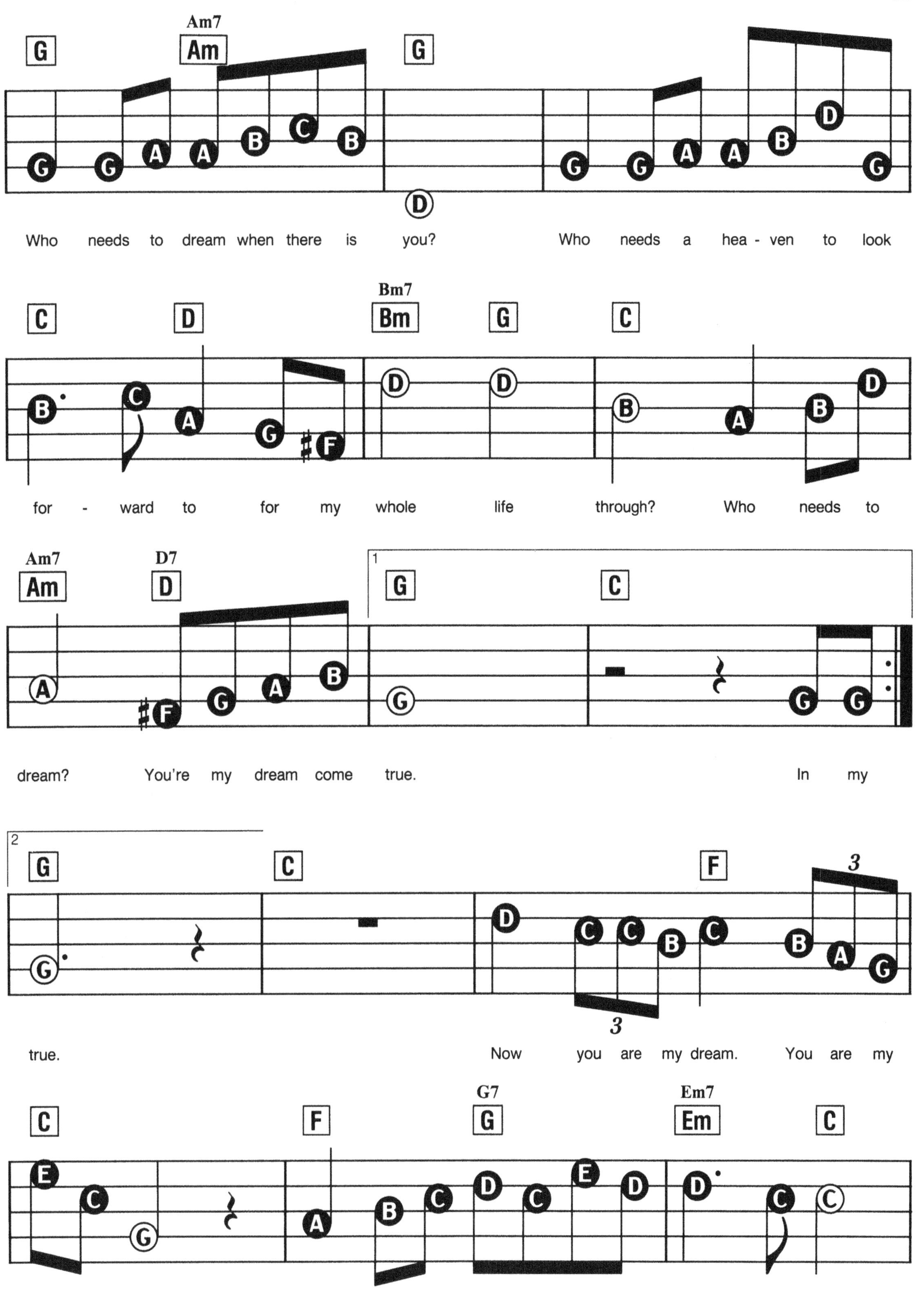
G Am7 Am G
Who needs to dream when there is you? Who needs a hea - ven to look
C D Bm7 Bm G C
for - ward to for my whole life through? Who needs to
Am7 Am D7 D 1 G C
dream? You're my dream come true. In my
2 G C F 3
true. Now you are my dream. You are my
3
C F G7 G Em7 Em C
on - ly dream. I'll hold you in my heart for - ev - er.

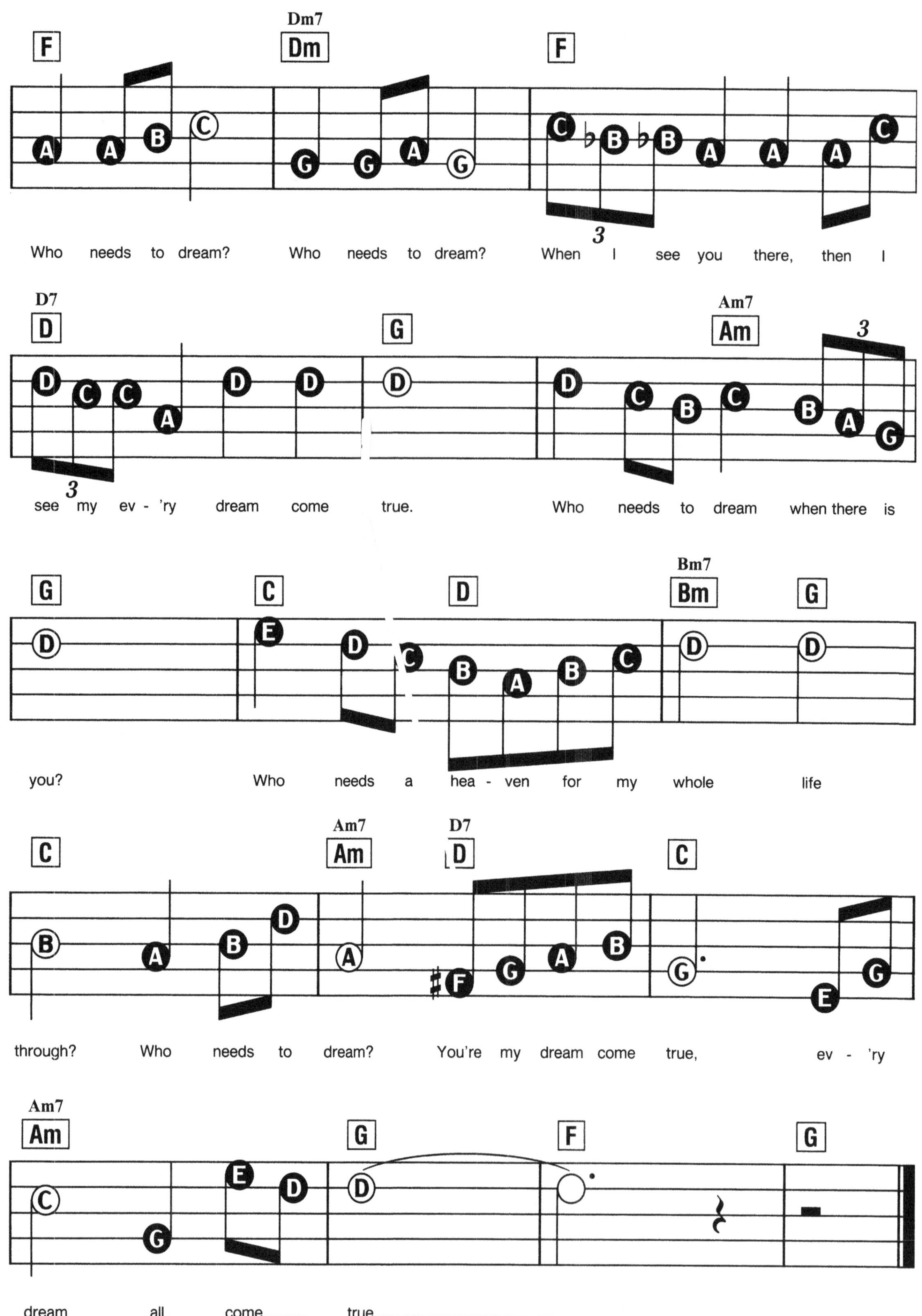
Dm7
F
Dm
F
A
A
B
C
G
G
A
G
C
B
B
A
A
A
C
3
Who needs to dream? Who needs to dream? When I see you there, then I
D7
D
G
Am7
Am
D
C
C
A
D
D
D
D
C
B
C
B
A
G
3
see my ev - 'ry dream come true. Who needs to dream when there is
Bm7
G
C
D
Bm
G
D
E
D
C
B
A
B
C
D
D
you? Who needs a hea - ven for my whole life
Am7
D7
C
Am
D
C
B
A
B
D
A
F
G
A
B
G
E
G
through? Who needs to dream? You're my dream come true, ev - 'ry
Am7
Am
G
F
G
C
G
E
D
D
dream all come true.